Case Book on Criminal Practice and Procedure

Case Book on Criminal Practice and Procedure

Roger A. Ramgoolam

Copyright © 2019 by Roger A. Ramgoolam.

Library of Congress Control Number: 2018915117
ISBN: Hardcover   978-1-9845-7446-6
               Softcover   978-1-9845-7445-9
               eBook   978-1-9845-7444-2

All rights reserved. No part of this book may be reproduced or transmitted in any form or by any means, electronic or mechanical, including photocopying, recording, or by any information storage and retrieval system, without permission in writing from the copyright owner.

Any people depicted in stock imagery provided by Getty Images are models, and such images are being used for illustrative purposes only.
Certain stock imagery © Getty Images.

Print information available on the last page.

Rev. date: 04/19/2019

To order additional copies of this book, contact:
Xlibris
1-888-795-4274
www.Xlibris.com
Orders@Xlibris.com
778680

CONTENTS

Acknowledgements vii
Table of Cases ix

Chapter One
Jurisdiction..1

Chapter Two
How a Person is Brought Before the Court 14

Chapter Three
Police Powers of Entry for the Purpose of Search and Seizure 36

Chapter Four
Role and Function of the Dpp 49

Chapter Five
Bail in Criminal Proceedings..72

Chapter Six
Court Process 88

Chapter Seven
Abuse of Process 109

Chapter Eight
The Plea... 139

Chapter Nine
Important Aspects of Summary Procedure 168

Chapter Ten
Summary Appeals... 188

Chapter Eleven
Triable Either Way Offences 205

Chapter Twelve
Committal Proceedings..222

Chapter Thirteen
Extradition 246

Chapter Fourteen
High Court Trials 279

Chapter Fifteen
The Jury and Verdict...313

Chapter Sixteen
Sentencing...339

Chapter Seventeen
Criminal Appeals From the High Court 364

ACKNOWLEDGEMENTS

This work was possible only with the input of many persons. They all helped out wherever they could by way of proofreading, advice on content and general encouragement. Many thanks go out in particular to my family and close friends who were there at the genesis of this work and then stood by me as it gained coherence. I wish here to state their names in no particular order of merit. I thank my close friends Justice Ronnie Boodoosingh and Mrs Boodoosingh for their inspiration and unflagging technical support. I thank the dedicated staff at the Hugh Wooding law school library for their professionalism and expertise in sourcing materials for the book. I thank Miss Miriam Samaru principal of the Hugh Wooding law school and Mrs Cheryl-Ann Jerome Alexander Senior Tutor both for their insistence on the highest possible standards of work and dedication to duty; the pursuit of these goals encouraged me greatly in my initial decision to compile this casebook.

I also wish to thank former students and now attorneys-at-law Russell Campbell and Aaron Seaton as well as my good friends and colleagues in the legal fraternity Chris Selochan, and Angelica Teelucksingh, who all read various chapters and provided valuable insights and criticisms. I also wish to thank my sister Delicia Hallman for her enthusiasm and encouragement in the early stages of the project which helped me keep focussed and organized.

This book was written when I was performing my duties as course director and tutor of both criminal practice and procedure and trial advocacy at the law school which meant long hours out my off time had to be sacrificed. Throughout it all my wife Sharon showed great understanding, patience and a sense of humour which eased the occasional difficult times. I thank her for standing by me and being such a source of strength.

My parents have always been supportive of me throughout my various journeys in life and in this venture it has been no different. I thank them.

I finally wish to thank my students, both past and present who it has been my privilege to teach (and to learn from). I hope this book plays an important part in the development of their legal careers.

TABLE OF CASES

Agdoma v Tomy (1968) 12 WIR 296 .... *175*

Aguillera, Ballai, Ballai and Ayow v The State Crim. App. Nos. 5, 6, 7, 8 of 2015 .... *345*

Ali v R (1969) 15 WIR 399 .... *367*

Albert v Lavin [1981] 1 All ER 628 .... *18*

Alderson v Booth [1969] 2 Q.B. 216 .... *25*

Ali v The Ag of Trinidad and Tobago Claim No. CV 2012-02695 .... *41*

Allette v Chief of Police (1965) 10 WIR 243 .... *168*

Attorney-General and Another v Aleem Mohammed (1985) 36 WIR 359 .... *66*

Attorney General v Whiteman [1992] 2 All ER 924 .... *32*

Attorney General v. Williams and Others (1997) 51 WIR 264 .... *38*

Attorney General's Reference (No 1 of 1990) [1992] 3 WLR 9 .... *109*

Bach v Ferreira (1965) 9 WIR 282Q *202*

Baksh v The Magistrate Mag. App. No. 107/82 .... *79*

Baksh and Brian Kuei Tung v Her Worship the Senior Magistrate Ejenny Espinet and The DPP CV2009-00868 .... *182*

Benedetto v R (2003) 62 WIR 63 298

Benjamin v. Commissioner of Police and AG [2014] UKPC 8 49

Bhagwan v Chester (1977) 25 WIR 187 106

Bharath v Cambridge (1972) 20 WIR 450 171

Bishop (Glenroy) v The State (2000) 60 WIR 370 300

Bolai v St Louis (1963) 6 WIR 453Q 21

Boolell v State of Mauritius [2012] 1 WLR 3718 133

Borneo v The State Cr. App: 7 of 2011 351

Bowen v Johnson 25 WIR 60 161

Bramble v R (1959) 1 WIR 473 230

Briggs v The State Cr. App No. T-013 of 2014 293

Brooks v Director of Public Prosecutions of Jamaica and
    another [1994] 2 All ER 231 235

Burgess v Thalia Silverton Mag. Appeal No. 98 of 2008 176

Cadogan v R (1963) 6 WIR 292 236

Cannonier v Director of Public Prosecutions Isaac and
    others v Director of Public Prosecutions (2012) 80 WIR 260
    373

Cauldero and another v The State [2000] 4 LRC 33 304

Chadee v Santana (1987) 42 WIR 365 207

Charles (Curtis), Carter (Steve) and Carter (Leroy) v The
State (1999) 54 WIR 455 .... *136*

Chevalier v Attorney-General and Another (1985) 38
WIR 240 .... *40*

Chief Constable of West Midlands Police v Gillard [1985]
3 All ER 634 .... *210*

Christie and Another v Leachinsky [1947] 1 All ER 567 .... *28*

Conliffe v Weekes Decision of the Supreme Court of
Barbados 1 March 1963 .... *89*

Connelly v DPP [1964] 2 All ER 401 .... *147*

Cox v Army Council [1963] AC 48 .... *1*

Cross v John Mag. App. No. 367/1963 .... *91*

Cummings (Steve) v The State; Paul (Rennie) v The State;
Polo (Horace) v The State (1995) 49 WIR 406 .... *334*

Cummins v Commissioner of Police Magisterial Appeal
No. 6 of 2011 .... *353*

Da Costa Hall v The Queen [2011] CCJ 6(AJ) *356*

Davis v The State Crim, Appeal No. 75 of 1988 .... *337*

D'Aguiar v PC Maurice Cox (1971) 18 WIR 44 .... *199*

Donnelly v Jackman [1970] 1 All ER 987 .... *14*

Doobay v Inspector of Police Decision of the High Court of
Guyana 4th & 16th March 1968 .... *97*

DPP v Bennett (1992) 157 JP 493 .... *101*

DPP v Chief Magistrate (No 2) (2003) 67 WIR 240 .... *226*

DPP v Humphrys [1977] A.C. 1 .... *140*

DPP V Nasralla [1967] 2 All ER 161 .... *155*

DPP v Nelson [2015] UKPC 7 .... *379*

DPP v Sullivan and Others (1996) 54 WIR 256 .... *218*

Duporte v The Queen [2015] UKPC 18 .... *323*

Elias and others v. Passmore and others [1934] 2 K.B. 164 .... *27*

Ferguson, Galbaransingh v The Attorney General of
  Trinidad and Tobago CV 2010 – 04144 .... *268*

Forbes v Maharaj (1998) 52 WIR 487 .... *198*

Frederick v Chief of Police (1968) 11 WIR 330 .... *10*

Flowers v R [2001] 1 LRC 643 .... *131*

Fuller v The Attorney General of Belize [2011] UKPC 23 .... *247*

George v Francois (1969) 15 WIR 394 .... *212*

Ghani and others v Jones [1969] 3 WLR 1158 .... *43*

Gomes v Government of Trinidad and Tobago; Goodyer v
  Government of Trinidad and Tobago [2009] 3 All ER 549 .... *253*

Green v Springer (1976) 28 WIR 9 .... *169*

Habib (Simon) v The State (1989) 43 WIR 391 145

Harrington v Roots [1984] 2 All ER 474 186

*Hastings and Folkestone Glassworks Ltd v Kalson [1948]
2 All ER 1013* 220

Hernandez v The State Cr. App. No. 63 of 2004 377

*Humphreys v Attorney General of Antigua and Barbuda
[2009] 4 LRC 405* 233

Hurnam v The State [2005] UKPC 49 72

Jagessar and Nandlal v The State (No 1) (1989) 41 WIR 342 54

*Jagmohan v The Commissioner of Prisons and the AG
CV 2013-04131* 272

Jaroo v Attorney General [2002] UKPC 5 44

John v R (1965) 8 WIR 302 225

John v The State Cr. App. No. 39 of 2007 386

Joseph v Mohammed (1964) 7 WIR 96 152

*Kadir and Ibrahim v The Commissioner of Prisons
CV 2007-2063* 256

Kenlin v Gardiner [1966] 3 All ER 931 16

King v The Queen [1969] 1 A.C. 304 47

*Knowles (Austin) and Others v Superintendent of Fox
Hill Prison and Others (2005) 66 WIR 1* 264

Knowles (Samuel) Jr v (1) The Government of the
  United States of America (2) The Superintendent of Prisons
  of the Commonwealth of the Bahamas [2006] UKPC 38 266

La Vende v The State (1979) 30 WIR 460 229

Lawrence v The Queen [2014] UKPC 2 322

Locabail (UK) Ltd v Bayfield Properties Ltd and Another
  [2000] 3 LRC 482 179

Lester (Kurt) v The State (1996) 50 WIR 452 279

Lewis v Commissioner of Police (1969) 13 WIR 186 196

Lewis v Irish (1966) 10 WIR 500 150

Liangsiriprasert v United States Government and Another
  [1990] 2 All ER 866 6

Maraj-Naraynsingh v The Attorney General of Trinidad and
  Tobago and The Director of Public Prosecutions [2010]
  UKPC 19 68

Melville v The State Cr App. No. T 10 of 2015 332

Mohammed v R (1965) 8 WIR 169 153

Nanan v The State [1986] A.C. 860 326

Nandlal v The State (1995) 49 WIR 412 121

Nicholls v Brentwood Justices [1991] 3 All ER 359 217

Nurse, De Four, De Merieux and Clarke v The Commissioner
  of Prisons and The AG of Trinidad and Tobago CA Nos.49,
  50,52,53 of 2007 275

*O'Hara v Chief Constable of Royal Ulster Constabulary
[1997] 1 All ER 129* 23

Paynter v Lewis (1965) 8 WIR 318 195

Partin v J D'Oliveira (1977) 24 WIR 261 190

Patrick and Small v R (1974) 26 WIR 518 309

Peters v The State Cr. App. No. 34 of 2008 111

*Pierre Simon Andre Sip Heng Wong Ng and another v
The Queen [1987] 1 WLR 1356* 8

*Pierre v The Commissioner of Prisons Claim No CV
2011-01865* 259

Pollard (George) v R (1995) 47 WIR 185 364

Pooran v The State Criminal App. No. 32 of 2015 359

R v Anderson (1868) 11 Cox Crim Cases 198 2

R v Angel [1968] 2 All ER 607 53

R v Assim [1966] 2 QB 249 92

*R. v Barrell (Victor Sidney), R. v. Victor Sidney Barrell,
R. v. Alan Henry Wilson (1979) 69 Cr. App. R. 250* 282

R v Beedie [1997] 2 Cr App Rep 167 148

R v Blackwell and others [1995] 2 Cr App Rep 625 320

*R v Birmingham Justices, ex parte Hodgson and another
[1985] 2 All ER 193* 208

R v Boyle [1954] 2 All ER 721 287

R v Chin-Loy (1975) 23 WIR 360 36

R v Croydon Justices, ex parte Dean [1993] 3 All ER 129 125

R (F) v Director of Public Prosecutions [2014] 2 WLR 190 63

R v General Council of the Bar, ex parte Percival [1990]
3 All ER 137 58

R v Gordon (1969) 14 WIR 21 178

R v Governor of Brixton Prison and Another Ex parte
Cuoghi [1998] 1 WLR 1513 262

R v Grays Justices, ex parte Graham [1982] 3 All ER 653 238

R v Heyes [1950] 2 All ER 587 139

R v Hines and King (1971) 17 WIR 326 184

R v Hogan (1960) 44 Cr App R 255 162

R v Horseferry Road Magistrates' Court, ex parte Adams
[1978] 1 All ER 373 232

R v Horseferry Road Magistrates Court, Ex parte Bennett
[1993] 3 WLR 90 119

R v Howell [1981] 3 All ER 383 19

R v Hussain Ex Parte Director of Public Prosecutions
(1965) 8 WIR 65 242

R v J (JF)[2014] 2 WLR 701 163

R v Johnson and Brown (1974) 22 WIR 470 94

R v Jones [2002] 2 All ER 113 310

R v Kent Justices Ex parte Machin [1952] 1 All ER 1123 205

R. v. Lake (1977) 64 Cr. App. R. 172 286

R v Latif; R v Shahzad [1996] 1 All ER 353 115

R v Lee [1984] 1 All ER 1080 383

R v Looseley; Attorney General's Reference (No 3 of 2000)
[2001] 4 All ER 897 126

R v Manchester City Stipendiary Magistrate, ex parte
Snelson [1978] 2 All ER 62 240

R v Manning (1959) 2 WIR 111 290

R v Maxwell [2011] 4 All ER 941 113

R v Medway [1976] 1 All ER 527 381

R. v Moghal (1977) 65 Cr. App. R. 56 284

R v Morais [1988] 3 All ER 161 281

R. v. Nelson (1977) 65 Cr. App. R. 119 291

R. v Novac (1977) 65 Cr. App. R. 107 283

R. v Pianka and Hilton (1975) 24 WIR 285 3

R v Podola [1960] 1 QB 325 144

R v Qureshi [2002] 1 WLR 518 329

R. v Reading Crown Court Ex p. Bello (1991) 92 Cr. App.
R. 303 81

R v Secretary of State for the Home Department Ex parte
Launder (No. 2) ; Launder v. Governor of Brixton
Prison and another [1998] 3 WLR 221 81

R v Smith (Wallace Duncan) (No 4) [2004] QB 1418 5

R v Tolera [1999] 1 Cr App R 29 142

R v Twiss [1918] 2 K.B. 853 316

R v. Vodden (1853) 169 ER 706 313

R v Waller [1910] 1 K.B. 364 52

R v West [1962] 2 All ER 624 241

R v West Norfolk Justices, ex parte Mc Mullen (1993) 157
JP 461 215

R v Whitehouse [1977] 3 All ER 737 384

R v Williams (Roy) [1977] 1 All ER 874 289

R v Wilmot (1933) 24 Cr App Rep 63 99

Ralph v A Magistrate (1968) 12 WIR 124 78

Rambarran v The Queen [2016] CCJ 2(AJ 369

Ramjohn v Johnson (1966) 10 WIR 159 95

Ramlogan (Arnold) v The State (2000) 58 WIR 374 317

Ramsarran v Attorney-General (2005) 66 WIR 280 34

Randall (Barry) v R (2002) 60 WIR 103...295

Re Barings plc [1999] 1 All ER 311 157

Re Harris (1984) 148 JP 584..83

Richards v R (1992) 41 WIR 263 159

Robbles v Glanville (1964) 7 WIR 220 214

Roberts v PC William Nurse Mag. App. 31 of 2002 201

Rowley v T A Everton & Sons Ltd [1940] 4 All ER 435 12

Sanker and Pitts v R (1982) 33 WIR 64...314

Scott and another v R; Barnes and others v R [1989] A.C.
    1242 302

Schiavo v Anderton [1986] 3 All ER 10..82

Sharma v Antoine and others [2007] 4 LRC 10 60

Sharma v Leacock (1970) 17 WIR 353..105

Spencer v Bramble (1960) 2 WIR 222 173,191

Stanley v Andrews (1963) 5 WIR 457 188

State v Forde No. CR 28 of 2004..128

State v Lezama H.C. Cr. No B069/10 74

State v Nicholas, Tan, Lewis Cr. S. No. 26/06 & No. 109
    of 2007...339

State v Scantlebury (1981) 27 WIR 103 85

Sutherland v The State (1970) 16 WIR 342 306

Tan v Cameron [1993] 2 All ER 493 130

Tappin v Lucas (1973) 20 WIR 229 64

Taylor v Khan (1969) 15 WIR 254 102

Thornhill v Attorney-General (1976) 31 WIR 498 30

Tibbetts v the Attorney General of the Cayman Islands
    [2010] 3 All ER 95 330

Vyse v Cpl Warwick POS Magisterial Appeal No. 14
    of 2009 193

Warren and others v Attorney General of the Bailiwick of
    Jersey [2011] 2 All ER 513 117

Wilson v The State Cr. App. No.31 of 2006 325

Woodcock v The Government of New Zealand [2003]
    EWHC 2668 249

Xavier v The State Cr A No. 78 of 1988 336

Yaseen and Thomas v The State (1990) 44 WIR 219 222

CHAPTER ONE

JURISDICTION

Jurisdiction relates to the court's power to try offences. The basis of the court's jurisdiction hinges on the principle of territoriality. The territoriality principle holds that crimes committed upon a state's territory are justiciable by the courts of that state. The concept of territory has expanded beyond the land territory of a state to include:

1. Internal waters
2. Territorial seas
3. The high seas
4. Airspace

CRIMINAL JURISDICTION OVER OFFENCES COMMITTED ON LAND

Principle

The courts have criminal jurisdiction over offences committed on a state's land territory.

Court-Martial Appeal Court and House of Lords

Cox v Army Council

[1963] AC 48

Facts

The appellant, while serving with the British Army in Germany, was charged before a district court-martial held in Germany with "committing a civil offence contrary to section 70 of the Army Act, 1955, that is to say, driving without due care and attention contrary to section 3 (1) of the Road Traffic Act. He was convicted and appealed his conviction.

Decision

Viscount Simonds held that with the exception of statutory provisions dealing with acts committed outside the United Kingdom, the criminal law of England applied only to acts committed on English territory.

CRIMINAL JURISDICTION OVER INTERNAL WATERS

Principle

Where a criminal act is committed on a ship which is in a state's internal waters, the coastal state has criminal jurisdiction over that act. In such an instance the flag state may also exercise criminal jurisdiction.

Court of Criminal Appeal, England

R v Anderson

(1868) 11 Cox Crim Cases 198

Facts

"A" committed an offence on a British flag ship 300 yards from shore in a tidal river leading from the open sea to the port of Bordeaux,

France. At the time of the offence the ship was about 45 miles up-river. The issue was whether the English courts had criminal jurisdiction in respect of the offence.

Decision

Bovill CJ held that the offence was committed in France, and that therefore the accused was subject to the laws of France. At the same time however, the offence was also committed on British territory, since the act took place on board a merchant vessel, flying the British flag. It followed that the accused was also subject to British law.

CRIMINAL JURISDICTION OVER TERRITORIAL WATERS

Principle

The coastal state's criminal jurisdiction extends to the state's territorial waters. This jurisdiction is not exclusive. It may be exercised in limited circumstances such as where the offence committed in the territorial waters was trafficking narcotics.

Court of Appeal of Jamaica

R v. Pianka and Hilton

Decision of the Court of Appeal of Jamaica, 12th June 1975

Facts

The appellants were foreigners and were seen aboard the motor boat SB. This boat was registered at Miami in the United States of America and was intercepted 3.8 miles from Rio Neuvo Bay, St Mary, and found to be carrying 60 bags of ganja. They were convicted in the Resident Magistrate's court for St Mary for unlawful possession of ganja and using a motor boat to convey ganja. On appeal against conviction it was contended, on behalf of the appellants, that the resident magistrate was without jurisdiction to try the appellants. The appellants' appeals against their convictions were dismissed.

Decision

Luckhoo JA held that a resident magistrate had criminal jurisdiction over the case since the court's jurisdiction extended to offences committed by a foreigner on a foreign ship within Jamaican territorial seas. The relevant legislation was the Resident Magistrates Law, 1891 and the Territorial Sea Act, 1971.

Luckhoo JA noted that:

> "...the appellants had received into their possession while on the territorial sea a dangerous drug the possession and conveyance of which were prohibited under the criminal law in the territory of Jamaica and its receipt and conveyance by the appellants in that event was prejudicial to the good order of Jamaica. The consequences of the crime therefore extended to Jamaica, and additionally was such as to disturb the good order of the territorial sea."

THE DIFFERENT THEORETICAL APPROACHES ON THE ISSUE OF WHETHER THE COURTS OF A STATE MAY EXERCISE CRIMINAL JURISDICTION

Principle

The court may exercise jurisdiction on the basis of the 'initiatory theory.' This posits that the crime is committed at the jurisdiction where the offender is located when he does the acts which constitute the essential physical element of the crime.

Court of Appeal

R v Smith (Wallace Duncan) (No 4)

[2004] QB 1418

Facts

The appellant established a merchant bank in England, of which he was the chairman and managing director. He was charged with one count of fraudulent trading and two counts of obtaining property by deception. The allegation was that, working from England and using a group of companies which he controlled, he had set up various bogus deals which boosted the size of the bank's profits. The appellant argued that the trial court in England had lacked jurisdiction because, although the deception had taken place in London, the obtaining had taken place outside the jurisdiction when the money was paid into a bank account in New York and the offences were thus committed in New York.

Decision

Lord Woolf CJ as part of his judgement discussed the application of the 'comity approach' also called 'the initiatory theory' which was that a crime is committed on the territory where the offender is located at the time when the offender does the acts which constitute the essential physical element of the crime. The court referred approvingly to dicta of Rose LJ in R v Smith (No 1) [1996] 2 Cr App R 1, which was to the effect that the reliance of international banking on increasingly sophisticated communications technology facilitated transnational fraud on an increasing scale. In light of this the court should not restrict itself to claiming criminal jurisdiction solely to instances where the unlawful obtaining actually took place in the territory where the court was located.

Principle

According to the 'terminatory' approach to criminal jurisdiction, the courts will exercise criminal jurisdiction over inchoate crimes committed abroad which are intended to result in the commission of criminal offences in England.

Judicial Committee of the Privy Council

Liangsiriprasert v United States Government and another

[1991] 1 AC 225

Facts

The appellant appealed to the Privy Council against the dismissal of his application for a writ of *habeas corpus ad subjiciendum* challenging an extradition order made against him by the Chief Magistrate of Hong Kong, at the request of the first respondent, the United States government.

The appellant contended *inter alia* that a conspiracy entered into abroad was not a common law crime unless either some overt act pursuant to the conspiracy took place within the court's jurisdiction.

Decision

The court acknowledged that generally, English criminal law was local in its effect and that the common law did not concern itself with crimes committed abroad. The reason for this was that the criminal law was developed to protect English society and not that of other nationals. In other words it was of no direct concern to English society if a crime was committed in another country.

Lord Griffiths held:

> "There has as yet, however, been no decision in which it has been held that a conspiracy entered into abroad to commit a crime in England is a common law crime triable in English courts in the absence of any overt act pursuant to the conspiracy taking place in England. There are, however, a number of dicta in judgments and academic commentaries suggesting that it should be so."

Lord Griffiths further held:

> "In DPP v Doot the respondents, American citizens, formed a plan abroad to import cannabis into the United States by way of England. Two vans in which cannabis was concealed were shipped from Morocco to Southampton. The cannabis in one van was discovered in Southampton and in the other van in Liverpool from whence it was intended to ship the vans to the United States. The respondents were charged with *inter alia*, conspiracy to import dangerous drugs. At the trial they contended that the court had no jurisdiction to try them on that count since the conspiracy had been entered into abroad."

The House of Lords decided that that a conspiracy to commit in England an offence against English law ought to be triable in England if it has been wholly or partly performed in England. Lord Griffiths also referred to the case of DPP v Stonehouse where the defendant, soon after insuring his life in England for the benefit of his wife, faked his death by drowning abroad. He was subsequently charged in England with attempting to obtain in England property by deception. He was convicted and the House of Lords decided that the charge was justiciable in England. The House emphasised that the effects of the defendant's actions were felt in England since following upon the reports of his faked death false claims would be made on the insurance companies located in the United Kingdom.

Lord Griffiths held:

> "Crime is now established on an international scale and the common law must face this new reality. Their Lordships can find nothing in precedent, comity or good sense that should inhibit the common law from regarding as justiciable in England inchoate crimes committed abroad which are intended to result in the commission of criminal offences in England."

JURISDICTION WHERE THE COURT SITS AS A TRIBUNAL OF FACT AND LAW

Principle

Those charged with returning a verdict in a criminal case (such as magistrates) have the duty to assess and determine the reliability and veracity of the witnesses who give oral evidence, and it is upon this assessment that their verdict will ultimately depend. If they have not had the opportunity to carry out this function as judges of the facts, they are disqualified from returning a verdict, and any verdict they purport to return must be quashed.

Judicial Committee of the Privy Council

Pierre Simon Andre Sip Heng Wong Ng and another v The Queen

[1987] UKPC 23

Facts

The trial of the defendants began before P and another magistrate and they continued hearing the case until the end of the prosecution's case and reserved judgment on a submission that there was no case to answer. Thereafter, pursuant to section 124 of the Courts Act 1945 the magistrate sitting with P was replaced by N. They determined that there was a case to answer and heard evidence and the submissions made on behalf of the defendants and co-defendants. The case was again adjourned and several months later P with another magistrate, B, gave judgment convicting the defendants and co-defendants. The Supreme Court of Mauritius dismissed the defendants' appeals against conviction holding that their right to a fair trial guaranteed by section 10(1) of the Constitution had not been infringed.

The defendants appealed to the Privy Council.

Decision

Lord Griffiths held:

> "The defendants, having been convicted by a magistrate who had heard none of the evidence in the case nor any of the submissions made on their behalf, complained that they had been denied the fair hearing of their cases guaranteed to them by section 10(1) of the Mauritius Constitution.
>
> This provides:
>
> 'Where any person is charged with a criminal offence, then, unless the charge is withdrawn, the case shall be afforded a fair hearing within a reasonable time by an independent and impartial court established by law.'
>
> "Their Lordships consider the defendants' complaint to be unanswerable. It should be said at once that the

Solicitor-General very properly did not seek to uphold their convictions."

Lord Griffiths went on to affirm the principle that it was a fundamental requirement of justice that a tribunal of fact hearing a case must have heard all the evidence. He stressed that the evaluation of oral evidence depends not only upon what is said but how it is said. Furthermore, a tribunal of fact charged with the responsibility of returning a verdict in a criminal case has a duty to assess and determine the reliability and veracity of the witnesses who give oral evidence. If the tribunal did not have the opportunity to discharge this function as judges of the facts, then they would be disqualified from returning a verdict. In fact, any verdict they purported to return in these circumstances must be quashed.

MAGISTRATES' JURISDICTION

Principle

When a magistrate's appointment is terminated, he becomes functus officio.

High Court of Justice, Grenada Appellate jurisdiction

Frederick v Chief of Police

(1968) 11 WIR 330

Facts

A person having been appointed in June 1966, to act as magistrate began the hearing of the case but was unable to complete it before his appointment was terminated. He was then appointed in December 1966, as an additional magistrate to complete the hearing of this case and others which had not been completed in June 1966. Counsel for the appellant submitted that the hearing should be commenced de novo because on the termination of the magistrate's acting appointment in June 1966, he had become *functus officio* and accordingly he had no jurisdiction to continue the hearing from the stage where it had been left incomplete in June 1966. The magistrate overruled this submission and continued the hearing of the case. The appellant was convicted and appealed.

Decision

A M Lewis CJ held that a person who is appointed as magistrate has the powers which are conferred on him by statute only so long as he remains the magistrate. However when the magistrate's appointment is terminated, he becomes *functus officio*, meaning that he is divested of his authority which he had as magistrate. The Chief Justice went on to state that on the facts, the magistrate had no authority to continue the hearing of the unfinished case. Instead, he ought to have started the case afresh. In these circumstances the unfinished trial was a nullity.

Appeal allowed. New trial ordered.

JURISDICTION AND STATUTORY LIMITATION

The concept of jurisdiction encompasses statutory limitation. In the case of summary offences statute provides that there is a specific time period within which a charge must be laid, failing which the courts will be unable to exercise jurisdiction to hear the offence.

Principle

In the case of a continuing offence, the statutory limitation does not, in general, apply. This is because so long as the offence continues, it is repeated from day to day. If for example the offence is the erection of dangerous machinery, the offence will be complete when the machinery is completely erected. Where the statutory requirement is that machinery should be kept securely fenced, then an offence is committed on every day on which it is not so fenced.

King's Bench Division

Rowley v TA Everton & Sons Ltd

[1941] 1 KB 86

Facts

The respondents were the owners of a quarry and operated a sand hopper and a crusher platform. These machines had been installed at dates prior to 29 August 1939, and, at and from that date, the whole of that machinery had been in operation. On 25 January 1940 and 29 January 1940, informations were laid against the respondents alleging that machines were not properly fenced in accordance with the requirements of the Metalliferous Mines Regulation Act 1872, and the Quarries General Regulations 1938, reg. 14, and that the respondents had failed to comply with these regulations on 31 October 1939 and 22 December 1939. The above Act required that an information be laid within 3 months from the time of the alleged commission of the offence.

Decision

Viscount Caldecote LCJ held that the information appeared to have been laid within three months from the time when the matter of the information arose, on the ground that the offence charged was that on a certain day the machinery in question was not kept securely fenced. His lordship was unable to accept the contention that, because the machinery had not been kept securely fenced on some days more than three months before the date of the information, the matter of the information had then arisen.

Humphreys J held:

> "I am of the same opinion. The argument of counsel for the respondents was certainly a startling one. The offence charged in these informations was the failure to comply with a bye-law which requires that certain dangerous machinery shall be securely fenced. It must be assumed that the allegation was that on a particular day--in fact, a particular day is mentioned in the information--it was found that the dangerous machinery was not securely fenced. Counsel for the respondents says: 'No offence is committed. The matter is statute-barred, because this man had been committing this offence on previous occasions over a period of 6 months.' I rather agree with counsel for the appellant that, if that is the result, the sooner the law is altered the better."

Humphreys J further held:

> "However, I do not think that that is the law or that it ever was the law. I do not think that it is in the least the meaning of the Summary Jurisdiction Act 1848, s 11, which provides practically what is provided in the Act with which we are dealing--namely, that the matter of complaint must have arisen within 6 months of the time when the proceedings are instituted. I am glad to find that this decision does not, in my opinion, conflict with any of the previous decisions of this court."

Appeal allowed with costs

CHAPTER TWO

HOW A PERSON IS BROUGHT BEFORE THE COURT

A person may be arrested or served with a summons to attend court.

At common law arrest is a legal concept which has two elements:

1. The physical element; and
2. The mental element

The physical element involves the use of force however slight. At the time of arrest the arrestor's intention must be to restrict the arrestee's freedom of movement, not to merely question him or her.

TOUCHING WITHOUT INTENTION TO ARREST

Principle

At common law, touching without the intention to arrest is an assault, except where the touch is trivial. In such circumstances the arrestee may be entitled to exercise his right of self-defence once excessive force is not used.

Divisional Court

Donnelly v Jackman

[1970] NZLR 98

Facts

The appellant was walking along the pavement when a police officer in uniform came up to him with a view to making enquiries about an offence which the officer had cause to believe the appellant might have committed. The appellant ignored the officer's repeated requests to stop and speak to him. At one stage the officer tapped the appellant on the shoulder, and shortly after the appellant tapped the officer on the chest.

It became apparent that the appellant had no intention of stopping. The officer then again touched the appellant on the shoulder with the intention of stopping him (but neither then nor previously had the officer any intention to arrest the appellant) when the appellant struck the officer with some force. The appellant was charged with and convicted of assaulting the officer in the execution of his duty. He appealed.

Decision

Talbot J held:

> "When one considers the problem: was this officer acting in the course of his duty, in my view one ought to bear in mind that it is not every trivial interference with a citizen's liberty that amounts to a course of conduct sufficient to take the officer out of the course of his duties. In my judgment the facts that the justices found in this case do not justify the view that the officer was not acting in the execution of his duty when he went up to the appellant and wanted to speak to him. Therefore the assault was rightly found to be an assault on the officer whilst acting in the execution of his duties, and I would dismiss this appeal."

Principle

Touching without an intention to arrest even where there is a genuine suspicion that an offence was being committed is technically an unlawful assault. In such a case the arrestee will be entitled to use self-defence.

Queen's Bench Division

Kenlin v Gardiner

[1966] 3 All ER 931

Facts

The appellants, both schoolboys, aged 14, were seen by two police officers in plain clothes going from house to house in a street. The officers became genuinely suspicious of their conduct, and identified themselves as police officers and showed the boys their warrant card. The boys did not believe the men were police officers and were frightened at being accosted by strange men.

Both boys attempted to run away and in so doing they hit the police officers. Both appellants were charged with assaulting the police in the execution of their duty contrary to Police Act 1964 section 51. The magistrates found that the boys had technically assaulted the respondents and convicted them, but granted them an absolute discharge. The justices stated a case for the Court of Appeal.

Decision

Winn LJ held that neither of the respondent police officers had been entitled in law to take hold of the first appellant by the arm, since this was executed not as an integral step in the process of arresting, but was done in order to merely detain and prevent an escape.

Winn LJ further held:

> "I regret to say that I think that there was a technical assault by each of the respondents. From which it follows that the justification of self-defence exerted or exercised by the appellants is not negatived by any justifiable character of the initial assault. It is plain in my own view that it was within the province of self-defence."

Appeals allowed. Convictions quashed.

ARREST WITH OR WITHOUT WARRANT

A person may be arrested with or without warrant. Both the common law and statute allow citizens and police officers to arrest without warrant while only police officers may arrest with warrant. At common law, in certain instances, a person may be apprehended for a breach of the peace for example a breach of the peace committed in a person's presence may justify an arrest. A breach of the peace may occur where an act is done which:

(1) actually causes harm or damage to property or

(2) is likely to cause harm or damage, or

(3) puts a person in fear of such harm or damage being done.

ARREST AT COMMON LAW FOR BREACH OF THE PEACE

Principle

At common law a private citizen or a police officer may execute an arrest for a breach of the peace.

Queen's Bench Division

Albert v Lavin

[1981] UKHL 6

Facts

The appellant caused a disturbance in a bus queue while attempting to board a bus. He was restrained by an off-duty police officer who was in plain clothes. A struggle ensued between the appellant and the officer, in the course of which the officer told the appellant that he was a police officer, which the appellant honestly, but unreasonably, disbelieved. The appellant continued to hit the officer and was arrested and charged with assaulting a police officer in the execution of his duty.

The appellant was convicted by magistrates on that charge. He appealed, contending, *inter alia*, that his belief that he was being subjected to an unjustified assault because of his genuine, albeit mistaken, belief that the officer was not a policeman was a good defence to the charge.

Decision

Hodgson J held:

> "…I would answer the questions we are asked as follows. (1) A constable who reasonably believes that a breach of the peace is about to take place is entitled to restrain a person without arrest if such is necessary to prevent a breach of the peace. In answering that question I have intentionally used the word 'restrain' rather than 'detain'. In the circumstances of this case the two words mean the same. I have used 'restrain' to make it clear that I look on the restraint as being a step which the officer was entitled to take to prevent a breach of the peace

and not as a detention primarily aimed at depriving a man of his liberty. (2) A person being restrained in the circumstances found by the magistrates to exist who does not accept that the person restraining him is a constable may be convicted of assault on a constable in the execution of his duty if he uses no more force than is reasonably necessary to protect himself from what he mistakenly and without reasonable grounds believes to be an unjustified assault and false imprisonment."

Appeal dismissed

Principle

A constable or an ordinary citizen has a power of arrest without a warrant where there is a reasonable apprehension of an imminent breach of the peace even though the person being arrested has not at that stage committed any breach.

Court of Appeal, Criminal Division

R v Howell

[1982] QB 416

Facts

The appellant, together with others, had been making a disturbance on the street after a party. After complaints made by neighbours, the police arrived and told the appellant and the others to leave or be arrested for breach of the peace. The appellant swore several times at two of the policemen who again warned him that he would be arrested for a breach of the peace if he did not leave.

The appellant continued to swear when one of the police constables took hold of the appellant, but before he could explain why he was arresting the appellant, the appellant struck him in the face and together with the others set on the two policemen. The appellant was convicted of an assault occasioning actual bodily harm on the police constable. He appealed against conviction on the grounds, *inter alia*, that his arrest was unlawful because no breach of the peace had been proved against him, and accordingly, he had been acting lawfully in escaping from a wrongful arrest in that he had used no more force than had been necessary.

Decision

Watkins LJ affirmed the power of arrest for a breach of the peace in certain instances, namely where:

(a) a breach of the peace was committed in the presence of the person making the arrest

(b) the arrestor reasonably believed that such a breach would be committed in the immediate future by the person arrested even though at the time of the arrest he had not committed any breach; or

(c) a breach had been committed and it was reasonably believed that a renewal of it was threatened.

Watkins LJ held:

> "…In those instances of the exercise of this power which depend on the basis of a belief that a breach of the peace is imminent, it must, we think we should emphasise, be established not only that it was an honest, albeit possibly mistaken, belief but that it was a belief which was founded on reasonable grounds."

Watkins LJ further held:

> "… we cannot accept that there can be a breach of the peace unless there has been an act done or threatened to be done

which either actually harms a person, or in his presence his property, or is likely to cause such harm, or which puts someone in fear of such harm being done. There is nothing more likely to arouse resentment and anger in him, and a desire to take instant revenge, than attacks or threatened attacks on a person's body or property."

Appeal dismissed

STATUTORY POWERS OF ARREST

Statutory powers may also allow arrest without a warrant for example a police officer has the power of arrest where a person is "found committing" an offence or where a police officer or a citizen has a reasonable suspicion that an indictable or arrestable offence has been committed. Property owners or their agents may also arrest a person where that person is "found committing" an offence against their property.

Principle

A police officer may arrest a person without warrant where that person was "found committing" an offence. In order to validly exercise the power of arrest the person must be arrested while actually committing the offence or arrested in "fresh pursuit."

Court of Appeal of Trinidad and Tobago

Bolai v St Louis

(1963) 6 WIR 453

Facts

The appellant was one of a number of persons seen coming from the direction of a ring where illegal cock-fighting had been going on. He subsequently got into a car. When challenged by the respondent, he explained that he was the driver of that car that he knew nothing about any cock-fighting and that he had taken no part in the game. But later, while he was still in the car, Cpl Franklyn came up with one Bachan whom he had captured and who was in his custody.

Bachan there and then stated he was its driver and that he had used it to carry some men, including the appellant, to the cock-fight. None of the police party could say that he actually saw the appellant at the cock-fighting ring at any time that afternoon. At most, he was seen by the respondent coming from that direction.

Decision

Wooding CJ in holding that the appellant was not found committing the offence for which he was arrested nor was he taken in fresh pursuit, stated that the facts revealed that none of the police party could say that he actually saw the appellant at the scene of the offence at any time that day. Taken at its highest all the prosecution could establish from the evidence was that the respondent was seen coming from the direction of the Gayel. The appellant was actually arrested while he was in a car, In these circumstances, the arrest could not have been justified on the basis that the appellant had been "found committing" an offence.

ARREST WITHOUT WARRANT

Arrest without warrant is justified upon reasonable suspicion that a breach of the peace is imminent. Reasonable suspicion is an honestly held belief based on reasonable grounds.

Principle

A police officer may execute an arrest where there are reasonable grounds for suspicion that an arrestable offence/indictable offence has been committed. Reasonable grounds for suspicion do not need to be based on the police officer's own observations but could be based on what he had been told, or on information which had been given to him anonymously.

House of Lords

O'Hara v Chief Constable of Royal Ulster Constabulary

[1997] AC 286

Facts

The appellant was arrested by a police officer in connection with a murder under s 12(1) (b) of the Prevention of Terrorism (Temporary Provisions) Act 1984 on suspicion of being a terrorist.

The appellant was eventually released two weeks later without being charged with any offence and he subsequently brought an action for damages against the chief constable for, *inter alia*, wrongful arrest.

At the trial, the officer gave evidence that prior to going to the appellant's house he had attended a briefing given by his superior officer at which he was told that the appellant had been involved in the murder and was told to arrest him. The judge accepted that the officer had suspected the appellant of having been concerned in terrorist acts.

The appellant appealed to the House of Lords, contending that section 12(1) (b) of the 1984 Act required that the reasonable grounds on which the arresting officer based his suspicion should exist in fact and that the objective test required proof of something more than just what was in the officer's mind. The chief constable contended that the order to arrest the appellant given to the officer by his superior officer was by itself sufficient to afford him a reasonable suspicion.

Decision

Lord Hope of Craighead emphasised that the arresting officer in this case had based his suspicion on a briefing delivered by his superior officer. It was not as though he been simply instructed to arrest the plaintiff, nor was it that he had been merely told that the plaintiff had been involved in the commission of criminal acts of terrorism.

Lord Hope of Craighead held:

> "My Lords, the test which s 12(1) of the 1984 Act has laid down is a simple but practical one. It relates entirely to what is in the mind of the arresting officer when the power is exercised. In part it is a subjective test, because he must have formed a genuine suspicion in his own mind that the person has been concerned in acts of terrorism. In part also it is an objective one, because there must also be reasonable grounds for the suspicion which he has formed. But the application of the objective test does not require the court to look beyond what was in the mind of the arresting officer. It is the grounds which were in his mind at the time which must be found to be reasonable grounds for the suspicion which he has formed. All that the objective test requires is that these grounds be examined objectively and that they be judged at the time when the power was exercised."

Lord Hope of Craighead further held:

> "…The question is whether a reasonable man would be of that opinion, having regard to the information which was in the

mind of the arresting officer. The information acted on by the arresting officer need not be based on his own observations, as he is entitled to form a suspicion based on what he has been told. His reasonable suspicion may be based on information which has been given to him anonymously or it may be based on information, perhaps in the course of an emergency, which turns out later to be wrong."

Appeal dismissed

LAWFUL ARREST

Principle

An arrest may be accomplished through the use of words only. This is known as a constructive arrest. The words used must be reasonably clear and must convey to the arrestee that his freedom of movement has been curtailed.

Divisional Court

Alderson v. Booth

[1969] 2 Q.B. 216

Facts

On the hearing of an information against the defendant for an offence contrary to section 1 (1) of the Road Safety Act, 1967 a question arose whether the defendant had been lawfully arrested. The police constable said to the defendant, "I shall have to ask you to come to the police station for further tests," and he voluntarily accompanied the constable to the station.

Decision

Lord Parker C.J. stated that in order to prove the offence charged it was necessary to prove that a specimen of blood had been taken following lawful arrest.

Lord Parker C.J. held:

> "Looked at in that way, I for my part have little doubt that, just looking at the words used here, 'I shall have to ask you to come to the police station for further tests,' they were in their context words of command which one would think would bring home to a defendant that he was under compulsion.

> "...I would only say this: that if what I have said is correct in law, it is advisable that police officers should use some very clear words to bring home to a person that he is under compulsion. It certainly must not be left in the state that a defendant can go into the witness-box and merely say, 'I did not think I was under compulsion.' If difficulties for the future are to be avoided, it seems to me that by far and away the simplest thing is for a police officer to say 'I arrest you'."

Appeal dismissed

SEARCH OF THE PERSON FOLLOWING LAWFUL ARREST

Principle

At common law a person who is lawfully arrested may be searched. Any property so taken might be retained by the police until the conclusion of proceedings under any such charge.

King's Bench Division

Elias and others v. Pasmore and others

[1934] 2 K.B. 164

Facts

In executing an arrest warrant the defendants P and K, two police inspectors, entered premises. In addition to arresting the suspect, they also seized a number of documents and removed them to the police station. The issue was whether the search and seizure of the documents was lawful.

Decision

Horridge J cited common law authorities in support of the proposition that the police had the right to search a person upon his arrest, and furthermore, that the police were entitled, upon a lawful arrest by them of a person, to take and detain property found in his possession which would form material evidence in the arrestee's prosecution for that crime, or any criminal charge.

Horridge J held:

> "As to the fourth proposition, that the police are entitled to retain property the taking of which is excused until the conclusion of any charge on which the articles are material, Wright J. says in the case of Reg. v. Lushington. Ex parte Otto (1): *'In this country I take it that it is undoubted law that it is within the power of, and is the duty of, constables to retain for use in Court things which may be evidences of crime, and which have come into the possession of the constables without wrong on their part. I think it is also undoubted law that when articles have once been produced in Court by witnesses it is right and necessary for the Court, or the constable in whose charge they are placed (as is generally the case), to preserve*

> *and retain them, so that they may be always available for the purposes of justice until the trial is concluded.'"*

RIGHTS UPON ARREST

A person who has been arrested has certain rights including the right to an attorney-at-law and the right to be informed of the reasons for his arrest.

Principle

If a policeman arrests someone without warrant on reasonable suspicion of committing a felony, or another crime of a sort which does not require a warrant, he must, in ordinary circumstances, inform the person arrested of the true ground of arrest.

House of Lords

Christie and Another v Leachinsky

[1947] UKHL 2

Facts

The police arrested the defendant without warrant but failed to inform him of the nature of the charge. The issue arose whether a police officer who entertains a reasonable suspicion of the commission of an offence was nevertheless under a duty to inform the suspect of the nature of the charge.

Decision

Viscount Simon stated the following propositions:

1. If a police officer (or private citizen) arrests without warrant on reasonable suspicion of a crime of a type which does not require a warrant, he must ordinarily inform the arrestee of the reasons for his arrest. This is because the arrestee is entitled to know these reasons.

2. If the citizen who is arrested in circumstances outlined in (1) above is not so informed, the police officer will normally be liable for false imprisonment.

3. The requirement that the person arrested should be informed of the reasons for his arrest is abrogated if the circumstances are such that he must know the general nature of the alleged offence for which he is arrested.

4. In informing the arrestee of the reasons, technical or precise language need not be used.

5. The arrestee who is responsible for a situation which makes it practically impossible for the arresting police officer to inform him of the reasons, e.g. by immediate counter-attack or by running away cannot thereafter complain that he was not so informed.

Viscount Simon held:

> "No one, I think, would approve a situation in which, when the person arrested asked for the reason, the policeman replied: 'That has nothing to do with you. Come along with me.' Such a situation may be tolerated under other systems of law, as, for instance, in the time of *lettres de cachet* in the eighteenth century in France, or in more recent days when the Gestapo swept people off to confinement under an overriding authority which the executive in this country happily does not in ordinary times possess. This would be quite contrary to our conceptions of individual liberty."

Principle

An arrested person has the right to consult a lawyer of his choice at the earliest opportunity.

Judicial Committee of the Privy Council

Thornhill v Attorney-General

[1979] UKPC 43

Facts

"T" was arrested by the police. He was detained from 5.30 pm on 17 October until 12.45 p.m. on 20 October 1973 before he was given his first effective opportunity to communicate with his lawyer, despite requests from his lawyer for access to him. By the time that "T" was allowed to speak with his lawyer he had been charged with eighteen offences. "T" subsequently applied for redress under section 6 of the Constitution of Trinidad and Tobago for breach of his right under section 2(c)(ii) of the Constitution to retain and instruct without delay a legal adviser and to communicate with him.

Decision

Lord Diplock approved of Georges J's analysis in the High Court of sections 1, 2 and 3 of the Constitution. Georges J had held that these sections proceed on the presumption that the human rights and fundamental freedoms referred to in sections 1 and 2 were already enjoyed by the people of Trinidad and Tobago under the law in force at the commencement of the 1962 Constitution.

Lord Diplock also cited the decision of the Privy Council in Ramesh Lawrence Maharaj v Attorney-General (No 2) which held that these said sections guaranteed protection against contraventions of the stated rights and freedoms by the State or other public authority endowed by law with coercive powers.

Lord Diplock held:

> "But section 2 also goes on to give, as particular examples of treatment of an individual by the executive or the judiciary which would have the effect of infringing those rights, the various kinds of conduct described in paragraphs (a) to (h) of that section. These paragraphs spell out in greater detail (although not necessarily exhaustively) what is included in the expression 'due process of law' to which Thornhill was entitled under section 1(a) as a condition of his continued detention and 'the protection of the law' to which he was entitled under section 1(b)."

Lord Diplock further stated:

> "Moreover, even if the treatment complained of by Thornhill had not been specifically described in section 2, the fact that section 1 uses terms of great breadth and generality to describe those rights and freedoms then existing for which (in conjunction with section 6) it provides legal protection in the future, is no ground for cutting down the amplitude of any of the descriptions of those rights and freedoms contained in section 1(*a*) to (*k*) by restricting them to rights for contravention of which the victim would before the commencement of the Constitution have had some legal remedy either in public law or private law which he could enforce in a court of justice."

His lordship concluded that an arrested person while in police custody enjoyed the right to communicate with his lawyer for the purpose of instructing him and obtaining his advice. This right was a matter of settled practice and was reflected in Appendix A to the Judges' Rules published in England in 1964 and adopted in identical terms by the judges of Trinidad and Tobago in 1965. It followed that Thornhill's constitutional rights had been contravened and he was entitled to a declaration to that effect.

Appeal allowed.

Principle

Where a person who has been arrested or detained has the legal right to communicate with a legal adviser, he should be informed of that right as soon as possible after his arrest, and in any event before any interrogation in custody takes place.

Judicial Committee of the Privy Council

Attorney General of Trinidad and Tobago and another v Whiteman

[1991] UKPC 16

Facts

The respondent was arrested and detained for a period in a police cell. He claimed that at no time during his detention was he informed of his right to communicate with a lawyer. He filed an originating motion under s 14 of the Constitution of Trinidad and Tobago claiming redress for alleged contraventions in relation to him of certain provisions of the Constitution.

Decision

Lord Keith of Kinkel held:

> "The language of a Constitution falls to be construed, not in a narrow and legalistic way, but broadly and purposively, so as to give effect to its spirit, and this is particularly true of

those provisions which are concerned with the protection of human rights. In this case the right conferred by s 5(2)(*c*)(ii) upon a person who has been arrested and detained, namely the right to communicate with a legal adviser, is capable in some situations of being of little value if the person is not informed of the right.

Many persons might be quite ignorant that they had this constitutional right or, if they did know, might in the circumstances of their arrest be too confused to bring it to mind. Section 5(2)(*h*) is properly to be regarded as intended to deal with that kind of situation as well as other kinds of situation where some different constitutional rights might otherwise be at risk of not being given effect and protection."

Lord Keith concluded that persons who have been arrested or detained have a constitutional right to be informed of their right to communicate with a legal adviser. He stated that this conclusion was based on both upon a proper construction of s 5(2) (*h*) of the Constitution of 1976 as well as on the basis of a settled practice existing when that Constitution was introduced. Lord Keith added that it was incumbent upon police officers to see that the arrested person was informed of his right in such a way that he understood it since he could be illiterate, deaf or unfamiliar with the language. He stressed that the mere exhibition of notices in the police station was insufficient in itself to convey the necessary right to communicate with a legal adviser to an arrestee.

Appeal dismissed.

Principle

A person arrested and detained has a constitutional right to retain, advise and consult an attorney-at-law whether or not the arrest

was for non-payment of a fine or in the ordinary course of police investigations.

Judicial Committee of the Privy Council

Ramsarran v Attorney-General

[2005] UKPC 8

Facts

The appellant was arrested by police officers for non-payment of a fine, which had in fact been paid some eighteen months before. Although he repeatedly protested that the fine had been paid, he was detained in custody for three days before a check on the records was carried out which verified his claim. In the proceedings which he subsequently brought, the court made a declaration that he had been wrongfully deprived of his liberty, contrary to the provisions of the Constitution of Trinidad and Tobago, and awarded him damages, to be assessed by a master.

The judge held, however, that he was not entitled to the other declarations which he sought: that there had been a breach of his right to retain and instruct a legal adviser on his arrest and to be informed of his right to do so. The Court of Appeal dismissed his appeal against this ruling and the appellant appealed to the Privy Council.

Decision

Lord Carswell affirmed that a person arrested on suspicion of having committed a criminal offence had a constitutional right to retain and instruct a legal adviser and to hold communication with him. This followed both from a proper construction of s 5(2) (c) of the constitution as well as on the basis of settled practice embodied in the Judges' Rules. He further affirmed the proposition that an arrested person also has the right to be informed of the existence of his right to legal advice.

Lord Carswell held:

> "In their lordships' view, the fundamental reason why s 5(2)(c) covers cases of non-payment of fines is that it is necessary to ensure that persons incorrectly arrested or detained for reasons other than suspicion of having committed a criminal offence have an effective and practical means of securing their release as soon as possible. That may be illustrated by the case before the Board. If the appellant had been informed of his right to legal advice and had been given the necessary facility to contact a lawyer, the lawyer could have lent his weight to a demand that the records be checked forthwith for payment of the fine, and could have made a speedy *habeas corpus* application if this did not secure the appellant's early release."

Advice that appeal be allowed

CHAPTER THREE

POLICE POWERS OF ENTRY FOR THE PURPOSE OF SEARCH AND SEIZURE

There is no general common law right to anyone to enter private premises without consent of the occupier. The Constitutions of all Commonwealth Caribbean territories also prohibit entry and search of private premises without the occupier's consent.

Entry of private premises may be justified where there is a need to:

1. Search for and seize evidence; and

2. Arrest a person

ISSUE OF A SEARCH WARRANT

At common law a search warrant is needed to search private premises. A magistrate or justice of the peace/clerk of the peace may issue a search warrant.

Principle

A search warrant may be addressed to a named constable or any constable.

Court of Appeal of Jamaica

R v Chin-Loy

Decision of the Court of Appeal of Jamaica, 31st January 1975

Facts

Section 61 of the Spirit Licence Law (Jamaica) authorises the issue, upon information given on oath to a Justice that there is cause for suspecting that alcoholic liquor is kept for sale on unlicensed premises, of a warrant directed to *any constable* to enter and search such premises.

Inspector S procured the issue of a warrant, directed to "All members ... of the Jamaica Constabulary Force, of Cross Roads in the parish of Saint Andrew", to search the appellant's premises.Under the Spirit Licence Law it was contended, *inter alia*, that the warrant was bad in law in that it was not directed to a named person, and that the apprehension of the appellant was unlawful with the consequence that the information laid against him was also bad in law.

Decision

Luckhoo P AG analysed s 61 (2) of the Spirit Licence Law, Cap 364 and held that the section authorised any constable to whom the warrant was directed by day or by night to enter the premises named in the information on oath, to take possession of such liquor and to apprehend the person in whose premises the liquor is found as well as every other person found in such premises who appears to have been employed in or assisting in the retailing of alcoholic liquor.

Luckhoo P AG held:

> "The warrant was directed to 'all members of the Jamaica Constabulary Force of Cross Roads in the parish of St Andrew'. In our view the words 'directed to ... any constable to enter and search' are to be given a wider meaning than the words 'any constable named' and would bear the wider meaning such as 'designated', 'specified', or 'identified' where the

search warrant was directed to 'any Lawful Constable of the parish of Kingston'.

Appeal dismissed.

Principle

In order for a search warrant to be issued the police officer must satisfy the magistrate or justice that there are reasonable grounds to suspect that the circumstances which justify the issuance of the warrant exist.

Judicial Committee of the Privy Council

Attorney General v Danhai Williams and Others

[1997] UKPC 22

Facts

Items were seized under the authority of a search warrant to search premises issued by a Justice of the Peace under section 203 of the Customs Act which stated:-

> "If any officer shall have reasonable cause to suspect that any uncustomed or prohibited goods…are harboured, kept or concealed in any house or other place in the Island… it shall be lawful for such Resident Magistrate or Justice by special warrant under his hand to authorise such officer to enter and search such house or other place, by day or by night, and to seize and carry away any such uncustomed or prohibited goods."

The redress sought by the motion was a declaration that the warrants were invalid, that the searches were unlawful and unconstitutional and that the seizure of the documents, files and other property was illegal or made without due process or an abuse of process.

Decision

Lord Hoffmann explained that the requirement that a warrant be issued by a Justice of the Peace allowed the independent scrutiny of the judiciary to protect the citizen against the excesses which would inevitably flow from allowing an executive officer to decide for himself whether the necessary conditions for entry into private premises were met. This scrutiny was of high constitutional importance.

His lordship went on to outline a Justice's legal obligation in issuing the search warrant. He held:

> "It must appear to him from information on oath that the officer has reasonable cause to suspect one or more of the matters there specified. It is not sufficient that the Justice is satisfied by the officer's oath that he suspects; it must appear to the Justice that his cause for suspicion is reasonable. The test is an objective one."

Lord Hoffman further stated:

> "Their Lordships do not underestimate the difficulty and delicacy of the task which is put upon Justices and other judicial officers to whom application is made for search warrants. The applicant is generally a police or other law enforcement officer who knows far more than the Justice about the investigation. The application is made *ex parte*; there is naturally a predisposition upon the part of the Justice to be helpful to the officer who is present and assures him that a search is necessary.

"...Nevertheless, if the constitutional safeguards are to have any meaning, it is essential for the Justice conscientiously to ask himself whether on the information given to him upon oath (in the case of section 203, either orally or in writing) he is satisfied that the officer's suspicion is based upon reasonable cause."

SEIZURE OF GOODS FOLLOWING A LAWFUL SEARCH

Principle

In lawfully searching premises, the police may seize goods which they were originally in search of or any other goods pertinent to another possible crime.

Court of Appeal of Trinidad and Tobago

Chevalier v Attorney-General and Another

Facts

The second respondent searched the appellant's premises under a search warrant for US dollars. A quantity of Venezuelan bolivars was seized as well as US dollars. It was submitted that the entry by the police into the home and the seizure by the second respondent of the foreign currency were effected without a search warrant or other order of the court.

Decision

Bernard JA cited a number of English authorities including Chic Fashion (West Wales) Ltd v Jones, King v R and Ghani v Jones in support of the proposition that when police officers enter into private premises with a search warrant they may lawfully seize any goods that they reasonably believe to be material evidence in relation to the crime for which they enter and also any other goods that show the owner of the premises to be implicated in some other crime, provided they act reasonably and detain the goods no longer than is necessary.

His lordship concluded that on the facts of the instant case, the police were entitled to seize the bolivars, even though they were not specified in the warrant, and to prefer charges against the appellant in relation to the said Bolivars, notwithstanding that they were not specified in the search warrant.

Appeal allowed.

RETENTION OF SEIZED GOODS

Seized goods may be retained by the police as evidence as long as necessary to prosecute the offence or some other offence.

Principle

Should the police wish to continue to detain lawfully seized property they must be able to justify their retention of it upon some ground which is clearly ascertainable.

Supreme Court of Trinidad and Tobago

Ali v The Attorney General of Trinidad and Tobago

Claim No. CV 2012-02695

Facts

The Claimant was questioned by the police in relation to several vehicles on his premises. The police took possession of one of his vehicles TBP2969 and he was charged with the offence of unlawful possession of same. The matter was subsequently dismissed in the Magistrate's Court but the police refused to return the said vehicle.

Decision

Rajkumar J held that the police were entitled, in the light of their suspicion that the chassis number had been tampered with, and that it contained personal documentation of persons other than the claimant, to seize the claimant's vehicle as evidence. The judge also stated that although the said vehicle was justifiably detained by the police in the absence of evidence of ownership by the Claimant he questioned the lengthy period of detention, noting that "after more than 5 years those alleged further investigations do not appear to have been a priority."

Rajkumar J held:

> "…the issues of right to possession and the relative strength of titles are equally applicable to the instant situation. Obviously, if in fact the vehicle were a stolen one, the plaintiff had no right to possession of it. But if after more than 5 years the police have not established that it is a stolen vehicle, then in the absence of evidence that there is a person with a right to it greater than that of the claimant, it must be returned to him. An allegation that the chassis appears to have been tampered with is not the same as establishing as a fact that it is a stolen vehicle."

The learned judge stated that the police had ample time (over 5 years) to establish that the vehicle was unlawfully obtained, or to ascertain "the true owner" and they had failed in this quest. It followed that the claimant's right to possession – his 'possessory title' had not been rebutted by evidence of superior title by anyone else. Furthermore the police could not now claim to retain the vehicle on the 'uncertain future contingency' that they could yet establish a superior title.

His lordship held:

> "Save for the suggestion that the chassis number had been tampered with, there was no properly concluded investigation to confirm that the instant vehicle had actually been stolen; far less was an alternative owner with superior legal title to the claimant's possessory title identified."

The court ordered the return of the seized vehicle within 7 days.

Court of Appeal

Ghani and others v. Jones

[1969] 3 WLR 1158

Facts

Police officers inquiring into a woman's disappearance searched, without a warrant, the house of her father-in-law. At their request he handed to them documents including the passports of himself, his wife and daughter, the plaintiffs living in the house. The police subsequently refused to return the documents. An action was brought for *inter alia* the delivery up of the passports and documents, and an injunction restraining their detention. The police claimed to have evidence to support their belief that the woman had been murdered.

They said that in the event of charges being preferred some of the documents seized would be of evidential value and others of potential evidential value. It was also claimed that the plaintiffs could help the police inquiries and that if they left the United Kingdom they might not return. No one had been arrested or charged with the murder.

Decision

Denning M.R. noted the state's case as being one where police officers, in investigating a murder, seized property without a warrant but did not make an arrest. The police subsequently retained the said property without the consent of the party from whom it was seized on the grounds that the property was of evidential value on a prosecution for murder.

His lordship held that the court had to consider the freedom of the individual and his right to privacy inasmuch as the individual's possessions were not to be seized except for the most compelling reasons. On the other hand, the court also had to consider society's interest in suppressing crime.

His lordship concluded that the police were not entitled to retain the seized items since although they had reasonable grounds for believing that a person had been murdered, they had failed to show reasonable grounds for believing that the seized passports and letters were material evidence to prove the plaintiff's involvement in the murder. The police were merely entitled to use photographs of the seized items as part of their case.

Principle

In order to establish the legality of the continued retention of goods seized by the police, it has to be shown that same was necessary to complete any investigations.

Judicial Committee of the Privy Council

Jaroo v Attorney General

[2002] UKPC 5

Facts

A motor car which the appellant had recently purchased in good faith was suspected by the licensing authorities of being a stolen vehicle. On their instructions he took the motor car to the police so that they could examine it and conduct such inquiries into its theft as they thought appropriate. After a suitable interval, having heard nothing from them, he asked the police to return the vehicle. Repeated requests to this effect met with no reply. Fourteen years later, the matter was heard by the Judicial Committee of the Privy Council.

Decision

Lord Hope of Craighead declared that while the police had extensive power to seize and detain property, the constitutional guarantee of due process meant that these powers had to be exercised lawfully and not arbitrarily.

Lord Hope held:

> "Their lordships consider that these observations explain what is meant, in the circumstances of this case, by the constitutional guarantee of due process. It means that the following requisites had to be satisfied by the police in order to justify their continued detention of the motor car. First, they must have had reasonable grounds when they insisted on detaining it for believing that it was a stolen vehicle. Second, they had to be in a position to show that its continued detention was reasonably necessary to complete their investigations or to preserve it for evidence."

His lordship cited dicta from Malone v Metropolitan Police Commissioner to the effect that when police wish to continue to detain lawfully seized property they must be able to justify their retention of it upon some clearly ascertainable ground. Lord Hope concluded however, that it had been an abuse of the court's process in this matter for the appellant to have proceeded with the case by way of a constitutional motion and therefore the appellant's claim for a declaration that his constitutional rights had been infringed had to be dismissed.

Lord Hope held:

> "But the situation which this case has revealed is far from satisfactory. There are two aspects of it which suggest that the appellant has not been dealt with fairly by the police. In the first place, they omitted to give him any explanation as to the reasons why they were continuing to detain the vehicle which he had handed over to them voluntarily. It was not until 27 June 1988, five weeks after the constitutional motion had been filed, that an explanation for its continued detention was given by Sgt Flemming in his affidavit. Secondly, fourteen years have now gone by since the appellant handed the vehicle over to them. It has still not been returned to him, nor has he or anyone else been charged with any offence in relation to it. Mr Dingemans was unable to say where the vehicle is now, if indeed it still exists. ..."

> "Their lordships consider that in these circumstances the conduct of the respondent cannot escape criticism. It is not disputed that the appellant was acting in good faith when he acquired the vehicle. He did all that was asked of him both by the police and by the licensing authorities. He had good reason to complain about the way in which the case was being dealt with by the police. The continued detention of the vehicle has not been explained, and after such a long period it is now inexplicable. Their lordships consider that it would be unfair for the appellant to have to bear the costs of the proceedings in these circumstances.

"The orders which were made against him for costs in the High Court and in the Court of Appeal will be set aside. There will be no order as to costs in the courts below and in proceedings before their lordships' Board."

Advice that appeal be dismissed.

SEIZURE OF GOODS FOLLOWING AN ILLEGAL SEARCH

Where goods are seized after an illegal search was conducted, they may still be admissible in evidence.

Principle

The court has a discretion to admit illegally obtained evidence.

Judicial Committee of the Privy Council

King v The Queen

[1969] 1 A.C. 304

Facts

By the Dangerous Drugs Law (Jamaica), section 21, any constable "named" in a warrant is authorised to enter, if need be by force, the premises named in the warrant and to search the premises and any persons found therein. The appellant was searched by a police officer acting under a search warrant obtained under section 21 of the Dangerous Drugs Law and ganja was found on him. The warrant was addressed to "Any lawful constable" and specifically named only one person "Joyce Cohen." The appellant was not taken before a justice to be searched in his presence.

Decision

Lord Hodson stated that the case before the court was that the appellant was searched by a police officer in pursuance of a search warrant, and ganja was found on him. The appellant, however, claimed that ganja was planted on him by the police officer who searched him.

The learned judge held that the warrant did not authorise search of any person, and in these circumstances the search without express authorization was not on the face of it justified by the warrant. Furthermore the warrant was defective since it was not issued in accordance with the terms of the relevant statutory provision which required that the warrant be executed by a named constable.

His lordship therefore stated that there was no legal justification for the search. This notwithstanding, the court could still exercise its discretion to decide whether the evidence though admissible, should be excluded in fairness to the accused. In fact the instant case was not one in which the evidence had been obtained by such objectionable conduct on the Crown's part that the court would exclude the evidence.

Appeal dismissed.

CHAPTER FOUR

ROLE AND FUNCTION OF THE DPP

The Director of Public Prosecutions (the DPP) performs a variety of functions within the criminal justice system. In Commonwealth Caribbean territories, the DPP is vested with constitutional powers and in most cases he exercises these powers free from external control. The DPP's most crucial functions include the institution and discontinuance of all criminal proceedings and the preferring of the indictment.

DPP'S POWER TO INSTITUTE OR DISCONTINUE CRIMINAL PROCEEDINGS

Principle

The DPP may request the police not to institute proceedings but he may not instruct them to do so.

Judicial Committee of the Privy Council

Benjamin v. Commissioner of Police and AG

[2014] UKPC 8

Facts

The appellant was charged with a summary offence relating to an endorsement on an application form for an Antigua and Barbuda passport. The DPP had however, previously instructed the police not to institute a criminal charge against the appellant; the police ignored the instruction and charged him. The appellant sought leave to apply for judicial review of the decision of the Commissioner of Police to charge him on the ground that he was charged by the police in defiance of a direction given by the DPP. The application for leave was dismissed and the appellant appealed the orders dismissing the application for leave to apply for judicial review. The Court of Appeal set aside the Judge's order. The Commissioner of Police appealed.

Decision

Lord Wilson in considering the issue of whether the Director of Public Prosecutions ('the Director') had a general power to prevent the police from instituting criminal proceedings stated that the relevant Constitutional provisions were central to the issue. The court dismissed the appellant's contention that section 88 of the Constitution expressly empowered the Director to instruct the police not to institute criminal proceedings.

His lordship held that the power of the Director to institute criminal proceedings conferred by subsection (1) (a) could not be construed as a power to prevent exercise of the power to do the same thing by any other person or authority. Lord Wilson also disagreed with the majority's reasoning in the Court of Appeal which held that implicit in the Director's power under section 88(1)(c) of the Constitution to discontinue proceedings was the power to prevent the police from instituting criminal proceedings.

Lord Wilson stated that while criminal proceedings could also be instituted by private persons and by authorities other than the police, for example the Inland Revenue and the Immigration Department, and, although such proceedings can be discontinued by the Director, it was not suggested that he had power to prevent private persons and those other authorities from instituting them. Logically, therefore, the suggested power to prevent could not be derived from the power to discontinue.

Lord Wilson further held:

"Is it indeed absurd for the power to discontinue not to be matched by a power to prevent? The Director exercises his power to discontinue by taking a formal, publicly visible, step in the proceedings which can (with whatever degree of difficulty)...be challenged by judicial review. An instruction by the Director to the police not to institute proceedings would also in theory be susceptible to judicial review but would often lack the public visibility which would alert potential applicants to the possibility of challenge.

"Sometimes a statute, for example section 4(1) of the Biological Weapons Act, provides that criminal proceedings cannot be instituted except with the Director's consent. In such circumstances he can indeed prevent the police from instituting proceedings by withholding consent. Although it can be said, strictly speaking, that such statutory provisions also apply to intended prosecutions otherwise than by the police, they sit uneasily with any general power of the Director to prevent the police from instituting proceedings. Nor does the machinery exist for any systematic exercise on his part of a general power to instruct the police not to institute criminal proceedings..."

"The Board's conclusion does not disable it from stressing the importance of a good, mutually respectful, working relationship between the police and the Director. Unresolved conflict between them of the sort exemplified in this appeal damages public confidence in the administration of justice. The Director can generally be expected to have a wider perception than the police of whether, for example, a proposed prosecution is in the public interest. The Director cannot instruct but he can request. The police would be wise to tread with care before deciding to reject a request by the Director not to institute proceedings."

Appeal allowed

THE DPP'S FIAT

There are certain offences for which the DPP's consent or fiat is required before the police can lay charges. These offences are specified by statute and include corruption and perjury.

Principle

No formal proof of the DPP's consent is necessary, unless objection is taken by the defence.

Court of Criminal Appeal

R v Waller

[1910] 1 K.B. 364

Facts

On the trial of a charge of being a habitual criminal, no formal proof was given of the consent of the DPP to the insertion of the charge in the indictment. An inspector of police produced a written consent purporting to be signed by the Director, but no evidence was given of the authenticity of the signature. No objection, however, was taken by the appellant at the trial to the absence of that proof. The defendant was convicted and appealed.

Decision

Lord Alverstone C.J. held that the giving of consent was a condition which had to be satisfied in fact, and unless it was in fact given, the indictment ought not to be allowed to go before the grand jury.

His lordship held:

> "But it is the duty of the clerk of assize to satisfy himself before the bill is presented to the grand jury that all the necessary steps preliminary to indictment have been taken, and, unless objection be taken by the prisoner that there was no consent in fact, it is to be presumed that the clerk of assize has discharged his duty in that respect."

Principle

Failure to obtain the DPP's consent to institute proceedings will result in any ensuing proceedings being rendered a nullity.

Court of Appeal Criminal Division

R v Angel

[1968] 2 All ER 607

Facts

The appellant pleaded guilty one count of gross indecency and two counts of buggery involving a boy of nine years of age. He appealed to the Court of Appeal on a point of law, viz, that the consent of the DPP to the prosecution had not been obtained pursuant to s 8 of the Sexual Offences Act 1967.

Section 8, so far as material, provided:

"No proceedings shall be instituted except by or with the consent of the Director of Public Prosecutions against any man for the offence of ... buggery with, or gross indecency with, another man ... where either of those men was at the time of its commission under the age of twenty-one ..."

Decision

Lord Parker CJ held that failure to obtain the consent of the Director of Public Prosecutions resulted in the entire trial, including the committal proceedings being a complete nullity. Accordingly, the conviction had to be quashed on the ground that the trial was a complete nullity.

Appeal allowed. Conviction quashed.

Principle

Failure to obtain the DPP's fiat where such is mandated by statute will result in subsequent proceedings being rendered null and void. This will not be the case where the DPP signs the indictment since consent will be implied.

Court of Appeal of Trinidad and Tobago

Jagessar and Bhola Nandlal v The State (No 1)

C.A/CRIM.44,45/88 (30th June 1989) Bernard C.J

Facts

J was indicted for corruptly receiving for himself on 22 December 1986, a Toyota 'Royal' saloon motor car (registration PAU 3465) as a gift or reward for dismissing criminal charges against N, an accused person, contrary to section 3(1) of the Prevention of Corruption Act (Ch. 11:11). N was, on the same indictment, charged with corruptly giving the motor vehicle to J on that day as a gift or reward for dismissing criminal charges preferred against him and heard and determined eventually by J, contrary to section 3(2) of that Act.

At the completion of the preliminary enquiry into the conspiracy charge against both applicants which was taken or at least determined before the bribery charges, the examining magistrate acting under the purported powers given to him in section 23(2) of the Act committed both J and N to the assizes to stand their trial for corruption.

The Indictable Offences (Preliminary Enquiry) Act. In particular sections 23 and 25 of this Act provide:

"Discharge: Committal for Trial

"23. (1) When all the witnesses on the part of the prosecutor and of the accused person, if any, have been heard, the magistrate shall, if upon the whole of the evidence, he is of opinion that no *prima facie* case of any indictable offence is made out, discharge him; and in such case any recognisance taken in respect of the charge becomes void.

"(2) If, upon the whole of the evidence, the magistrate is of opinion that a *prima facie* case for any indictable offence (whether an offence with which the accused is charged or otherwise) is made out, he shall grant his warrant for the commitment of the accused person to prison, there to be detained until brought to trial upon any indictment which may be preferred against him, or until discharged in due course of law...

"Proceedings Subsequent to Committal

"25. (1) After the preliminary enquiry has been concluded and the warrant of commitment for trial has been made out, the magistrate shall, without delay, transmit to the Director of Public Prosecutions the complaint, the depositions of the witnesses, the documentary exhibits thereto, the statement (if any) of the accused person, the warrant of commitment for trial, and the recognisances entered into. All exhibits other than documentary exhibits, shall, unless the magistrate otherwise directs, be taken charge of by the police and shall be produced by them at the trial.

"(2) Subject to this Act, the depositions and other documents received from the magistrate by the Director of Public Prosecutions shall be kept by him until the indictment (if any) to which they relate is filed, and shall then be transmitted to the Registrar of the Supreme Court, who shall keep them and produce them to the court at the trial of the accused person.

"(3) A person committed for trial may be indicted for any offence for which he was committed for trial or for any offence which, in the opinion of the Director of Public Prosecutions, is disclosed by the depositions."

The Acting DPP acting under section 25 of the Act (and under her constitutional powers) indicted both accused on the charges enumerated earlier. It was contended that the indictment was bad since the consent of the DPP to the prosecution had not been obtained in accordance with section 10 of the Prevention of Corruption Ch.11:11 Act which provided that: "a prosecution for an offence under [the] Act shall not be instituted except by or with consent of the Director of Public Prosecutions."

Decision

Bernard CJ stated that the appellant's submission was that the committal was bad since it was in breach of section 10 of the Prevention of Corruption Act. Notwithstanding section 23(2) of the Indictable Offences (Preliminary Enquiry) Act, the examining magistrate had no power whatsoever to commit either of the applicants for bribery. In acting as he did he usurped his powers. Furthermore, the course adopted both by the magistrate and the Director of Public Prosecutions was unauthorised by law. The correct procedure would have necessitated first obtaining the consent of the Director of Public Prosecutions in accordance with section 10 of the Prevention of Corruption Act.

His lordship also summarised the State's position as being that section 23 of the Indictable Offences (Preliminary Enquiry) Act fully empowered the examining magistrate to act as he did. Furthermore, section 25 empowered the Director of Public Prosecutions and section 90(3)(*a*) of the Republican Constitution also empowered her to adopt the course which she did. The Prevention of Corruption Act was designed to control and deal effectively with this mischief; but that since accusations of the sort could be made willy-nilly, no prosecution of the kind could be proceeded with by a third party without the sanction of the Director of Public Prosecutions. That was the purport and intent of the Act. On the evidence and the law there was no contravention of the spirit and intendment of section 10 of the Prevention of Corruption Act.

Bernard CJ held:

> "We do not doubt, of course, that in appropriate cases the spectre of section 10 of the Prevention of Corruption Act (Ch. 11:11) must, of necessity, loom large and that indeed, observance thereof is of prime importance and necessity;... Be that as it may, on a proper construction of the conjoint effect of section 23(2) and 25(3) of the Indictable Offences (Preliminary Enquiry) Act, this cannot be to the exclusion of or without regard, in our view, to the right of an examining magistrate, in an appropriate case, to commit for bribery

subject, of course, to the equivalent right and power of the Director of Public Prosecutions to act or not thereon; that is to say to lay the indictment for bribery or not which she, in the exercise of her undoubted powers, considers proper and appropriate.

Otherwise, in our view, sections 23(2) and 25(3) (which, incidentally, were later in time on the Statute Book than section 10 of the Prevention of Corruption Act, Ch. 11:11) would either be meaningless or, at least, have failed to achieve the desired object which Parliament undoubtedly intended by these 'reform' provisions."

Bernard CJ concluded that he agreed with the State's contentions and held that there had not been any breach of the policy or spirit of section 10.

Applications for leave to appeal refused.

THE DPP'S DECISION IS SUBJECT TO JUDICIAL REVIEW

The DPP in exercising his discretion whether to prosecute persons or not has a duty to act fairly. As such, the exercise of the DPP's discretion is subject to judicial review.

Principle

Whether judicial review of a prosecuting authority should be granted depends on the substantive issues of irrationality and/or procedural irregularity which may be proved.

Queen's Bench Division

R v General Council of the Bar, ex parte Percival

[1991] 1 QB 212

Facts

The applicant, who was the head of a set of barristers' chambers, accused another member, who was the financial and general administrator of the chambers, of mishandling chambers money and reported him to the Bar Council as being in breach of para 6 of the Code of Conduct for the Bar of England and Wales. The applicant's complaint was referred to the Professional Conduct Committee of the Bar Council, to which, pursuant to r 2 of its rules, was delegated the power "to investigate and sift complaints ... to prefer charges ... and be responsible for prosecuting any such charges" before a disciplinary tribunal.

The committee decided that the barrister should be charged with a breach of proper professional standards under para 8. The applicant, who considered that the barrister should have been charged with the more serious charge of professional misconduct under para 7, applied for judicial review of the committee's decision.

Decision

Watkins LJ held that the discretion of a prosecuting authority was reviewable. Furthermore it was not right that strictly defined limits should be set to the judicial review of a body which can broadly be described as a prosecuting authority. Instead, each case had to be considered on its facts.

Watkins LJ held:

> "The test we have had to apply in deciding whether or not the decision of the PCC is flawed is obviously not whether were we in their position we would have come to the same decision as they did....What we believe cannot be controverted is that the PCC acted within a broad discretion, which undoubtedly

they had, on correct principles and with impartiality and fairness. Even if they did in fact change their minds following the receipt of Mr Read's opinion we would not regard them in the particular circumstances as having acted unreasonably or perversely or otherwise wrongly in the exercise of their discretion in that respect..."

Application dismissed

Principle

Judicial review of a prosecutorial decision, although available in principle, is a highly exceptional remedy.

Judicial Committee of the Privy Council

Sharma v Antoine and Others

[2006] UKPC 57

Facts

The Chief Justice was granted leave to seek judicial review of the decision to prosecute him on a charge of attempting to pervert the course of public justice. The central issue before the Privy Council was whether the decision to prosecute the Chief Justice should be examined by way of judicial review or whether the criminal process should be allowed to take its course.

Decision

Lord Bingham of Cornhill and Lord Walker of Gestingthorpe acknowledged that a decision to prosecute was susceptible to judicial review, though it was a highly exceptional remedy. The court cited the case of R v DPP, ex p Kebilene where it was held that the applicant for judicial review in such cases had to establish dishonesty, mala fides or some exceptional circumstance.

The Board noted that judicial review was also granted in cases where the decision was not to prosecute. This was allowed on the basis that in such a case the aggrieved person could not raise his or her complaint at a criminal trial or on appeal, and judicial review therefore afforded the only possible remedy.

Lord Bingham of Cornhill and Lord Walker of Gestingthorpe held:

> "In Wayte v United States Powell J described the decision to prosecute as 'particularly ill-suited to judicial review'. The courts have given a number of reasons for their extreme reluctance to disturb decisions to prosecute by way of judicial review.
>
> They include:
>
> (i) 'the great width of the DPP's discretion and the polycentric character of official decision-making in such matters including policy and public interest considerations which are not susceptible of judicial review because it is within neither the constitutional function nor the practical competence of the courts to assess their merits'
>
> "(ii) 'the wide range of factors relating to available evidence, the public interest and perhaps other matters which [the prosecutor] may properly take into account'
>
> "(iii) the delay inevitably caused to the criminal trial if it proceeds
>
> "(iv) 'the desirability of all challenges taking place in the criminal trial or on appeal'

> "In addition to the safeguards afforded to the defendant in a criminal trial, the court has a well-established power to restrain proceedings which are an abuse of its process, even where such abuse does not compromise the fairness of the trial itself."

> "(v) the blurring of the executive function of the prosecutor and the judicial function of the court, and of the distinct roles of the criminal and the civil courts."

Lord Bingham of Cornhill and Lord Walker of Gestingthorpe held that on the facts of the present case there was no evidence that improper pressure was exerted on the police and therefore the Chief Justice's complaints (if any) could be fairly resolved within the criminal process. Furthermore, a full hearing of the application for judicial review, if unsuccessful, might possibly have compromised the fairness of any subsequent criminal trial.

Baroness Hale of Richmond, Lord Carswell and Lord Mance held that this was a case in which all issues should be resolved in one set of proceedings. They further stated that there were potential disadvantages for all concerned, including the public, should long and probably public judicial review proceedings followed by criminal proceedings ensue.

Baroness Hale of Richmond, Lord Carswell and Lord Mance held:

> "A criminal judge would we think be better placed to manage the different potential issues, such as whether the decision to charge was politically influenced, whether there is evidence fit to be left to the jury (both matters for him at separate stages of any trial) and, if the case gets that far, how the evidence should be left to the jury."

Principle

The court in examining the decision not to prosecute is not vested with a broad jurisdiction to exercise its own judgment and second guess the Director's decision and direct reconsideration of the decision simply because the court itself would have reached a different conclusion. The remedy is "highly exceptional."

High Court of England and Wales

R (F) v Director of Public Prosecutions

[2013] EWHC 945 (Admin)

Facts

The claimant sought judicial review of the decision of the DPP to refuse to initiate a prosecution for rape on the basis that, whilst the claimant's credibility was secure, even if she were believed the evidence would be insufficient to establish a realistic prospect of conviction for any offence.

Decision

Lord Judge CJ held that the court examining the decision not to prosecute was not vested with a broad jurisdiction to exercise its own judgment, and second guess the Director's decision, simply because the court itself would have reached a different conclusion. The remedy of judicial review was therefore highly exceptional.

Lord Judge CJ held:

> "Without suggesting a comprehensive list, the decision not to prosecute may be shown to follow a perverse decision to disregard compelling evidence or inexplicably to ignore the relevant prosecutorial policy or policies, or a combination of

both. It may, although as far as we know there have never been any such examples, follow some impropriety or abuse of power by those entrusted by the Director with the relevant responsibility. It may also be based on an error of law. If so it would be open to this court to require the decision to be reconsidered and the law correctly applied."

Claim allowed

THE DPP'S POWER TO DISCONTINUE CRIMINAL PROCEEDINGS

The DPP has the power to discontinue criminal proceedings either through the issuance of a Nolle prosequi (common law) or discontinuance (constitutional).

Principle

A letter signed by the DPP is sufficient to discontinue criminal proceedings.

Court of Appeal of Guyana

Tappin v Lucas

Decision of the Court of Appeal of Guyana, 2nd May 1973

Facts

Upon a matter coming before a magistrate, the latter read a letter in open court purporting to have been signed by the DPP in which the latter stated that he had discontinued the proceedings launched by the appellant by virtue of art 47 (1) (c) of the Constitution of Guyana. Thereupon the magistrate made an order for the discontinuance of the criminal proceedings and discharged the respondent. The appellant appealed against the order of the magistrate.

Decision

Bollers CA held:

> "When the Director exercises his powers under art 47 (2) (a), (b) or (c), he is required under (3) to do so 'in person or through other persons acting under and in accordance with his general or special instructions'. This language does not specify that he is required to appear in person in court, nor is there any hint that any such persons" authorised by him to act on his behalf are to appear in person in court."

His lordship noted that the appellant had not questioned the bona fides of the authority of the DPP's signed letter and held that under art 47 of the Constitution the Director of Public Prosecutions could exercise his powers under the Constitution not only by a physical appearance in court but by letter.

Bollers CA held:

> "In the light of the historical background adverted to above, the interpretation of the wording of art 47 of the 1966 Constitution reached ought to leave little room for doubt, and that is, that the Director of Public Prosecutions exercises his powers in person under the article when he writes a letter to the magistrate signifying his decision that criminal proceedings against an accused person be discontinued."

Appeal dismissed

THE DPP'S POWERS WHERE THE ACCUSED HAS BEEN DISCHARGED FOLLOWING COMMITTAL PROCEEDINGS

Statute in some territories provides that should the magistrate discharge the accused following committal proceedings, the DPP may, following his consideration of the evidence led at the committal proceedings, seek a judge's warrant to arrest the accused and commit him for trial.

Principle

A person discharged by a magistrate at the conclusion of a preliminary enquiry into an indictable offence is not entitled by reason of the audi alteram partem rule to be heard before a judge's warrant is issued.

Court of Appeal of Trinidad and Tobago

Attorney-General and Another v Aleem Mohammed

(1985) 36 WIR 359

Facts

The respondent was charged with murder. After a preliminary enquiry he was discharged by the magistrate. He later filed an originating motion in which he sought a declaration that he was entitled to be heard in any application by the State to obtain a warrant from a judge for his arrest and committal for trial of the said murder. The trial judge made a declaratory order in the terms requested. The AttorneyGeneral and the DPP appealed against that order.

Section 23(5) and (6) of the Indictable Offences (Preliminary Enquiry) Act ("the Act") states:

"(5) In every case in which a magistrate discharges an accused person on a preliminary enquiry, he shall, if required to do so by the Director of Public Prosecutions, transmit forthwith to him the record of the proceedings, and if the Director of Public Prosecutions, on perusing and considering the evidence, is of opinion that the accused ought not to have been discharged, he may apply to a judge of the High Court for a warrant for the arrest and committal for trial of the accused person.

"(6) If the judge is of opinion that the evidence, as given before the magistrate, was sufficient to put the accused person on his trial, he may issue a warrant for the arrest of the accused person and for his committal to prison for trial, there to be kept until discharged in due course of law or admitted to bail, and every person so proceeded against shall be further prosecuted in the like manner as if he had been committed for trial by the magistrate by whom he was discharged."

Decision

Kelsick CJ stated that the presumption that the *audi alteram partem* rule applies to judicial acts or proceedings may be rebutted and excluded by an express enactment or where the intention of Parliament to that effect is made clear by implication that the enforcement powers may be exercised *ex parte*. Furthermore a *prima facie* right to prior notice and opportunity to be heard may be excluded by necessary implication. An application of the maxim *expressio unius, exclusio alterius* may deny a right to notice and hearing in a context where the statute or rules are silent but the maxim ought not to be applied when its application having regard to the subject matter to be applied leads to inconsistency or injustice.

His lordship concluded that from an examination of the Act and after applying the relevant principles of statutory interpretation it was apparent that the legislature by implication clearly did not intend that the accused person should be heard by the judge either before or after the issue of the warrant of arrest and committal. Accordingly the requirements of natural justice did not apply at the stage of the proceedings where the judge issued the warrant.

Appeal allowed

THE DPP'S DELAY IN FILING THE INDICTMENT

Principle

The constitutional right to be brought promptly before an appropriate judicial authority contains an obligation which arises upon initial arrest or detention and does not continue or arise anew so as to apply upon a magistrate's subsequent committal of a defendant for trial.

Judicial Committee of the Privy Council

Maraj-Naraynsingh *v* The Attorney General of Trinidad and Tobago and The Director of Public Prosecutions

[2010] UKPC 19

Facts

The appellant was arrested and detained on 30 November 2004 and was charged, together with other persons, with murder. All three accused were brought promptly before the Acting Deputy Chief Magistrate of Trinidad and Tobago who held a preliminary inquiry on various days between 3 December 2004 and 14 March 2005. On 14 March 2005 the learned Magistrate committed the appellant and R to stand trial for murder at the next sitting of the assizes.

The appellant was remanded in custody. Under the Indictable Offences (Preliminary Enquiry) Act (No 12 of 1917 as amended) it was the Chief Magistrate's duty to send the complaint, depositions, exhibits, other evidence and warrant of committal to the DPP "without delay". The DPP's South Office received this material, comprising some 358 pages, on or about 25 May, and forwarded it to the DPP on or about 6 June 2005.

The DPP was on vacation from 25 August, returning on 20 September. In an affidavit, he explained that he was, in particular in the light of the magistrate's decision and comments, anxious to review the evidence with the greatest of care, and so took a longer time than usual to make up his mind. On 21 and 22 November two different attorneys instructed by the appellant wrote to the DPP, taking issue with the alleged delay in filing an indictment and threatening proceedings.

On 24 November the DPP replied to both attorneys indicating that the indictment would be filed during the week 28 November to 2 December 2005. An indictment against the appellant and R was in fact signed on 25 November and was filed on 1 December 2005. On 30 November 2005 the Appellant applied *ex parte* for leave to apply for judicial review, seeking an order of mandamus directing the DPP to prepare and file the indictment as well as various declarations, including a declaration that her constitutional rights had been infringed by reason of delay on the part of the DPP.

Leave to apply for judicial review was granted on the same day, and on 2 December 2005 the Appellant filed a claim form. The Appellant was tried for the murder in January 2006. She was acquitted and released from custody on 26 January 2006. The Appellant filed a claim for a declaration that the Appellant's rights under s.5 (2)(c)(iii) of the Constitution (as well as ss. 4(a), (b) and 5(2)(a)) had been infringed and a claim for damages, including aggravated and/or exemplary damages. Section 4(a) of the Constitution recognises the right of the individual to *inter alia* "liberty, security ... and the right not to be deprived thereof except by due process of law", and s. 4(b) the right of the individual to "the protection of the law".

Section 5(2) reads:

"..... Parliament may not-

"(a) authorise or effect the arbitrary detention, imprisonment or exile of any person

"(b) ...

"(c) deprive a person who has been arrested or detained-

"(i) of the right to be informed promptly and with sufficient particularity of the reason for his arrest or detention;

"(ii) of the right to retain and instruct without delay a legal adviser of his own choice and to hold communication with him;

"(iii) of the right to be brought promptly before an appropriate judicial authority;

"(iv) of the remedy by way of *habeas corpus* for the determination of the validity of his detention and for his release if the detention is not lawful."

The claim was dismissed by the judge and the Court of Appeal and the appellant appealed to the Privy Council. She confined the appeal to the alleged breach of s.5(2)(c)(iii).

Decision

Lord Mance held that para (iii) of s.5 (2) (c) (the right to be brought promptly before an appropriate judicial authority) related on its face to a single time. It would make no sense to regard it as applying continuously during any period when a person was under arrest or in detention but would apply upon initial arrest or detention.

Lord Mance further held:

> "Para (iii) is not the only provision in s. 5(2)(c) to focus on the time of initial arrest or detention. In para (i), the right to be informed promptly and with sufficient particularity of the reason for arrest or detention, does so exclusively. In para (ii), the right 'to retain and instruct without delay' a legal adviser of his own choice arises upon and from the moment of initial arrest or detention, although the right 'to hold communication with him' refers to a period thereafter. In para (iv) the right to the remedy of *habeas corpus* for the determination of the validity of his detention and for his release if the detention is not lawful arises upon and from the initial arrest or detention, although it too no doubt continues thereafter."

Lord Mance concluded that s.5(2)(c)(iii) contained an obligation which arose upon initial arrest or detention and did not continue or arise anew so as to apply upon a magistrate's subsequent committal of a defendant for trial.

Appeal dismissed

CHAPTER FIVE

BAIL IN CRIMINAL PROCEEDINGS

Bail is an integral part of the criminal justice system. It is noteworthy that it is also a constitutional right in some jurisdictions. Statute in various jurisdictions allows the grant of bail when a person has been charged as well as following conviction and appeal. Statute may also allow the police to grant bail at the police station. A Judge may grant bail following a Magistrate's refusal to grant bail, or he may vary the conditions of bail. The Magistrate has a duty to inform a defendant of his right to apply to a Judge in chambers for bail.

BAIL CRITERIA

A court has regard to various factors when contemplating the grant of bail. These include the defendant's age, employment status, antecedents and ability to provide a surety.

Principle

While the seriousness of the offence and the severity of the penalty likely to be imposed on conviction may provide grounds for refusing bail, they are not always determinative of the issue.

Judicial Committee of the Privy Council

Hurnam v The State

[2005] UKPC 49

Facts

A magistrate granted bail to the appellant after having considered the seriousness of the charges, the risk of interference with witnesses and the risk of the appellant absconding. The Director of Public Prosecutions appealed to the Supreme Court, seeking to have the magistrate's order for release set aside. The Supreme Court allowed the appeal and set aside the magistrate's order. The appellant was granted special leave to appeal to the Privy Council, which also admitted the appellant to bail on the same terms ordered by the magistrate.

Decision

Lord Bingham of Cornhill held that factors such as the seriousness of the offence and the severity of the penalty likely to be imposed on conviction were factors relevant to the issue of whether in all the circumstances, it was necessary to deprive the applicant of his liberty.

His lordship held:

> "The reasoned judgment of the magistrate cannot be faulted. He did not overlook, minimise or discount the seriousness of the offences with which the appellant was charged. But he did not, rightly, treat this as a conclusive or all but conclusive reason for refusing bail. Instead, he addressed, rightly, the wider question whether, given the seriousness of the alleged offences, it was necessary to refuse bail in order to serve one of the ends for which detention before trial is permissible.
>
> *Appeal allowed*

THE SURETY

An accused person may be granted bail on the condition that he provides a surety. The purpose of the surety is to ensure the defendant's court attendance on the specified dates. The court should explain to the surety his obligation to ensure the defendant's attendance to court; including the consequence of a failure to honour that obligation.

Principle

A judicial discretion has to be exercised in deciding whether to approve a particular person as a surety. In determining whether to approve a surety, regard must be paid to (amongst other things)

(i)   *the surety's profession, occupation, trade or business;*

(ii) *his character and his previous convictions, if any; and*

(iii) *his proximity, whether of kinship, place or residence or otherwise, to the person for whom he is to be a surety.*

High Court Trinidad and Tobago

The State v Mervyn Lezama

H.C. Cr. No B069/10

Facts

The applicant was granted bail with a surety by a High Court judge but was unable to get the necessary approval by the Registrar. He subsequently filed a fresh application to the High Court seeking to have this court approve his common law wife as his surety.

The Bail Act Chap 4:60 at s. 16 provides:

> "(1) This section applies where a person is granted bail in criminal proceedings on condition that he provides a surety for the purpose of securing his surrender to custody.
>
> "(2) In considering the suitability of a proposed surety referred to in subsection (1), the Court shall—
>
>> "(a) have regard amongst other things, to—
>>
>>> "(i) the surety's profession, occupation, trade or business;
>>>
>>> "(ii) his character and his previous convictions, if any; and
>>>
>>> "(iii) his proximity, whether of kinship, place or residence or otherwise, to the person for whom he is to be a surety; and
>>
>> "(b) require the surety to make a statutory declaration in the form set out in the Second Schedule."

Decision

The Hon. Mr Justice Rajiv Persad held that the party entrusted (whether a Clerk of the Peace, Registrar, Magistrate or Judge) with the discretion whether to approve a particular person as a surety has to exercise that discretion judicially. In particular the party exercising that discretion must have regard to the matters outlined in Section 16 (2) of the Bail Act, including (i) the surety's profession, occupation, trade or business; (ii) his character and his previous convictions, if any; and (iii) his proximity, whether of kinship, place or residence or otherwise, to the person for whom he is to be a surety."

Justice Persad held further:

> "...In other words the effect of Section 16 (5) of the Bail Act is to mandate that where a High Court sets bail in a particular sum with a surety to be approved by the Registrar of the Supreme Court, for example, a person seeking to be approved as Surety by the court making the order will not be entitled to come before the High Court for such an approval unless he can establish that the Registrar of the Supreme Court has declined to take the recognizance because he/she is not satisfied with the surety's suitability.
>
> "Similarly the effect of Section 16(5) is to mandate that if a Magistrate makes an order setting Bail with a surety in a particular sum to be approved by the Clerk of the Peace, it will not be open to the party seeking to have a particular surety approved by the same Magistrate who made the order for bail, unless he can establish that the Clerk of the Peace has declined to take the recognizance because the clerk was not satisfied with the surety's suitability."

His lordship commented on the practice employed by bailors of using a single piece of property to secure bail for multiple parties. He stated that:

> "As a general rule a person can use a piece of property to secure bail for more than one person if and only if the surety has the approval of the Court. If a person does not get the approval of the Court a criminal offence is committed per section 19 of the Bail Act Chap 4:60. In the normal course of things once the approval of the Court is sought there should be no objection to a piece of property being used to secure bail for more than one person once the court is satisfied that the value of the unencumbered property can cover the value of the bail for each."

Other considerations may arise if the property has been used to secure multiple bails. Then, the court must ensure that the person seeking to be approved is not a professional bailor. Equally concerns may arise where a property is mortgaged in which case the decision maker must ensure that the property has enough value outside the mortgage obligations to cover the bail sum. In this case the applicant seeking to be approved was able to satisfy the Court that out of the three persons for whom bail had been taken previously, all had been either discontinued and or revoked thereby freeing herself of the previous obligations."

The learned judge sounded a note of caution to persons who wished to have a bailor approved. He stated that the process of approving bail was one that must be done with expedition. In this regard, failure by a declarant to disclose relevant material up front may be a compelling reason for a decision maker to refuse to approve a particular surety. Failure to make the relevant disclosure will be especially critical where it turns out that the person seeking approval may have taken bail for others not necessarily with the same deed and not disclosed it. This is because the non-disclosure may lead to a strong inference that the person may be a "professional bailor".

THE SHOW CAUSE APPLICATION

Principle

It is a matter of judicial obligation for a magistrate, before committing any person to imprisonment, to call upon him to show cause why he should not be committed for non-payment of the bond which has been declared to be forfeited.

Court of Appeal of Trinidad and Tobago

Ralph v A Magistrate

Decision of the Court of Appeal of Trinidad and Tobago, 11th April 1967

Facts

The condition for discharge of a bail bond not having been satisfied, a magistrate declared the bond to be forfeited and summarily ordered payment of the bond, or in default thereof, a term of imprisonment. The bailor did not attend court and no opportunity was given him to be heard before the making of the order. In his reasons the magistrate said that it was unnecessary to send to the appellant a summons to show cause why the bond should not be forfeited.

The bailor appealed.

Decision

Wooding CJ noted the relevant statutory provisions:

1) Section 123 (1) of the Summary Courts Ordinance provides that where a recognisance is conditioned for the appearance of any person before a summary court, that court may, if the recognisance appears to it to be forfeited, declare it to be so.

2) Section 124 (1) provides that where any recognisance is declared to be forfeited the magistrate having jurisdiction over the matter of the complaint may, forthwith or at any time after such declaration, issue a warrant or commitment against any person liable under such recognisance for any term not exceeding that prescribed by the Ordinance.

Wooding CJ held:

> "Having regard to the fact that an order for the payment of the amount of the forfeited bond is guarded by a term of imprisonment, it is contrary to natural justice to make any such order without first calling on the person concerned to show cause why it ought not to be made. It may well be that if a person is called upon that person will be able to show either that the person who should have appeared was dead or immobilised by a recent accident or serious illness, thereby making it quite impossible for him to appear. In any such case, more especially if the surety signing the bond presented himself on the day appointed for the appearance of the defendant and explained the cause of the absence, it would be a relevant circumstance to be taken into account before deciding to issue a commitment warrant. It is, therefore, a matter of judicial obligation for a magistrate, before committing any person to imprisonment, to call upon him to show cause why he should not be committed for non-payment of the bond which has been declared to be forfeited."

Principle

A bailor must show good and sufficient cause at a show cause hearing why the recognizance, into which he had entered for the due appearance of a defendant in the magistrate's court, should not be forfeited.

Court of Appeal of Trinidad and Tobago

Baksh v The Magistrate

Mag. App. No. 107/82

Facts

The appellant had entered into a recognizance for the appearance of the defendant in a summary matter. On one of the dates of hearing the defendant and appellant failed to appear and the court issued a warrant for the arrest of the defendant. The court also issued a summons to show cause to the appellant to show cause why the recognizance should not be forfeited. Following the show cause hearing the court forfeited the entire amount of the recognizance and ordered the appellant to pay this sum and in default of payment that distress was to be levied on the appellant's goods.

The appellant appealed against this order

Decision

Braithwaite J held that the Court of Appeal had the jurisdiction to assess the evidence given before the magistrate to draw its own inferences from that evidence and to form its own opinion as to whether or not the appellant had shown good and sufficient cause why the recognizance into which he had entered for the due appearance of the defendant in the magistrate's court should not be forfeited.

Braithwaite J held:

> "...it is only by keeping in close touch with the bailed prisoner that a surety can be sure that he is and remains in a position to guarantee the appearance of that prisoner when his matter comes on for hearing...It is our view that it is also the duty of the surety to keep himself informed of the date of each adjourned hearing and not to rely on the memory of the defendant or of anyone else."

Appeal dismissed.

FORFEITURE OF THE RECOGNISANCE

Principle

The failure of the accused to surrender when required triggers the court's power to forfeit the recognisance but the court, before deciding what should be done, must enquire into the question of fault on the surety's part.

Court of Appeal

R. v Reading Crown Court Ex p. Bello

(1991) 92 Cr. App. R. 303

Facts

A surety was ordered to forfeit one half of the recognisance put up by him as surety for an accused who did not appear in court when required to do so. The surety applied for judicial review of the decision but the application was refused. The surety appealed this decision.

Decision

Parker LJ held that in cases where the defendant failed to appear in court, the onus would rest on the surety to satisfy the court that the full recognizance should not be forfeited. In instances where the surety was unrepresented, the court should assist the surety by giving him the opportunity to call evidence and advance argument in relation to them. If the court was satisfied that the surety was blameless throughout it would be proper to remit the whole of the amount of the recognisance.

His lordship stated further that if the accused and the surety were on the way to court when both of them were seriously injured in a motor vehicular accident and taken to hospital then the justice of the case would not require that any part of the recognisance be forfeited.

Appeal allowed

NON-APPEARANCE OF THE DEFENDANT WHO IS ON BAIL

Principle

When the accused who has been granted bail fails to appear for his hearing but then eventually appears, he should be given an opportunity either to purge his contempt or to mitigate the consequences of it.

Queen's Bench Division

Schiavo v Anderton

[1987] QB 20

Facts

The defendant was charged with obtaining property by deception and was bailed to appear before a magistrates' court. He failed to appear on the appointed date and a warrant for his arrest was issued by the court. He was arrested and charged under s 6(1) of the 1976 Act with failing to surrender to custody.

Decision

Watkins LJ held:

> "An offence under s 6 of the 1976 Act is not a contempt of court, although it may be said to bear some relation to it in the

sense that a person who commits it has acted in defiance of an essential condition of his bail, namely that he surrender so as to appear before the court at a place and at a time appointed.

The invariable procedure for dealing with a contempt of court in the Crown Court is for the judge of his own motion to do so at a time during or usually at the end of the trial of an accused, being careful to ensure in the interests of fairness that the contemnor has an opportunity either to purge his contempt or to mitigate the consequences of it with the assistance, if fitting and desirable, of a solicitor and barrister."

BAIL APPLICATIONS

Principle

When dealing with a bail application, a magistrate is not necessarily functus officio at the moment he stops speaking. One has to look at the circumstances of each case and ask oneself whether, in practical terms, the occasion in question had come to an end.

Queen's Bench Division

Re Harris

(1984) 148 JP 584

Facts

A stipendiary magistrate granted bail following committal of the applicant for trial at the Crown Court, although initially minded to refuse bail on the ground that the appellant was likely to commit further offences. Thereafter, on leaving the dock, the applicant passed a disparaging remark to a policeman.

This caused the magistrate to change his mind and he remanded the applicant in custody. The applicant applied for a writ of *habeas corpus* on the ground that the magistrate was *functus officio* when he ordered the applicant to be remanded in custody and therefore his detention was unlawful.

Decision

Goff LJ framed the issue as being whether at the time the magistrate ordered that the applicant be remanded in custody, he was *functus officio* and held that at the moment the magistrate stopped speaking he was not *functus officio*. He gave an example to illustrate this as when a magistrate, right after indicating that he was minded to grant bail upon certain conditions, which he then specified, but then a few moments later added that he was minded to add a further condition.

His lordship further held that one had to look at the circumstances of each case and ask oneself whether, in practical terms, the occasion in question had come to an end, in deciding whether the court was *functus officio*. On the facts of the present case, the fact that the applicant was only just leaving the dock, that the magistrate had only just finished speaking before he did so, indicating the form of order he was prepared to make the magistrate was not *functus officio*. It was open to him then, to add another condition to bail, had he thought fit to do so. It was equally open to him, having regard to the circumstances, not to make an order of bail at all.

Application for habeas corpus refused but an application for bail on behalf of applicant granted

BAIL ON APPEAL FROM CONVICTION IN THE HIGH COURT

Principle

Bail on appeal from conviction in the High Court will be granted where the defendant would be exposed to the almost certain consequence of serving the sentence before having the appeal determined.

Court of Appeal of Guyana

The State v Scantlebury

Decision of the Court of Appeal of Guyana, 6th November 1976.

Facts

LS was sentenced to six months' imprisonment. She petitioned the Court of Appeal for admission to bail pending the hearing of her appeal against conviction and sentence in the High Court. She sought bail on the following grounds: (a) her own ill-health, (b) her husband's ill-health; (c) great hardship on her family; and (d) the real likelihood that her appeal would come on for hearing after she would have served her sentence.

Decision

Haynes C held that on the facts of this case, grounds (a), (b) and (c), separately or cumulatively, would not support a grant of bail, though cumulatively, they might allow bail to be granted in other particular circumstances. The learned judge went on to add that it was possible that an appellant's state of health might be, in certain circumstances, a ground on which to grant bail. As far as a spouse's health was concerned, special circumstances had to exist to justify a grant of bail.

Haynes C further held:

> "I think, however, that the fourth ground deserves careful consideration. Undoubtedly, this court has the jurisdiction to admit an appellant to bail pending the determination of an appeal. It is accepted law that it is a matter of discretion. An appellant has no common law or statutory or constitutional right to bail.
>
> But like all other discretionary powers it must be exercised judicially. If appellants are admitted to bail freely on appeals from the verdict of juries, a dangerous situation could arise inimical to the public interest.
>
> "In England, under the Court of Criminal Appeal Act 1907, a similar statutory discretion to admit an appellant to bail existed until its repeal. A study of the many judgments of the Court of Criminal Appeal there would indicate the considerations by which that court did so and its successor is guiding itself in the exercise of this discretion. These authorities are clear that the circumstances must be 'exceptional' to justify the grant of bail to persons convicted by juries…"

The learned judge outlined what could constitute 'exceptional circumstances'. This included where the conviction appeared plainly wrong so that the appeal had every prospect of success or where the sentence was a short one and it was administratively impossible to hear the appeal before the termination of the sentence. Another instance would be where the appellant would have served most or a very substantial part of the sentence by the time the appeal was to be heard.

Haynes C held that on the facts of the present case:

> "…But this court is aware that the offence for which the appellant has been convicted, not infrequently is punished by fines of varying severity. While nothing that this court says in this ruling should be interpreted as accepting or suggesting that the appeal has a fair chance of success either as to the conviction or as to the sentence, having regard to the nature of the offence and the very short sentence imposed, it is felt that this is a fit case to admit her to bail. It must be wrong that she should be exposed to the almost certain consequence of, in effect, serving her sentence before having her appeal determined. And it is certainly very likely, if not certain, that this will occur if bail is refused."

Petitioner admitted to bail pending hearing and determination of her appeal.

CHAPTER SIX

COURT PROCESS

Criminal proceedings in the courts are initiated by:

1. The complaint

2. The information

3. The indictment

These documents contain the same basic information, such as the accused's name and alias, the date of the offence, the place of the offence and the law allegedly contravened.

AMENDMENT OF DEFECTS

There may be defects in the contents of process which may or may not render them invalid. The law may allow these defects to be corrected through amendment. Not all defects may be cured. Some defects are so serious that they render the process invalid.

Principle

An application to amend which substitutes a different offence from the one charged is seldom permissible, especially where the original charge was for an offence created under a different Act.

Full Court of the Supreme Court of Barbados

Conliffe v Weekes

Decision of the Supreme Court of Barbados 1 March 1963

Facts

The respondent was charged before a magistrate exercising summary jurisdiction on an information for unlawfully and maliciously inflicting bodily harm on the appellant contrary to s 17 of the Offences against the Person Act, 1868. At the close of the evidence for the prosecution counsel for the appellant sought to amend the information by deleting the words "inflicting bodily harm" and inserting the word "wounding." The magistrate refused to allow the amendment, and as the evidence did not disclose the offence of inflicting grievous bodily harm, he dismissed the case.

Decision

Stoby CJ stated that the appellant's case was that the magistrate had jurisdiction to allow the amendment asked for by virtue of s 109 (1) of the Magistrates' (Jurisdiction and Procedure) Act, 1956 [B], which provided:

> 'No objection shall be allowed to any information or complaint, or to any summons or warrant to procure the presence of the accused or defendant, for any defect in it in substance or in form, or for any variance between it and the evidence adduced on behalf of the informant or complainant at the hearing of the information or complaint.'

Stoby CJ noted that the respondent's case was that s 109 (1) did not permit an amendment where a different offence from to the one charged was disclosed by the evidence. The court referred to Section 5 (1) of the Indictments Act, 1915 [UK] which states:

'Where before trial or at any stage of a trial it appears to the court that the indictment is defective the court shall make such order for the amendment of the indictment as the court thinks necessary to meet the circumstances of the case unless, having regard to the merits of the case, the required amendment cannot be made without injustice'."

Stoby CJ stated that on the authority of R v Harden this section was interpreted to mean that if the indictment was defective in matters of description or in any other respects of a similar nature, the amendment will be allowed at any stage of the proceedings. Where, however, the amendment is applied for at a late stage of the proceedings and goes beyond the correction of a mis-description of the original offence and substitutes a different offence from the one originally charged then an amendment is seldom permissible.

Stoby CJ concluded that if s 5 (1) of the Indictments Act, 1915 [UK] would seldom permit an amendment at a late stage which substitutes a different offence from the one charged then a similar view ought to be taken with respect to s 109 (1) of the Magistrates' (Jurisdiction and Procedure) Act, 1956 [B]. The learned judge stated that this view did not create any hardship. In any given case whether the magistrate granted an amendment or not necessarily depended on the circumstances of the case, the nature of the amendment applied for and the stage which the case had reached at the time of the application.

It followed that on the facts of the present case, the appellant had concluded the evidence he wished to call, the amendment required was for an offence known to the law whereas the charge was for an offence not provided for in the Offences against the Person Act, 1868.

In these circumstances the magistrate was correct in deciding not to allow an amendment.

Appeal Dismissed

Principle

Amendments to the date will be allowed provided the charge was laid within the statutory limitation period.

Court of Appeal of Trinidad and Tobago

Cross v John

Mag. App. No. 367/1963

Facts

At the hearing before the magistrate an amendment was sought by the appellant so that the complaint should read 4 Mar 1960, instead of 5 Mar 1960. This application was refused, for the reason that it was made more than six months after the date of the alleged offence.

Decision

Mc Shine JA held that on the authority of Meek v Powell it was correct to hold that where an amendment does not charge a different offence and a defendant is not prejudiced by the mere alteration of a date it is within the discretion of the magistrate to allow the amendment. The learned judge also cited R v Wakeley in support of the proposition that an information preferred within the statutory limitation period may be amended after the expiry of that period provided that the date substituted is within the period.

Mc Shine JA noted that the information in the present case was laid on 14 April 1960, while the amendment requested was that the date of the offence be changed to 4 Mar 1960, instead of 5 Mar 1960. It followed that the new date sought by the amendment did not transgress the principle that an amendment is permissible so long as the charge was laid within the six month statutory period of limitation. His lordship concluded that since there was no question of the respondent being deceived or misled the court would allow the amendment sought.

Appeal dismissed

JOINDER OF COUNTS

Where the facts of the individual offences are so related, whether in time (or by other factors) that the interests of justice are best served by their being tried together, then they can properly be the subject of counts in one indictment and can, subject always to the discretion of the court, be tried together.

Principle

The court has jurisdiction to try two defendants together on an indictment containing two separate counts, each being a count against one defendant alone.

Court of Criminal Appeal

R v Assim

[1966] 2 QB 249

Facts

The appellants appealed on the ground "that the court had no power in law to try two defendants on an indictment containing only two counts, one being against the appellant alone for maliciously wounding X, and the second count being against his co-defendant alone for assaulting Y". It was submitted that, in consequence of this alleged misjoinder, the whole trial was a nullity.

Decision

Sachs J held that where the matters which constituted the individual offences of the several offenders were on the available evidence so related, whether in time or by other factors, that the interests of justice were best served by their being tried together, then they could be joined as separate counts in one indictment and tried together. Such a rule included cases where there was evidence that several offenders acted in concert but was not limited to such cases.

His lordship emphasised that it was essentially a matter for the discretion of the court whether several offenders could be properly be tried together in a single trial. In such cases the onus rested on the trial judge to scrutinize matters closely with the same degree of care that was applied in dealing with the question whether a single person could be tried with several offences before the same jury.

Appeal Dismissed.

DEFECTS DUE TO DUPLICITY

The rule against duplicity states that a complaint/information/ count must contain only one offence/charge otherwise it will be bad for duplicity. This rule is also statutory in some jurisdictions. There are however certain situations where apparently duplicitous process will not run afoul of the rule.

Principle

A charge will not be duplicitous where it contemplates one activity even though such activity involves more than one act.

Court of Appeal of Jamaica

R v Johnson and Brown

Decision of the Court of Appeal of Jamaica, 20th December 1974

Facts

The applicants, J and B, were seen by two constables, F and SJ, running from certain premises towards a motor car which they entered, B getting into the driver's seat and J into the passenger seat. As the car reversed F called out: "Police, stop." J put his head out of the left front window, pointed a firearm at F and SJ who were then some 16 feet away, and fired two shots at them. The car continued to reverse and crashed into the bank at the side of the road.

J and B ran from the car. F and SJ gave chase, and as they did so B spun around, pointed a gun at the two constables and fired two shots at them.

J and B were each indicted on a single count with shooting at the two constables with intent. On appeal against their convictions it was contended on their behalf that the counts which charged each of them with shooting at the constables were bad for duplicity since each of those counts charged more than one offence.

Decision

Luckhoo P (Ag) stated that the case for the appellants was that the prosecution was contending that when each applicant allegedly shot at each constable separate and distinct offences were committed with respect to each constable and that even if it were accepted that the two shots which were fired by each applicant were fired *at* the two constables that transaction would be two separate and distinct acts and not one activity.

Luckhoo P (Ag) cited with approval the case of Jemmison v Priddle where an information charging the unlawful taking and killing of two red deer without licence was held by the English Divisional Court not to be bad for duplicity because it was legitimate to charge in a single charge one activity even though that activity may involve more than one act. The court in Jemmison reasoned that since the killing of the deer occurred within a very few seconds of time and all in the same geographical location, then the unlawful activities were actually a single activity, and that made it proper for the prosecution to join them in a single charge.

Luckhoo P (Ag) held:

> "We respectfully agree with the Lord Chief Justice's conclusions so clearly stated. We think the case of Jemmison v Priddle on that point to be applicable to the question raised in the instant appeal as to the validity of the first two counts of the indictment and hold that those counts are not bad for duplicity."

Appeal Dismissed

Principle

Where there are two separate acts arising out of a single incident and either one or the other act is itself capable of constituting the offence charged, then these acts may be charged in a single information provided they are charged conjunctively.

Court of Appeal of Trinidad and Tobago

Ramjohn v Johnson

Decision of the Court of Appeal of Trinidad and Tobago, 2nd February 1967

Facts

Section 66 (1) of the Summary Offences Ordinance says:

> "Every person having in his custody or possession any weapon, instrument, stick, bottle, stone, or other thing intended for the purpose of committing a felony or misdemeanour shall be deemed a rogue and vagabond...."

The appellant went into his bedroom and, returning with a stick, he asked the respondent to leave his house, adding that if he did not do so he would beat him. He continued to threaten the respondent but his wife took away the stick. Thereupon, he went into his kitchen and returned with a cutlass. He resumed his threats. He threatened to beat and chop the respondent if he did not leave; and, pressing his demand, he went towards the respondent with the cutlass, moving it up and down while his wife stood her ground between them. The appellant was prosecuted by the respondent for having a stick *and* a cutlass in his possession intended for the purpose of wounding the respondent. He was convicted. On appeal it was contended that the information was bad for duplicity.

Decision

Fraser JA held that s 66 (1) created the offence of being in possession of weapons intended for crime and the section also prescribed different ways in which the offence could be committed. A defendant could also be charged with being in possession of any one of the several weapons mentioned in the section but he could only properly be charged with being in possession of two or more weapons provided his possession of the weapons was contemporaneous. In this case the appellant was not shown to be in contemporaneous possession of the two weapons.

Fraser JA held further that where the evidence disclosed the doing of two separate acts either one or the other being in itself capable of constituting the offence charged, a defendant may be convicted for the offence if the separate acts arose from a single incident and were charged conjunctively. On the facts, the appellant was charged with being in possession of a stick *and* a cutlass with intent to wound the respondent. The evidence disclosed that the events between the respondent and the appellant were sufficiently uninterrupted so as to constitute a single incident. The appellant had armed himself with a stick and threatened the respondent. His wife intervened and disarmed him. It was at this stage that he went to his kitchen and returned armed with a cutlass. In such a case, either one or the other of these two acts was adequate to constitute the offence charged.

Appeal dismissed

Principle

Where a statute creates separate offences which were committed as part of one single continuous act then if the offences are charged conjunctively the information will not be duplicitous.

High Court of Guyana

Doobay v Inspector of Police

Decision of the High Court of Guyana, 4th & 16th March 1968

Facts

Section 36 of the Colonial Medical Service Ordinance, Cap 134 [G], provides as follows:

> "Anyone who wilfully and falsely pretends to be, or takes or uses the name or title of, a physician, doctor of medicine ... or general practitioner, or any name, title, addition, or description,

implying that he is registered under this Ordinance or that he is registered by law as a physician ... or a practitioner in medicine, shall, on conviction thereof, be liable to a penalty not exceeding one hundred dollars."

The appellant was found to have a sign-board on his premises which read:

"Dr J C Doobay, MDIH, FSAUI, Physician"

and among his papers were found three sheets of paper on which the above description was repeated together with the words "Practitioner of Medicine".

The particulars of the charge read as follows:

> "Joseph Chateau Doobay between Tuesday, 4th and Thursday, 6 January 1966 at Georgetown in the Georgetown Judicial District, did wilfully and falsely use the name and title of a physician implying that he is recognised by law as a physician."

Decision

Bollers CJ held that the words, namely, using the name of a physician and using the title of a physician created two offences and not two modes of committing a single act. The learned judge cited *R v* Clow in which the appellant was charged with causing death by dangerous driving contrary to s 1 (1) of the Road Traffic Act, 1960 (UK). The particulars of offence alleged that the appellant caused death by the driving of a motor vehicle on a road at a speed and in a manner dangerous to the public having regard to all the circumstances of the case. The Court of Criminal Appeal concluded that the charge was valid and not bad for duplicity. The basis of the decision in Clow was that separate offences could be charged conjunctively provided it was one indivisible act committed by the defendant or one single incident. On the facts of Clow, the single incident was the driving of the appellant which caused the death of a person.

Bollers CJ also noted that the case of Simon v Reid followed R v Clow. In Simon v Reid, the respondents had been charged for assembling together and taking part in a public lottery contrary to s 5 of the Gambling and Betting Ordinance (T). It was held that two separate offences were implicit in the charge namely:

> (1) assembling for the purpose of gambling and (2) gambling. However, as both offences arose out of a single incident and the respondents had been charged conjunctively and not disjunctively, the information was not duplicitous.

Bollers CJ concluded that on the facts of this case, the act of the appellant in saying that on 4 January 1966, that he was Dr Doobay and displaying a signboard outside the door of his home both on that day and on the subsequent days when the other decoys were attended by him and when the police arrived at his home, was one single, continuous act on his part and therefore the two offences of using the name of a physician and using the title of a physician could properly be charged conjunctively

Principle

The test to determine whether a statutory provision creates two offences is if a person may do one act without doing the other, then two separate offences are created. The information will be duplicitous if the separate offences are charged in the alternative.

Court of Criminal Appeal

R v Wilmot

(1933) 24 Cr App Rep 63

Facts

By the Road Traffic Act, 1930, s 11(1):

"If any person drives a motor vehicle on a road recklessly, or at a speed or in a manner which is dangerous to the public, having regard to all the circumstances of the case, including the nature, condition, and use of the road, and the amount of traffic which is actually at the time, or which might reasonably be expected to be, on the road, he shall be li-able ... (b) on conviction on indictment to imprisonment for a term not exceeding six months or to a fine, or to both such imprisonment and fine."

The appellant was convicted on a count of an indictment charging him with dangerous driving, contrary to s 11(1) of the Road Traffic Act, 1930, the particulars of the offence being stated as follows:

"CW, on the 25th day of October 1932, on a certain road ... in the county of Lincoln, drove a motor car recklessly, or at a speed or in a manner which was dangerous to the public, having regard to all the circumstances of the case, including the nature, condition and use of the road and the amount of traffic which was actually at the time, or which might reasonably have been expected to be, on the said road."

Decision

Lord Hewart CJ held that the information was bad for duplicity. He cited the case of R v Surrey Justices, Ex parte Witherwick where it was held that where a statute created separate offences then a person may do one act without doing the other. In such a case, an information which charged a defendant in the alternative was bad for duplicity since the defendant could not then know with precision with what he was charged.

Conviction quashed

STAUTORY PROVISIONS CHARGING DIFFERENT MODES OF COMMITTING AN OFFENCE

Principle

In determining whether a statutory provision creates multiple offences or different modes of committing a single offence the court should consider the nature of the offence.

Queen's Bench Division

DPP v Bennett

(1993) 157 JP 493

Facts

Section 170 of the Road Traffic Act 1988 provides:

"(1) This section applies in a case where, owing to the presence of a motor vehicle on a road, an accident occurs by which - (a) personal injury is caused to a person other than the driver of that motor vehicle . . . (2) The driver of the motor vehicle must stop and, if required to do so by any person having reasonable grounds for so requiring, give his name and address and also the name and address of the owner and the identification marks of the vehicle . . . (4) A person who fails to comply with subsection (2) . . . above is guilty of an offence . . ."

The defendant, a taxi driver, while driving on a road injured a pedestrian and was charged with having "failed to stop, and on being required by a person having reasonable grounds for so requiring, failed to give his name and address and the name and address of the owner and the identification marks of the vehicle," contrary to section 170(4) of the Road Traffic Act 1988. He was convicted by justices and appealed to the Crown Court. At the close of the case for the prosecutor, on a submission, the Crown Court held that the information was bad for duplicity in that two offences were charged against the defendant, namely, failing to stop and failing to give his name and address.

Decision

Beldam LJ stated that the issue before the court was whether the Crown Court were correct in deciding that section 170(2) provided for two possible factual allegations, each of which separately constituted an offence under section 170(4), and that therefore the summons was bad for duplicity. The learned judge held that subsection (2) contained a requirement to stop and, if required to do so, to give a name and address. In order, therefore, to comply with subsection (2), it was necessary to fulfil the first and if required the second of those duties. It followed that the information laid against the defendant did not charge more than one offence and was not bad for duplicity. The section created only one offence.

Appeal allowed

Principle

Where a statute creates different modes of committing an offence, then it does not create separate offences. In such a case it will not be duplicitous to charge separate modes disjunctively provided the wording of the charge follows strictly the language of the statute.

Court of Appeal of Trinidad and Tobago

Taylor v Khan

Decision of the Court of Appeal of Trinidad and Tobago, 7th October 1969

Facts

J K was charged on a summary complaint which alleged that he wilfully secreted or kept a postal packet containing jewellery in the course of transmission by post and which ought to have been delivered to some other person, contrary to s 45 (a) of the Post Office Ordinance which provided as follows:

"45. Any person who fraudulently retains, or wilfully secretes or keeps, or detains, or, when required by an officer of the Post Office, neglects or refuses to deliver up:

(a) any postal packet which is in course of transmission by post and which ought to have been delivered to any person, ... shall be guilty of a misdemeanour...."

On the matter coming before the magistrate for hearing the respondent submitted that this information was bad for duplicity for the reason that the expression 'secreted or kept' in the information stated that two offences had been committed, and that it was bad in law to charge in one complaint more than one offence. The respondent submitted that 'to secret' was one offence, while 'to keep' was another offence.

The magistrate dismissed the case and the prosecution appealed.

Decision

Mc Shine CJ noted that the appellant's submission was that the expression 'secreted or kept' in the information was merely alternatively descriptive of one offence. The learned judge formulated the issue as being whether the expression 'wilfully secretes or keeps, or detains' merely amounted to one offence or to three offences.

Mc Shine CJ held:

"In our judgment this information was not void for duplicity. In our view one, and only one, offence was charged. Whether it was considered to be 'secreted or kept' or both expressions, and described alternatively in the complaint, we are of the view that the magistrate erred in holding that the prosecution should elect upon which charge it would proceed, whether for secreting or for keeping. He further erred in dismissing the complaint when he thought that two offences were charged in the one information and that made the information bad for duplicity. In the final analysis this appeal will be allowed. The matter will be remitted to be tried *de novo* by another magistrate. The respondent will pay the costs of this appeal."

Appeal allowed

THE CONSEQUENCES OF BEING CONVICTED ON DUPLICITOUS PROCESS

Where a duplicitous charge is not amended and the defendant is convicted, different consequences may flow depending on the jurisdiction. In Guyana the conviction is invalid. In Trinidad, the Court of Appeal may allow the charge to be amended and uphold the conviction. In St Lucia, the conviction is valid.

Principle

A conviction on a duplicitous charge will not necessarily be quashed on appeal. It will be quashed if it can be shown that the defence might be prejudiced or embarrassed in any way by the duplicitous charge.

Court of Appeal of Trinidad and Tobago

Sharma v Leacock

Decision of the Court of Appeal of Trinidad and Tobago, 3rd November 1970

Facts

The appellant was convicted of larceny of certain articles alleged to be the property of the Trinidad and Tobago Electricity Commission. In a search of the appellant's house, a bolt cutter, an electric soldering iron, two double end spanners, three pieces of angle iron and three brackets were found. These articles had been stolen from the Commission during the period 1967 to 1970 and were actually missed at different times. The information was worded in this way:

"that the appellant sometime during the period 1967 to 25 April 1970, at Syne Village stole the articles in question, namely: a bolt cutter, a soldering iron, two double end spanners and three pieces of angle iron, together valued $54.68."

Decision

Phillips JA held:

> "The question, therefore, is whether it can be said that this information charges the commission of more than one offence and whether that fact alone is sufficient to entitle the appellant to succeed. In other words, should this court quash the conviction? It must be remembered first of all that when he appeared before the magistrate the appellant did not take this point in limine.

> "It was said that counsel took the point at the end of the case for the prosecution. There was no question of any adjournment being sought for the purpose of preparing for trial or relieving any embarrassment suffered by counsel. However, the case went on and the appellant gave evidence.

Phillips JA stated that the fact that an indictment was duplicitous did not automatically mean that a conviction should be quashed on appeal. The conviction should be quashed if it can be shown in all the circumstances that the defendant might have been prejudiced or embarrassed in his defence. Furthermore, an appeal on the grounds of duplicity would not necessarily fail if the point was not raised at the earliest possible time.

The learned judge concluded that in the present case it had not been shown that the appellant was in any way prejudiced by the duplicity. The appellant had been entitled, to ask for separation of the charges, but he elected not to.

Principle

The error of duplicity is a fundamental one with the result that a conviction on a duplicitous complaint will be invalid and must be quashed. The conviction should not be quashed where a statutory provision exists which saves the validity of the conviction in cases where it is not shown that an appellant was or might have been prejudiced in his defence.

Court of Appeal of Guyana

Bhagwan v Chester

(1977) 25 WIR 187

Facts

The appellant was convicted on summary charges for breaches of inter alia s 8 (2) which read:

> "Every person who knowingly and wilfully prints or publishes, or causes to be printed or published, or either as a proprietor or otherwise, sells or delivers out, any newspaper,

relating to which a declaration containing the matters and things required by this Act to be therein contained, has not been duly signed, made, and delivered when and so often as by this Act is required, or any other matter or thing required by this Act to be done or performed has not been accordingly done or performed, shall be liable...'

On appeal to the Guyana Court of Appeal, it was contended that the charge (under s 8 (2)) for printing without making a declaration was bad for duplicity inasmuch as the particulars of offence alleged that the appellant "knowingly and wilfully printed or caused to be printed" Dayclean.

Decision

Haynes C. held that the issue to be decided was whether the words 'print or caused to be printed' related to one indivisible process, one act, one activity, one transaction or to different acts, activities and separate transactions. In other words did these words describe one offence which could be committed in different ways or two offences of a different nature? Are the constituent facts of printing and causing to be printed the same or different.

The learned judge concluded that 'to print' and 'to cause to be printed' related to two different activities, and so were separate and different offences. It followed that the words in s 8 (2): "every person who knowingly and wilfully prints or publishes or causes to be printed or published" created four separate offences and therefore the eight informations were bad for duplicity in charging for two offences in the alternative.

Haynes C went on to cite certain Guyanese decisions namely Wilson and Hassan Ali v Burnett and Hunt; Burnett and Hunt v Wilson and Ali which declined to follow Sharma v Leacock, a judgment of the Court of Appeal of Trinidad and Tobago. The learned judge approved of the principle established in those Guyanese cases which was to the effect that since the error of duplicity was a fundamental one a conviction on a duplicitous complaint would be invalid and must be quashed, as there was no statutory provision which would allow the conviction to be upheld.

Appeals allowed

CHAPTER SEVEN

ABUSE OF PROCESS

The defence may apply for a stay on the grounds that there has been an abuse of the court's process. The application may be made as a preliminary submission or after the prosecution has closed its case. The burden of proof lies on the applicant.

APPLICATIONS FOR A STAY: LEGAL REQUIREMENTS

Principles

a) Proceedings should be stayed only in exceptional circumstances.
b) An applicant for a stay due to delay must show on the balance of probabilities that owing to the delay he will suffer serious prejudice to the extent that no fair trial can be held.

COURT OF APPEAL

Attorney General's Reference (No 1 of 1990)

[1992] QB 630

Facts

The Attorney-General referred to the Court of Appeal under section 36 of the Criminal Justice Act 1972 the questions whether proceedings upon indictment could be stayed on the grounds of prejudice resulting from delay in the institution of those proceedings even though that delay had not been occasioned by any fault on the part of the prosecution, and, if so, what degree of likelihood and seriousness of prejudice was required to justify a stay of such proceedings.

Decision

Lord Lane CJ discussed the principles relating to the court's discretionary power to grant a stay. He held that stays whether imposed on the grounds of delay or for any other reason should only be granted in exceptional circumstances. Stays should rarely be granted in the absence of any fault on the part of the complainant or prosecution. Furthermore, delay due to the complexity of the case or contributed to by the actions of the defendant himself should never be the foundation for the grant of a stay.

Lord Lane CJ went on to discuss the relevant burden and standard of proof. He held:

> "In answer to the second question posed by the Attorney General, no stay should be imposed unless the defendant shows on the balance of probabilities that owing to the delay he will suffer serious prejudice to the extent that no fair trial can be held, in other words that the continuance of the prosecution amounts to a misuse of the process of the court."

The learned judge stated that when assessing whether there was likely to be serious prejudice the court needed to consider certain matters. The first was the trial judge's power (whether statutory or common law) to regulate the admissibility of evidence. Then there was the matter of the trial process itself which should ensure that all relevant factual issues arising from delay were placed before the jury as part of the evidence for their consideration. Finally, the court should have regard to the judge's powers to give appropriate directions to the jury before they considered their verdict.

THE BURDEN OF PROOF

The burden of proof on the applicant for a stay is a heavy one. The court will only grant a stay in exceptional circumstances, even where there is a constitutional right to a speedy trial.

Principles

1. *Where there is no express right to a speedy trial or trial within a reasonable time (as in the Trinidad and Tobago Constitution) then common law principles are to be applied in order to determine whether the trial would be a fair one.*

2. *The burden lies on the applicant to show that he has suffered prejudice which leads to unfairness that cannot be cured by the trial judge's actions/directions.*

COURT OF APPEAL OF TRINIDAD AND TOBAGO

Peters v The State

Cr. App. No. 34 of 2008

Facts

The appellant sought a stay on the grounds that due to inordinate delay (24 years and eight months between the date the appellant was charged and the trial) her trial constituted an abuse of process of the court. The application was refused at the trial of the matter and she was convicted and appealed. It was not disputed that the appellant had contributed to nearly one half of the total delay (nearly 13 years).

Decision

P. Weekes JA first considered the state of the law where there was an express constitutional right to trial without undue delay or within a reasonable time. The learned judge held that in such a case, complaint by way of constitutional motion was the more appropriate remedy. Where there was no express right to a speedy trial or trial within a reasonable time (as in the Trinidad and Tobago constitution) then common law principles were to be applied in order to determine whether the trial would be a fair one.

P Weekes JA held that the central issue in the appeal was whether the appellant would have suffered serious prejudice to the extent that no fair trial as expressly granted by the constitution of Trinidad and Tobago was possible owing to the delay. The learned judge held that it was not sufficient for the applicant to show prejudice simpliciter. The applicant for a stay had to show he had suffered prejudice which leads to unfairness that cannot be cured by the trial judge's actions/directions.

The learned judge held that:

> "The prosecution neither manipulated nor misused the process of the court to deprive the appellant of any protection provided by law…She enjoyed fully all protections provided as she underwent the trial process. Any prejudice she may have suffered by virtue of prosecutorial delay was not such as to render a fair trial possible especially given the trial judge's directions."

JURISDICTION TO GRANT A STAY

Principle

A stay may be granted by the Court of Appeal but will not be granted if applied for the first time at the Privy Council. The Court of Appeal may also quash a conviction on the grounds of an abuse of process and decline to order a re-trial.

Supreme Court
R v Maxwell

[2010] UKSC 48

Facts

The appellant was convicted of murder and two robberies. At trial the main prosecution witness was C. An investigation subsequently revealed that the police had systematically misled the court, the Crown Prosecution Service and counsel by concealing and lying about benefits received by C and his family. The conclusion of the investigation was that a number of police officers had conspired to pervert the course of justice. The police had deliberately withheld information from the court; they had colluded in C's perjury at the trial; they had lied in response to inquiries following the conviction and had perjured themselves in the course of the defendant's first application for leave to appeal against conviction. The appellant's conviction was quashed but the Court of Appeal ordered a re-trial. The appellant appealed to the House of Lords against this order.

Decision

Lord Dyson stated that the court had the power to stay proceedings in two categories of case, namely (i) where it would be impossible to give the accused a fair trial, and (ii) where it offended the court's sense of justice and propriety to be asked to try the accused in the particular circumstances of the case. In the first category of case, if the court concluded that an accused could not receive a fair trial, it would stay the proceedings without more. No question of the balancing of competing interests arose.

In the second category of case, the court was concerned to protect the integrity of the criminal justice system. In such a case, a stay would be granted where the court concluded that in all the circumstances a trial would offend the court's sense of justice and propriety. The learned judge further held that the gravity of the alleged offence was a factor of considerable weight for the court to weigh when deciding whether to stay proceedings on the grounds of abuse of process. This was because society had a greater interest in having an accused retried for a grave offence than for a relatively minor one.

Regarding the issue of whether a re-trial should have been ordered the learned judge stated that the issue of whether the interests of justice required a retrial was broader than the question whether it was an abuse of process to allow a prosecution to proceed (whether or not by retrial).

Lord Dyson further held:

> "...The only justification for refusing a retrial on the grounds of the misconduct in such a case would be to mark the court's disapproval of that historical misconduct and to discipline the police. But that is not the function of the criminal courts...."

Lord Dyson concluded:

> "...In deciding what the interests of justice required, the Court of Appeal were right to respect the strength of the public interest in seeing that that those against whom there is *prima facie* admissible evidence that they are guilty of crimes, especially very serious crimes, are tried. This public interest is all the greater where, as in the present case, there is compelling evidence of guilt...."

In dismissing the appeal the learned judge held that there was a strong case for ordering a retrial and it had not been shown that the Court of Appeal had erred in law in deciding to order a retrial.

Appeal dismissed

HEADS UNDER WHICH A STAY MAY BE GRANTED

Principle

A judge may exercise his discretion to stay proceedings due to an abuse of process which amounts to an affront to the public conscience.

House of Lords

R v Latif and Shahzad

[1996] UKHL 16

Facts

The appellant submitted that an informer and customs officers by subterfuge incited him to commit the offence and then lured him into the jurisdiction. It was submitted that in those circumstances it was an abuse of process to institute criminal proceedings against the appellant and that the proceedings should be stayed.

Decision

Lord Steyn acknowledged that though entrapment was not a defence under English law Shahzad would probably not have committed the offence in question but for the conduct (which included criminal conduct) of the informer and the customs officers.

Lord Steyn held on this issue:

> "...If the court always refuses to stay such proceedings, the perception will be that the court condones criminal conduct and malpractice by law enforcement agencies. That would undermine public confidence in the criminal justice system and bring it into disrepute. On the other hand, if the court were always to stay proceedings in such cases, it would incur the reproach that it is failing to protect the public from serious crime."

The learned judge stated that in cases where there was an alleged abuse of process and the court concluded that a fair trial was not possible, it would stay the proceedings. However on the facts of the present case, a fair trial was possible, and the appellant had received a fair trial. He also stated that the judge had to weigh in the balance the public interest in ensuring that those that were charged with grave crimes should be tried and the competing public interest in not conveying the impression that the court would adopt the approach that the end justified any means.

Lord Steyn held:

> "...The conduct of the customs officer was not so unworthy or shameful that it was an affront to the public conscience to allow the prosecution to proceed. Realistically, any criminal behaviour of the customs officer was venial compared to that of Shahzad. In these circumstances I would reject the submission that the judge erred in refusing to stay the proceedings."

Appeals dismissed

Principles

a) A stay will be granted where the court concludes that in all the circumstances a trial will "offend the court's sense of justice and propriety".

b) The question whether the interests of justice require a retrial is broader than the question whether it is an abuse of process to allow a prosecution to proceed (whether or not by retrial).

Judicial Committee of the Privy Council

Warren and others v Attorney General of the Bailiwick of Jersey

[2011] UKPC 10

Facts

The appellants applied for a stay of the proceedings on the grounds of abuse of process. The basis of the application was that crucial evidence on which the prosecution wished to rely had been obtained as a result of serious prosecutorial misconduct. They appealed to the Privy Council against the refusal to stay the proceedings for abuse of process.

Decision

Lord Dyson stated that the courts of England and Wales had to perform a balancing test in deciding whether to stay proceedings where it was claimed that the continuation of the proceedings would compromise the moral integrity of the criminal justice system to an unacceptable degree. This "balancing" test that took into account factors such as the seriousness of any violation of the defendant's (or even a third party's) rights; whether the police had acted in bad faith or maliciously, or with an improper motive; whether the misconduct was committed in circumstances of urgency, emergency or necessity; the availability or otherwise of a direct sanction against the person(s) responsible for the misconduct; and the seriousness of the offence with which the defendant was charged'.

The learned judge conceded that the police had been unquestionably guilty of grave prosecutorial misconduct in the instant case. They had acted in the knowledge that the Attorney General and the Chief of Jersey Police had not given authority to install the audio device without the consent of the relevant foreign authorities and would not do so; and that the foreign authorities had refused their consent. The police had therefore misled the Attorney General, the Chief of Police and the authorities of three foreign states.

There were factors to be balanced against this misconduct; namely the offence with which the appellants were charged was very serious. Secondly, the ringleader Mr Warren was a professional drug dealer. Thirdly, to some extent the unwise advice of Crown Advocate Jowitt mitigated the gravity of the misconduct of the police since the officers must have felt encouraged and heartened by that advice. Fourthly, there was no attempt to mislead the Jersey court since it was always understood by the police that the circumstances in which the evidence was obtained would be revealed to the court which would then decide whether to refuse to admit the evidence.

Fifthly, this was a case where real urgency was needed. The Jersey police were understandably anxious to secure the evidence as to the nature of the drugs. They were dealing with experienced and sophisticated criminals, who could be expected to second guess the police tactics. It was in these circumstances that the police cut corners and acted unlawfully.

Lord Dyson held:

> "The commissioner had to undertake a difficult balancing exercise. Some judges might have granted a stay; others, like the commissioner, would have refused one. The Board finds

it impossible to characterise the decision to refuse a stay in this case as perverse or one which no reasonable judge could have reached."

Appeals dismissed

Principle

Where process of law is available to return an accused to face trial through extradition procedures, the courts will stay proceedings if the accused had been (with the knowledge of the police, prosecuting or other executive authorities) forcibly brought within the jurisdiction in disregard of those procedures.

House of Lords

R v Horseferry Road Magistrates Court, Ex parte Bennett

[1994] 1 AC 42

Facts

The defendant, a citizen of New Zealand who was alleged to have committed criminal offences in England, was traced to South Africa by the English police and forcibly returned to England. There was no extradition treaty between the two countries, and although special arrangements could be made for extradition in a particular case under section 15 of the Extradition Act 1989 no such proceedings were taken. The defendant claimed that he had been kidnapped from the Republic of South Africa as a result of collusion between the South African and British police and returned to England, where he was arrested and brought before a magistrates' court to be committed to the Crown Court for trial.

Decision

Lord Griffiths stated that the case before the court was not one where there was a suggestion that the appellant could not have a fair trial, nor that it would have been unfair to try him if he had been returned to the United Kingdom through extradition procedures. The learned judge stated further that the court would exercise its power to interfere with the prosecution in the present case on the basis that the judiciary accepted a responsibility for the maintenance of the rule of law. This included a willingness to oversee executive action and to refuse to countenance a serious abuse of power that threatened either basic human rights or the rule of law.

Using the context of extradition, Lord Griffiths illustrated the power of the courts to maintain the rule of law. He stated a hypothetical situation wherein should a practice be developed in which the police or prosecuting authorities of the United Kingdom ignored extradition procedures and secured the return of an accused by a mere request to police colleagues in another country they would be flouting the extradition procedures and depriving the accused of the safeguards built into the extradition process for his benefit. In such a case it would be unthinkable that the court should declare itself to be powerless and decline to intervene. The courts in such a situation can declare that such behaviour is an abuse of process and thus stay a prosecution.

On the issue of a magistrate's jurisdiction to entertain an abuse of process application, **Lord Griffiths** held:

> "I would accordingly affirm the power of the magistrates, whether sitting as committing justices or exercising their summary jurisdiction, to exercise control over their proceedings through an abuse of process jurisdiction. However, in the case of magistrates this power should be strictly confined to matters directly affecting the fairness of the trial of the particular accused with whom they are dealing,

such as delay or unfair manipulation of court procedures. Although it may be convenient to label the wider supervisory jurisdiction with which we are concerned in this appeal under the head of abuse of process, it is in fact a horse of a very different colour from the narrower issues that arise when considering domestic criminal trial procedures. I adhere to the view…that this wider responsibility for upholding the rule of law must be that of the High Court and that if a serious question arises as to the deliberate abuse of extradition procedures a magistrate should allow an adjournment so that an application can be made to the Divisional Court which I regard as the proper forum in which such a decision should be taken."

Appeal allowed

STAY GRANTED WHEN SEPARATE PROCEEDINGS ARE BROUGHT FOR OFFENCES ARISING OUT OF A SINGLE CRIMINAL TRANSACTION

Principle

Where an accused commits a number of offences arising out of a single criminal transaction, these counts should be tried in a single proceeding. It may be unfair to the accused to try the accused in separate proceedings.

Court of Appeal of Trinidad and Tobago

Nandlal v The State

C.A. Crim. 99/1988

Facts

The appellant had three criminal cases listed against him in the Chaguanas Magistrate's Court, before Magistrate J. He corruptly gave the magistrate a motor car, and the sum of $440,000 to dismiss the cases. The magistrate did so. The appellant and S R were subsequently found 'Guilty' at a trial on indictment for corruption. The appellant was sentenced to two years on the count for corruption, and ten years on the conspiracy count. These sentences were to run concurrently. Following conviction and sentence on the first indictment the appellant was served with a second indictment containing a number of offences including conspiracy.

He claimed that this caused him severe prejudice as the verdict on the first indictment constituted the rejection by the jury of the appellant's defence and resulted in the trial of the second indictment being nothing more than a charade. In effect he claimed that this had deprived him of the opportunity of having all the charges against him considered in a manner which would not have been oppressive to him, either by applying to have some of the charges stayed, or (after having been found 'Guilty') by having the totality of the proceedings against him brought to finality.

Decision

Sharma JA firstly decided that even if it was proper to hold two preliminary inquiries, because the receipt of the car and the money had taken place in two different magisterial jurisdictions it was still difficult to see the necessity for the DPP to have preferred two separate indictments and to hold separate trials, since when the time came to indict the appellant, the question of jurisdiction was no longer an issue.

The learned judge further substantiated his point that a second indictment was not necessary by pointing out that several of the witnesses who testified on the corruption charge, were also witnesses on the conspiracy charge. Even if there were additional witnesses on the conspiracy charge, this would still not have amounted to a good reason for separate indictments. The learned judge concluded that the strategy adopted by the Director of Public Prosecutions, was clearly misconceived since what was done was to take essentially one transaction and split it into several counts.

Sharma JA held:

> "What, however, has driven us mainly to this conclusion is the fact that, even on the basis that each act was a distinct one of corruption, even on the basis that it was justifiable to have separate indictments, why did the Director of Public Prosecutions only serve the second indictment after the appellant had been found 'Guilty' and sentenced on the first indictment (in which he was charged with corruption)?
>
> ...The answer to the question earlier posed is, we submit, to be found by asking another. Is it not proper for any reasonable tribunal to infer that the Director of Public Prosecutions' intention was to await the outcome of the trial on the first indictment before the director took any further action? We think that this can justifiably be borne out by the chronology of the indictments and events."

The learned judge ruled that the DPP's approach resulted in serious prejudice to the appellant. Having been found guilty on the first indictment, he was then put in the invidious position of having to go through another trial, on the second indictment on the so-called 'second act of corruption'. In these circumstances the second trial amounted to nothing more than a charade.

Furthermore, although the appellant had already been sentenced to two years in prison and a fine of $20,000 had been imposed (such being the maximum penalty), he was entitled to feel that the matter was over and done with.

However in the end he was sentenced to two more years in the second trial on the second act of corruption. The result was that he was sentenced to four years for an offence the maximum of which was two years. If both counts had been charged in the first indictment, the judge would have quite properly passed the maximum sentence and even if he were minded to sentence on the second count for corruption he would no doubt have ordered the sentences to run concurrently.

Sharma JA concluded:

> "By serving the second indictment after the conviction and sentence on the first indictment, the Director of Public Prosecutions effectively deprived the appellant of the opportunity of an important choice of having all the charges considered in such a way that would not have been oppressive to him, either by asking that some of the counts be stayed or, on being found 'Guilty' upon trial of the several counts on the same indictment, to have the question of sentence before the same tribunal dealt with in a way which would have brought finality to these sordid proceedings."

Appeal allowed. Convictions quashed; proceedings stayed.

STAY GRANTED FOLLOWING A BROKEN PROMISE NOT TO PROSECUTE

Principle

The prosecution of a person who had received a promise, undertaking or representation from the police that he would not be prosecuted was capable of being an abuse of process.

Queen's Bench Division

R v Croydon Justices, ex parte Dean

[1993] QB 769

Facts

The applicant, together with two other men, was arrested on suspicion of murdering a man. The applicant did not take part in the actual killing but after it had taken place he went to the scene of the crime with the other two men and assisted in destroying the victim's car. He was subsequently interviewed by the police and made statements containing potentially important evidence against the principal offender who was subsequently charged with murder.

The applicant agreed to be a prosecution witness and was then released. In a subsequent interview, the police officers interviewing him stated that he was a prosecution witness and had the protection of the police. He later went to the scene of the crime with the police and described how the victim's car had been destroyed. However, before he was charged he made further statements to the police identifying articles belonging to the other defendants which he had seen on the floor of the victim's car.

At the committal proceedings, counsel for the applicant submitted that there was an abuse of process of the court because the applicant had received an undertaking from the police that he would not be prosecuted in connection with the killing. It was submitted that since the defendant had clearly been given the impression, for a period of over five weeks, that he was not going to be prosecuted for the offence with which he was charged, it was clearly an abuse of process for him to be prosecuted subsequently.

Decision

Staughton LJ held that the prosecution of a person who had received a promise, undertaking or representation from the police that he will not be prosecuted is capable of being an abuse of process. The learned judge stated that George Dean was given to understand, over a considerable period, that he was to be a prosecution witness, on the understanding that he was not himself to be prosecuted for any offence in connection with the murder, though the was not expressly promised any immunity.

Staughton LJ held:

> "...In my judgment, particularly having regard to the fact that Dean was only 17 at the time (although not, as he has since admitted, a stranger to crime), it was clearly an abuse of process for him to be prosecuted subsequently. The impression created was not dispelled for over five weeks, during which period he gave repeated assistance to the police. This case can, I think, be regarded as quite exceptional. The justices were bound to treat it as one of abuse of process. I would quash the committal of George Dean for the offence."

Application allowed

STAY GRANTED ON THE BASIS OF ENTRAPMENT

Principle

Entrapment is not a defence at common law though it may form the basis of a claim for abuse of process.

House of Lords

R v Looseley; Attorney General's Reference (No 3 of 2000)

[2001] UKHL 53

Facts

The appellant appealed with leave of the Appeal Committee of the House of Lords from the order of the Court of Appeal dismissing his appeal against his conviction The appellant had pleaded guilty following a ruling by the trial judge who (i) refused to stay the proceedings as an abuse of the process of the court, and (ii) refused to exclude the evidence of an undercover police officer.

Decision

Lord Nicholls of Birkenhead noted that Entrapment was an instance where a misuse of executive power could occur. He ruled that it was unacceptable that the state through its agents should lure its citizens into committing acts forbidden by the law and then seek to prosecute them for doing so. Lord Nicholls noted whereas in some instances a degree of active involvement by the police in the commission of a crime is generally regarded as acceptable, there were limits to what was acceptable.

The learned judge cited an instance where an undercover policeman repeatedly badgers a vulnerable drug addict for a supply of drugs in return for excessive and ever increasing amounts of money. Where the addict is prosecuted for yielding to the pressure, and supplies drugs, this result would be objectionable since the crime committed by the addict could be characterised as artificial or state-created crime. To prosecute in such circumstances would be an affront to the public conscience.

Lord Nicholls held:

> "Thus, although entrapment is not a substantive defence, English law has now developed remedies in respect of entrapment: the court may stay the relevant criminal

proceedings, and the court may exclude evidence... Exclusion of evidence from the trial will often have the same result in practice as an order staying the proceedings."

Lord Nicholls concluded that ultimately the overall consideration was whether the conduct of the police or other law enforcement agency was so seriously improper as to bring the administration of justice into disrepute.

Appeal dismissed

STAY GRANTED ON THE GROUNDS OF UNJUSTIFIED DELAY

Principles

a) *Where there has been an application for a stay on the basis of unjustified delay the stay will be refused where the State was not substantially or wholly responsible for the delay.*
b) *The applicant for a stay on the grounds of unjustified delay must provide evidence of actual prejudice that would be suffered by the continuation of the trial.*

High Court of Justice Trinidad and Tobago

The State v Murray Joseph Forde

No. CR 28 of 2004

Facts

The accused faced a retrial on an indictment for murder. The offence was alleged to have taken place in 2002. The indictment was filed on 16th July, 2004 and the first trial of the accused took place from 1st March, 2005 to 26th April, 2005. The jury failed to agree and a retrial was ordered. The retrial started some 8 years after the first trial concluded. The Defence filed a motion to stay the latest proceedings on the basis of abuse of process.

The defence claimed that he would be seriously prejudiced at the re-trial due to the failing memory of the state's witnesses as well as his himself.

Decision

Browne Antoine J decided that the accused had not proved he had suffered any prejudice due to his failing memory since he had placed no evidence before the court to establish either that he had a medical condition or that this medical condition had affected his memory. The learned judge also noted that during the *voir dire* the attorney for the accused was able to obtain sufficient instructions from the accused to allow him to cross-examine and put instructions to all the State's witnesses. This showed that the accused would not be prejudiced should the re-trial continue.

In relation to the length of the delay **Browne Antoine J** held:

> "There has been a delay of 8 years between the first and second trials. This delay is considerable. The preparation of the notes of evidence accounts for 3 years and 7 months of the delay. The rest of the period of delay, that is 4 years and 4 months can be accounted for by the unavailability of defence attorney or the change in defence attorneys for various reasons. In these circumstances I do not find that the State was substantially or wholly responsible for the delay. This was the main ground upon which the application for a stay was founded and this ground wholly fails."

Principle

Delay is not always the fault of the prosecution. The more protracted the delay, the more likely it is that fault will be attributed to the prosecution.

Judicial Committee of the Privy Council

Tan v Cameron

[1992] UKPC 18

GTS appealed with leave of the Court of Appeal in Hong Kong refusing his application for a perpetual stay of the criminal prosecution brought against him.

Decision

Lord Mustill ruled on the effect that a lengthy delay would have on the fairness of the trial. He held:

> "Naturally, the longer the delay the more likely it will be that the prosecution is at fault, and that the delay has caused prejudice to the defendant, and the less that the prosecution has to offer by explanation, the more easily can fault be inferred. But the establishment of these facts is only one step on the way to a consideration of whether, in all the circumstances, the situation created by the delay is such as to make it an unfair employment of the powers of the court any longer to hold the defendant to account. This is a question to be considered in the round, and nothing is gained by the introduction of shifting burdens of proof, which serves only to break down into formal steps what is in reality a single appreciation of what is or is not unfair."

Appeal dismissed

TIMING OF THE APPLICATION FOR A STAY

Principles

a) *The application for a stay based on abuse of process should be made early preferably at the trial stage. A failure to do so will make it difficult for a defendant to later prove that he was denied a speedy trial.*
b) *In a case where both the prosecution and the defence's cases were simple, the possibility of prejudice to the defence from even lengthy delay will be substantially reduced.*

Judicial Committee of the Privy Council

Flowers v R

[2001] 1 LRC 643

Facts

The appellant based his appeal in part on the long delay between the date on which he was charged with the capital murder on 6 April 1991 and the date of the commencement of his third trial on 13 January 1997. Section 20(1) of the Constitution of Jamaica provides:

"Whenever any person is charged with a criminal offence he shall, unless the charge is withdrawn, be afforded fair hearing within a reasonable time by an independent and impartial court established by law."

Decision

Lord Hutton considered the appellant's submission that it was oppressive and an abuse of process to try him on a charge of capital murder after he had faced that charge on two previous occasions and after two juries had failed to reach agreement. He concluded that the appellant's failure to raise the issue of delay before the courts in Jamaica was a factor which weighed against the appellant's submission, though in exceptional cases the Board would quash a conviction after earlier abortive trials by reason of delay or oppression even though the issue had not been raised in the local courts.

Lord Hutton concluded that notwithstanding the lengthy period of delay between the charging of the appellant and his third trial, the conviction of the appellant should not be quashed by reason of that delay or on the grounds of oppression or abuse of process. This was because the case made against the appellant was a relatively simple one and his defence was also a simple one. It followed that the possibility of prejudice to the defence from the very lengthy delay can be substantially discounted.

Appeal allowed in part

APPLICATION FOR A STAY WHERE THERE IS A CONSTITUTIONAL RIGHT TO A SPEEDY TRIAL/A TRIAL WITHIN A REASONABLE TIME

Principle

In deciding whether the reasonable time requirement under the Constitution has been breached, it is necessary to consider a number of factors namely:

i. *the length of the delay.*
ii. *if the delay is one which, on its face is a real concern, it is necessary for the court to look into the detailed facts and circumstances of the particular case. It is necessary for the contracting state to explain and justify any excessive lapse of time.*
iii. *Other factors to consider are the complexity of the case, the conduct of the defendant and the manner in which the case has been dealt with by the administrative and judicial authorities.*

Judicial Committee of the Privy Council

Boolell v State of Mauritius

[2006] UKPC 46

Facts

The appellant, PB, was on 24 March 2003 convicted by the Intermediate Court of on an information containing one count of swindling. He appealed to the Supreme Court on a number of grounds, on all of which the court found against him. The appellant appealed to the Privy Council on the ground that there was a breach of his constitutional rights to a fair trial within a reasonable time, as guaranteed by section 10(1) of the Constitution. Section 10(1) of the Constitution of Mauritius contains a guarantee that where a person is charged with a criminal offence "the case shall be afforded a fair hearing within a reasonable time by an independent and impartial court established by law.

The appellant relied on the very long delay which took place between the date when the first statement under caution was taken from him and the eventual disposition of the case by the finding of guilt by the Intermediate Court.

Decision

Lord Carswell held in relation to delay:

> "Their Lordships accordingly consider that the following propositions should be regarded as correct in the law of Mauritius. (i) If a criminal case is not heard and completed within a reasonable time, that will of itself constitute a breach of section 10(1) of the Constitution, whether or not the defendant has been prejudiced by the delay. (ii) An appropriate remedy should be afforded for such breach, but the hearing should not be stayed or a conviction quashed on

account of delay alone, unless (a) the hearing was unfair or (b) it was unfair to try the defendant at all."

The learned judge referred approvingly to the principles established in In Dyer v Watson which were material to determining the reasonableness of the time taken to complete the hearing of a criminal case. These principles were as follows:

1. First consider the period of time which has elapsed. Unless that period is one which, on its face gives grounds for real concern it is almost certainly unnecessary to go further since the threshold of proving a breach of the reasonable time requirement is a high one, not easily crossed. But if the period which has elapsed is one which, on its face and without more, gives ground for real concern, two consequences follow.

2. First the court should look into the detailed facts and circumstances of the particular case. Secondly, it is necessary for the contracting state to explain and justify any lapse of time which appears to be excessive. There are three areas as calling for particular inquiry. The first area is the complexity of the case. The more complex a case, the greater the number of witnesses, then the longer the time which must necessarily be taken to prepare it adequately for trial and for any appellate hearing. But with any case, however complex, there comes a time when the passage of time becomes excessive and unacceptable.

The second matter is the conduct of the defendant. A defendant cannot properly complain of delay of which he is the author. This includes making spurious applications and challenges, changing legal advisers, absenting himself and exploiting procedural technicalities.

The third matter considered by the court is the manner in which the case has been dealt with by the administrative and judicial authorities. States cannot blame unacceptable delays on a general want of prosecutors or judges or courthouses or on chronic under-funding of the legal system. It is incumbent upon states so to organise their legal systems as to ensure that the reasonable time requirement is honoured.

In relation to the facts of the instant case, Lord Carswell held:

> "In their Lordships' opinion it is undeniable that the delay in completing the trial was caused to a considerable extent by the actions of the defendant. It is quite apparent from consideration of the history of the proceedings that he deliberately made numerous attempts to exploit and abuse the legal system, making inappropriate use of his legal knowledge and experience....The defendant's contribution to the delay may be an important factor, but before dismissing his complaint of delay as a breach of his constitutional rights the appellate tribunal is obliged to look at the whole picture."

Appeal allowed in part. Declaration that defendant's right to fair trial within reasonable time infringed.

APPLICATION FOR A STAY WHERE THERE IS A RE-TRIAL

Principles

a) *It is common practice, though not a rule of law, for the prosecution to offer no evidence where two juries have disagreed.*
b) *An application for a stay on the grounds of abuse of process should be raised before the trial judge and the Court of Appeal. The Privy Council would generally be reluctant to allow the issue to be raised for the first time before them.*
c) *Where the application for a stay is based on delay, the delay cannot be looked at in vacuo but must bear relation to local conditions and circumstances and the public interest.*

Judicial Committee of the Privy Council

Charles (Curtis), Carter (Steve) and Carter (Leroy) v The State

[1999] UKPC 24

Facts

On 1 August 1987 the three appellants were arrested and taken into custody. They appeared before the magistrate on 4 August 1987 but were not committed for trial until 11 August 1988. On 5 December 1991 the appellants were all convicted of murder. Two and a half years later on 15 June 1994 all the convictions were quashed by the Court of Appeal on the ground of misdirection by the trial judge in his summing up. A retrial was ordered and the second trial began on 11 April 1995.

On 25 April 1995 the jury concluded that they could not agree on a verdict. The prosecution still insisted on continuing and the appellants appeared before the judge and jury on 19 September 1996 (some nine years one month after the incident and two and a quarter years after a retrial was ordered). An application was made on behalf of Leroy Carter that the proceedings should be stayed on the ground that to try them for the third time after such a long delay was an abuse of the process of the court. The application was refused and the trial began. On 30 September 1996 all the defendants were convicted and sentenced to death.

The Court of Appeal dismissed an appeal on behalf of all three appellants on 25 September 1997. Almost 12 years after the incident, the court was asked to set aside the convictions on the ground that it was an abuse of process to try the accused for the third time in 1996.

Decision

Slynn LJ noted that the common practice was for the prosecution to offer no evidence where two juries had disagreed. In the instant case, only one jury was unable to reach a verdict. The learned judge also identified a second ground of complaint raised; namely that the appellants should not have been put on trial for the third time after so many years when one conviction had already been quashed and when one jury had been unable to agree on a verdict. Slynn LJ affirmed that it may be contrary to due process and unacceptable as a separate ground from delay that the prosecution having failed twice should continue to try to secure a conviction.

On the issue of when the applicant for a stay ought to make the necessary application, Slynn LJ ruled that:

> "Here, the issue was raised squarely before the judge even though it was not raised before the Court of Appeal. In the circumstances their Lordships accept that since the matter was raised before the trial judge the appellants are entitled to raise the issue before them on this appeal."

Slynn LJ summarised the basis of the defence assertion that they had suffered prejudice due to the delay. Steve Carter, for example, said that he could not remember precisely where they were, whether inside or outside the house, when they first saw Ward, that he could not say what he planned to do with the cutlass after he ran after Ward, that he could not recall having given certain statements to a police inspector, and that he could not remember where his brother was when Steve Carter first saw Ward. Another witness (Mc Dowald) said that he had seen three men running when he gave evidence at the trial, whereas he was recorded as having told the magistrate that he saw two men running, a matter which he himself at the trial could not recall.

The learned judge further held that claims to delay cannot be looked at *in vacuo* but must bear relation to local conditions and circumstances and the public interest. In other words it would be incorrect to look at the issue of delay in Trinidad and Tobago in the context of conditions and practices in England. On the facts of this case, Slynn LJ concluded that the delay was 'considerable and disturbing.'

Slynn LJ concluded

> "Their Lordships recognise that the trial judge has a margin of discretion in these cases and that they will not readily interfere with the exercise of this discretion. After careful consideration, however, they are satisfied that the combination of these two factors required the trial judge in this case to stay the third trial. For the prosecution to continue was wrong in principle and constituted a misuse of the criminal process."

Appeal allowed

CHAPTER EIGHT

THE PLEA

When a defendant first appears in court, the charge is read and he is called upon to enter a plea. Pleas are typically guilty and not guilty although pleas of autrefois acquit/convict or pardon may also be entered.

ENTERING THE PLEA

Principles

a) In the High Court, the plea of guilty must be entered personally.

b) Once an accused has been put in charge of a jury he can only be convicted or discharged by the verdict of the jury.

Court of Criminal Appeal

R v Heyes

[1951] 1 KB 29

Facts

On arraignment the appellant pleaded not guilty to charges of stealing and receiving. During the opening of the case for the prosecution, the appellant's counsel said that he (the appellant) wished to change his plea to guilty of receiving and asked that the jury should return a verdict accordingly. The recorder said that that was not necessary and he passed sentence without a verdict being returned.

Decision

Lord Goddard CJ noted that the transcript of the shorthand note of the proceedings did not indicate that the appellant himself was asked to plead. It merely contained a statement that his counsel said that he wished to plead guilty.

The learned judge held:

> "That is not enough. A prisoner must himself plead. After the jury had heard that the appellant wished to withdraw his plea and admit his guilt, the proper proceeding was to direct them to return a verdict."

Conviction quashed

THE DOCTRINE OF ISSUE ESTOPPEL AND CRIMINAL TRIALS

Principle

Issue Estoppel has no application to criminal trials.

House of Lords

DPP v Humphrys

[1977] A.C. 1

Facts

The respondent was charged with driving a motor vehicle while disqualified. The only issue at the trial was whether a police officer was correct in identifying the respondent as the driver of a motor bicycle on that day. In evidence, in answer to a question the respondent denied driving any motor vehicle during 1972. He was acquitted. Later he was charged with perjury, the allegation being that at the first trial he had wilfully made a statement which he knew to be false, viz., that he did not drive any motor vehicle during 1972.

The same police officer was a prosecution witness, with others, at the second trial. The judge, rejecting a plea of issue estoppel raised by the defence, allowed the police officer to give evidence again identifying the respondent as the driver of the motor bicycle. The respondent was convicted. The Court of Appeal allowed his appeal on the ground that the doctrine of issue estoppel applied. The Crown appealed.

Decision

Viscount Dilhorne held that the respondent in the present case was not at the second trial being tried for a crime in respect of which he had previously been acquitted or convicted, nor was he tried for a crime of which he could have been convicted on the first indictment. The offence of perjury was not the same or substantially the same as the offence he had been acquitted of, and the evidence necessary to support the second indictment was not evidence which proved that he had been driving while disqualified. Reliance by the respondent on autrefois acquit did not therefore suffice to sustain the conclusion of the Court of Appeal."

The learned judge stated that:

> "In my opinion issue estoppel has not and never has had a place in English criminal law and it is very undesirable that it should have."

His lordship subsequently concluded that a prosecution for perjury alleged to have been committed at an earlier trial at which the accused has been found not guilty of another offence did not place the accused in double jeopardy.

Appeal allowed. Conviction of perjury restored.

PLEAS OF GUILTY AND THE NEWTON HEARING

Principle

If the defendant wishes to ask the court to pass sentence on any other basis than that disclosed in the Crown case, it is necessary for the defendant to make that quite clear. If the Crown does not accept the defence account, and if the discrepancy between the two accounts is such as to have a potentially significant effect on the level of sentence, then consideration must be given to the holding of a Newton hearing to resolve the issue.

Court of Appeal

R v Tolera

[1998] EWCA Crim 1219

Facts

The appellant pleaded guilty to an offence of possession of a class "A" drug (heroin) with intent to supply. Following a Newton hearing, he was sentenced to five years' imprisonment. He was also recommended for deportation and a forfeiture order was made. He was granted leave to appeal sentence by the full court.

Decision

Lord Bingham of Cornwall CJ considered the procedure to be adopted where there was a discrepancy between the basis upon which a defendant pleaded guilty and the case presented by the Crown. The learned judge decided that where the defendant asked the court to pass sentence on any other basis than that disclosed in the Crown case, it was necessary for the defendant to make that quite clear. If the Crown did not accept the defence account, and if the discrepancy between the two accounts is such as to have a potentially significant effect on the level of sentence, then consideration had to be given to the holding of a Newton hearing to resolve the issue.

The learned judge further elaborated upon the procedure, stating that when a defendant gives an account of the facts of an offence to a probation officer which later forms part of a pre-sentence report, and those facts differ from the facts presented by the Crown (usually by glossing over, omitting or misdescribing the more incriminating features of the offence), the sentencing judge will not ordinarily pay attention (for purposes of sentence) to any account of the crime given by the defendant which conflicts with the Crown case.

However should the defendant want to rely on the pre-sentence report by asking the court to treat it as the basis of sentence, then the defendant should expressly draw the relevant paragraphs to the attention of the court and ask that it be treated as the basis of sentence. In such cases it was very desirable that the prosecution should be forewarned of this request and then the issue can be resolved if necessary by calling evidence.

Lord Bingham also noted that where the defendant, having pleaded guilty, advanced an account of the offence which the prosecution does not, or feels it cannot challenge, but which the court feels unable to accept, whether because it conflicts with the facts disclosed in the Crown case or because it is inherently incredible and defies common sense, it was desirable that the court should make it clear that it does not accept the defence account and why. In this case, failing any other resolution, a hearing can be held and evidence called to resolve the matter. This hearing would ordinarily involve calling the defendant and the prosecutor asking questions to test the defendant's evidence, exploring matters which the court wished to be explored.

FITNESS TO ENTER A PLEA

A defendant who is unable to properly instruct his attorney-at-law or to fully comprehend the nature and consequences of the plea, or the court proceedings will be unfit to plead to the charge.

Principle

The question of fitness to plead is determined by a jury in a Podola hearing.

Court of Criminal Appeal

R v Podola

[1960] 1 Q.B. 325

Facts

The appellant appeared before the court on a charge of capital murder. Before arraignment counsel for the appellant told the judge that he wished to call evidence which raised the preliminary issue whether he was fit to plead to the indictment. He alleged that he was suffering from hysterical amnesia and had completely lost his memory the day after his arrest.

Decision

Lord Parker C.J. outlined the process used by the court to try the preliminary issue. He stated that the trial of the preliminary issue was taken in two stages.

1. The jury should be directed to consider the whole of the evidence and to answer the question 'Are you satisfied upon that evidence that the accused person is insane so that he cannot be tried upon the indictment?'

2. If the contention that the accused is insane is put forward by the defence and contested by the prosecution, there is a burden upon the defence of satisfying the jury of the accused's insanity. In such a case, as in other criminal cases in which the onus of proof rests upon the defence, the onus is discharged if the jury are satisfied on the balance of probabilities that the accused's insanity has been made out.

3. Conversely, if the prosecution alleges, and the defence disputes, insanity, there is a burden upon the prosecution of establishing it.

ENTERING A PLEA OF GUILTY TO MURDER

Principle

An accused person on a capital charge must be represented by an attorney before he is arraigned. Even where the accused is so represented, a judge must satisfy himself that the accused person was fit to plead at the time of his arraignment before he accepts a plea of guilty to murder.

Court of Appeal of Trinidad and Tobago

Habib (Simon) v The State

C.A. Crim. 102 of 1988

Facts

The appellant was charged with murder. When he appeared before the trial judge, he was not represented by an attorney. He was arraigned and, following upon his arraignment, he pleaded guilty to the charge. Thereafter, the trial judge inquired of the appellant whether he wished to have him appoint an attorney on his behalf, either before or after the allocutus. The appellant said, 'No'. Following upon the allocutus the trial judge then asked the appellant whether he had anything to say on his behalf, except to say that he was guilty. The appellant said, 'No'. The trial judge accordingly passed the mandatory sentence. The appellant appealed to the Court of Appeal against his conviction for murder.

Decision

Bernard CJ stated that generally, if on arraignment on a charge of murder an accused person pleads guilty, that plea is a good plea. A plea of guilty to a capital charge may be entered by reason of sheer bravado, because the accused truly wished to confess his crime, or due to unfitness to plead.

His lordship decided that should the accused person be unrepresented, the trial judge should, before his arraignment, ensure that he was represented, and he must do so even if the accused person declines legal representation. The reason for this is because judge must satisfy himself that the accused person would have had the benefit of instruction and advice by an attorney who would take steps to ensure that the question of his fitness to plead would be resolved.

Bernard CJ concluded:

> "As the record shows in this case, quite apart from the fact that he was not represented by an attorney as he should have been, one cannot say that at the time the appellant had been arraigned and the indictment had been read to him that he was in fact fit to plead. As we said, there was a fundamental breach of procedure in this case. The breach went to the root of the matter and was such as to render the trial of the appellant a nullity."

Appeal allowed. Order for retrial.

THE PLEA OF AUTREFOIS

At common law, the rule against double jeopardy holds that a person may not be tried a second time for the same offence in respect of which he was in jeopardy of being convicted, was convicted or acquitted in a previous trial.

Principle

The plea of autrefois would be inapplicable where the essential ingredients of the offences were not the same. The plea of autrefois in a second trial is not necessarily available even where the facts in the two trials have much in common.

House of Lords

Connelly v Director of Public Prosecutions

[1964] 2 AC 1254

Facts

Arising out of an armed raid two indictments were preferred against the appellant, one charging him (together with three others) with the murder of H, the second charging him (together with three others) with robbery with aggravation. At the trial of the first indictment for murder the appellant put forward two defences, an alibi and alternatively that he did not have the necessary intent to murder. All four accused were found guilty of murder. On appeal, the appellant's conviction of murder was set aside. The appellant was subsequently tried on the second indictment and convicted of robbery with aggravation. He appealed against this conviction.

Decision

Lord Morris of Borth y Gest stated that the correct principle to be applied was that it did not matter that facts being tried on the second indictment were precisely the same as those which were tried in the first. The court is concerned with charges of offences or crimes. The test was therefore, whether such proof as is necessary to convict of the second offence would establish guilt of the first offence or of an offence for which on the first charge there could be a conviction.

His lordship then applied this principle to the facts and concluded:

> "...the question is whether proof that there was robbery with aggravation would support a charge of murder or manslaughter. It seems to me quite clear that it would not. The crimes are distinct. There can be robbery without killing. There can be killing without robbery. Evidence of robbery does not prove murder or manslaughter. Conviction of robbery cannot involve conviction of murder or manslaughter. Nor does an acquittal of murder or manslaughter necessarily involve an acquittal of robbery. Nor on a charge of murder or manslaughter could a man be convicted of robbery. That the facts in the two trials have much in common is not a true test of the availability of the plea of autrefois acquit."

Appeal dismissed

Principle

A second prosecution of a more serious offence based on substantially the same facts as an earlier prosecution should be barred.

Court of Appeal

R v Beedie

[1997] EWCA Crim 714

Facts

The appellant was the landlord of a bedsit where a young woman had died of carbon monoxide poisoning, caused by a poor maintenance of a gas fire. The appellant pleaded guilty in the magistrates' court to an offence contrary to s 33 of the Health and Safety at Work Act 1974. The appellant was subsequently charged with manslaughter on the basis of the above facts.

At trial, his plea of autrefois convict was rejected by the trial judge and the appellant accordingly pleaded guilty. The appellant appealed, contending that the judge was wrong in rejecting his plea of autrefois convict and in refusing to stay the proceedings for manslaughter.

Decision

Rose LJ held that the majority in Connelly v DPP defined autrefois narrowly when they held that it occurred where a second indictment charged the same offence as the first. He also held that on the facts of the instant case, even though it was in the public interest that there was a prosecution for manslaughter this did not give rise to special circumstances.

His lordship concluded:

> "In our judgment there being, as we have indicated, no special circumstances in the present case, it is one in which the general rule should have prevailed. A stay should have been ordered because the manslaughter allegation was based on substantially the same facts as the earlier summary prosecutions, and gave rise to a prosecution for an offence of greater gravity, no new facts having occurred..."

Appeal allowed. Conviction quashed.

AUTREFOIS AND ALTERNATIVE OFFENCES

Principle

Statute may provide that in the event that the court does not convict for the principal offence the court may nevertheless convict of an alternative offence. Where following an acquittal of the principal offence, the evidence also fails to establish that the defendant was in jeopardy of conviction for the alternative offence the plea of autrefois acquit will not succeed where the defendant is put on trial for the alternative offence.

Court of Appeal of Trinidad and Tobago

Lewis v Irish

Decision of the Court of the Appeal of Trinidad and Tobago, 3rd June 1966

Facts

The respondent was charged with unlawful possession. The case was part heard before a magistrate and adjourned to a later date. In the interim, further inquiries were made, and a charge of larceny of the same property was laid. The magistrate subsequently dismissed the charge of unlawful possession, and in relation to the larceny charge, accepted a plea of autrefois acquit. The prosecution appealed.

S.73 (5) of the Summary Courts Ordinance states:

"Where an offence under s 36, 37, 44, or 45 of the Summary Offences Ordinance is charged and the evidence establishes the commission of the offence of larceny of any kind or of receiving property knowing the same to have been stolen, the defendant shall not be entitled to have the complaint dismissed but he may be convicted of such larceny or of receiving property knowing the same to have been stolen and punished accordingly."

Decision

Phillips JA considered the appellant's submission that the above-quoted statutory provision did not expose any person charged with the offence of unlawful possession to the danger of conviction for larceny since these are offences of an entirely distinct nature. The learned judge compared the relationship between the offences of unlawful possession and larceny with that existing between other offences in connection with which the issue of autrefois often arose such as murder and manslaughter, wounding with intent and unlawful wounding, manslaughter by reckless driving and dangerous driving. With these latter examples, liability for one offence involves the commission of the other.

His lordship held:

> "We consider the submission of the acting Solicitor-General to be sound and that the answer to the question posed must depend upon whether or not the necessary condition for the application of the subsection can be said to have existed, namely, whether or not the evidence given in the unlawful possession case established the commission of the offence of larceny by anyone (and not necessarily the respondent). From a perusal of that evidence it becomes manifest that it did not. We accordingly hold that the respondent was never in jeopardy of being convicted of larceny....
>
> "...In our judgment, therefore, the learned magistrate came to the wrong conclusion in this case. In the result we allow the appeal, set aside the magistrate's order of dismissal, and order that the case be heard *de novo* before another magistrate."

Appeal allowed

Principle

Where there is an acquittal of a more serious offence, there is no bar to further proceedings on a lesser alternative offence.

Court of Appeal of Trinidad and Tobago

Joseph v Mohammed

Decision of the Court of Appeal of Trinidad and Tobago, 15th January 1964

Facts

By s 55 of the Road Traffic Ordinance Cap 16 No 3 [T]: "Where a person is charged summarily before a magistrate with an offence under…s 46 [reckless or dangerous driving] and the magistrate is of the opinion that the offence is not proved, then, at any time during the hearing or immediately thereafter, the magistrate may, without prejudice to any other powers possessed by him, direct or allow a charge for an offence under s 47 [driving without due care and attention or without reasonable consideration for other users of the road] to be preferred forthwith against the defendant and may thereupon proceed with that charge…".

The appellant preferred separate informations against the respondent for dangerous driving and driving without due care and attention. The charge of dangerous driving was heard first and dismissed. The charge of driving without due care and attention was then proceeded with, but a magistrate upheld the respondent's plea of autrefois acquit and dismissed the charge. The prosecution appealed.

Decision

Phillips JA stated that the issue under consideration was whether the respondent when he was tried for the offence of dangerous driving under s 46 was in jeopardy of being convicted on that charge of the offence of driving without due care and attention. The learned judge concluded that the respondent was not in jeopardy since it was not a case similar to a case of murder, where a person charged with murder is at common law liable on the same indictment to be convicted of the lesser offence of manslaughter.

His lordship concluded:

> "I think enough has been said to show that a charge of careless driving is something distinct from dangerous driving, and when the respondent was acquitted of the charge of dangerous driving he was never in jeopardy of being convicted of the charge of careless driving. In those circumstances, we hold that the decision of the magistrate was wrong and should be set aside."

Appeal allowed

Principle

Where statute allows a jury to find an accused guilty of a lesser summary offence and the accused is convicted of this offence after summary trial, this conviction will bar further criminal proceedings for the greater indictable offence.

Court of Appeal of Trinidad and Tobago

Mohammed v R

Decision of the Court of the Appeal of Trinidad and Tobago, 12th February 1965

Facts

The appellant was charged indictably with the offence of manslaughter and summarily with the offence of dangerous driving. At the close of the preliminary inquiry into the charge of manslaughter a magistrate found that no *prima facie* case was made out and discharged the appellant. He was thereupon convicted on his plea of guilty to the summary charge of dangerous driving. Following his conviction a judge considered the evidence given at the preliminary inquiry and ordered that the appellant be arrested and committed to stand his trial at the Assizes on a charge of manslaughter.

On his subsequent arraignment on an indictment for manslaughter the appellant pleaded autrefois convict contending that he ought not to be prosecuted further since he was already convicted of the lesser offence of dangerous driving. On the direction of the trial judge this plea was rejected by the jury and the appellant was convicted of manslaughter and sentenced to a term of imprisonment. The appellant appealed his conviction.

Decision

Phillips JA agreed with the appellant's submission that the evidence necessary to support the indictment for manslaughter would have been sufficient to procure a legal conviction for the offence of dangerous driving.

Philips JA held:

> "At the time of the first trial of the appellant for dangerous driving the alleged offence of manslaughter was already complete, and it appears to us that it would be investing the executive authorities of the state with powers that could easily become an instrument of oppression if, in circumstances in which it is open to them to prosecute an offender for either of two possible offences, having elected to proceed on the less serious charge and obtained a conviction thereon, they

should then be allowed to prosecute the offender on the graver charge. This, in our opinion, is contrary to both the letter and spirit of the existing law of this country."

The learned judge concluded that the appellant's plea of autrefois convict should have been upheld by the trial judge.

Appeal allowed

Principle

Where on a charge of murder the judge leaves to the jury two possible verdicts of murder or manslaughter and the jury brings in a verdict of not guilty of murder, but are unable to agree sufficiently as to manslaughter, autrefois acquit will not bar a subsequent trial for manslaughter on the same evidence.

Judicial Committee of the Privy Council

Director of Public Prosecutions v Nasralla

[1967] UKPC 3

Facts

At the trial of the accused on a charge of murder the judge left to the jury the two possible verdicts of murder or manslaughter. The jury brought in a verdict of not guilty of murder, but were unable to agree sufficiently as to manslaughter and did not bring in a verdict on that issue.

The case was adjourned for the accused to be tried for manslaughter. The Court of Appeal subsequently ruled that the accused could not be tried for manslaughter since to do so would breach section 20 of the Constitution, which bears the marginal note "Provisions to secure protection of law". This states at sub-s (8):

"No person who shows that he has been tried by any competent court for a criminal offence and either convicted or acquitted shall again be tried for that offence or for any other criminal offence of which he could have been convicted at the trial for that offence…"

The Crown appealed that decision.

Decision

Lord Devlin held that in order to maintain a plea of autrefois acquit a verdict of acquittal of the offence charged was required. This was not the case in this matter as there was a disagreement on the verdict for manslaughter.

Lord Devlin concluded:

> "…In the present case they were directed by the judge to consider both murder and manslaughter and they evidently did so. When asked for their verdict on manslaughter they did not answer…They said that they or the necessary majority of them were unable to agree …What is required for the plea of autrefois acquit is proof of acquittal of manslaughter…"

Appeal allowed

THE TEST TO DECIDE WHETHER A SUBMISION OF AUTREFOIS WILL SUCCEED

Principle

A plea of autrefois is not bound to succeed even where, to a great extent, the same facts will be explored in both the former and the subsequent proceedings. The test to be applied is whether the question to be answered in the subsequent proceedings is in fact materially different than that in the former proceedings.

Court of Appeal Civil Division

Re Barings plc and others (No 2); Secretary of State for Trade and Industry v Baker and others

[1999] 1 All ER 311

Facts

The Secretary of State for Trade and Industry issued proceedings against B and nine other former directors of companies in a group, seeking disqualification orders under s 6 of the Company Directors Disqualification Act 1986. B applied for a stay of the proceedings on the ground that the prosecution of the proceedings against him would infringe the principle of double jeopardy (or the collateral attack principle).

He argued that he had already successfully resisted disciplinary proceedings brought against him by the Securities and Futures Authority (the SFA) in which the same, or substantially the same charges were made against him as were made by the Secretary of State in the disqualification proceedings. In the alternative he argued that in the circumstances, the prosecution of the proceedings against him would be unfair, unjust and oppressive.

B's application was dismissed and he applied for leave to appeal.

Decision

Chadwick LJ held that the overriding consideration was the need to preserve public confidence in the administration of justice. The court was therefore entitled to stay proceedings where to allow them to continue would threaten its own integrity, or to state it another way, where to allow proceedings to continue would bring the administration of justice into disrepute among right thinking people.

His lordship reasoned that before the court could stay the disqualification proceedings regard would be had to the nature of the SFA proceedings as well as the disqualification proceedings and the interrelation between them. It would be crucial in this regard to examine whether the issues in the disqualification proceedings were the same, or substantially the same, as those which had already been investigated and adjudicated upon in the SFA proceedings.

The learned judge upon an examination of the disqualification proceedings observed that the disqualification proceedings involved an investigation into the very matter which was held not to be relevant in the SFA proceedings--namely what responsibility did Mr Baker have as a director of BB & Co, for the insolvency of BB & Co.

Chadwick LJ concluded:

> "The relevant question will be whether Mr Baker's acts or omissions fell so far short of the competence required of a director of BB & Co that the court ought to reach the conclusion that he is unfit to be concerned in the management of a company--that is to say, any company. That is not at all the same question as that which the tribunal had to consider--namely whether Mr Baker was a fit and proper person to remain on the SFA register."

Waller LJ stated that the appellant's submission was based on the principle of double jeopardy by reason of the proceedings instituted by the SFA, backed by the assertion that the continuation of the disqualification proceedings would subject Mr Baker to unacceptable injustice, oppression and unfairness. The learned judge also stated that the appellant would not necessarily succeed simply because he was able to show that to a great extent the same facts would be explored in the disqualification proceedings as were explored in the SFA tribunals.

Waller LJ concluded:

> "(1) As explained by Chadwick LJ and the judge, the question to be answered in the different proceedings is in fact materially different. The SFA is concerned with whether the conduct is such as to render a director unfit to be registered in accordance with the SFA rules. A finding that he was or a finding that he was not cannot necessarily answer the question which arises under disqualification proceedings which is whether he is fit to be a director of any company..."

Swinton Thomas LJ held that even though the underlying facts of the charges brought by the SFA and the Secretary of State were the same, the status, the issues and the consequences of the two sets of proceedings had very important differing features.

Application for leave to appeal dismissed

Principle

In order to rely upon autrefois convict, it must be shown that there was a conviction and sentence at the first trial.

Richards (Lloydell) v R

[1992] UKPC 28

Facts

The appellant was charged with murder. When he was arraigned, he pleaded guilty to manslaughter and counsel for the Crown said that he accepted that plea. The case was then adjourned to enable character witnesses to be called in mitigation. When the hearing was resumed the Director of Public Prosecutions entered a *nolle prosequi* and the appellant was subsequently charged again with murder. Following a trial before a judge and jury the appellant was convicted of murder and sentenced to death. His appeal to the Court of Appeal on the ground that his trial was a violation of section 20(8) of the Constitution of Jamaica (protection against double jeopardy) was dismissed and he appealed by special leave to the Privy Council.

Decision

Lord Bridge of Harwich identified the central issue raised by the appeal as being whether a plea of autrefois convict can be sustained by anything less than evidence that the offence with which the defendant was charged had already been the subject of a complete adjudication against him by a court of competent jurisdiction comprising both the decision establishing his guilt (whether it be the decision of the court or of the jury or the entry of his own plea) and the final disposal of the case by the court by passing sentence or making some other order such as an order of absolute discharge. The learned judge also noted that section 20(8) of the Jamaican Constitution embodied the common law doctrines of autrefois convict and autrefois acquit.

His lordship concluded:

> "…when a plea of guilty to a lesser offence than that charged has initially been accepted by the prosecutor with the approval of the court, there can, it appears to their Lordships, be no finality in that 'acceptance' until sentence is passed."

Advice that appeal be dismissed

DISMISSAL ON THE MERITS

In order to rely on a plea of autrefois acquit the previous dismissal must have been one which followed a full adjudication. This is termed a dismissal on the merits and can be compared to a mere technical acquittal.

Principle

Where the defendant appears and pleads not guilty and the prosecutor leads no evidence this results in a dismissal on the merits.

Court of Appeal of Guyana

PC Bowen v Johnson

25 WIR 60

Facts

An indictable information was laid against the respondent. By consent the charge was taken summarily, and a plea of not guilty was entered. The matter was adjourned for a peremptory fixture and the respondent appeared, but the prosecution was not ready to proceed because its witnesses were absent. The prosecutor, offering no explanation for their non-appearance, made no application for an adjournment and the magistrate marked the case-jacket "struck out". He then discharged the respondent, indicating later on in his reasons for decision that his striking out "amounted to a dismissal on the merits".

The appellant swore to a second information in respect of the same charge against the respondent who again pleaded not guilty. On this occasion, however, counsel on her behalf entered a special plea of autrefois acquit, his contention being that the respondent had been acquitted on that very charge when the case-jacket was marked "struck out" by the trial magistrate. The court accepted the respondent's plea of autrefois acquit and an appeal by the prosecution to the Full Court of the Supreme Court was dismissed. The prosecution appealed to the Court of Appeal.

Decision

HAYNES C acknowledged that the common law plea of autrefois rested upon an adjudication on the merits. The learned judge agreed that a complaint could be dismissed although no evidence was led in cases where the prosecution deliberately offered no evidence or because the witnesses did not attend and there was no adjournment. He rejected the contention, however, that at common law a dismissal upon no evidence being offered could not be a dismissal upon the merits.

Haynes C held:

> "I would hold it could be. It would be strange if offering no evidence at all should place the prosecution in a better position than offering insufficient evidence."

Appeal dismissed. Decision of the Full Court affirmed.

Principle

In order to rely on autrefois, the first adjudication must have been before a court of competent jurisdiction.

Court of Criminal Appeal of England and Wales

R v Hogan

[1960] 2 QB 513

Facts

The appellants, who had escaped from prison, had been punished by the visiting committee of justices under the Prison Rules 1949 by forfeiture of privileges, earnings, loss of remission, etc. The issue arose as to whether there could be a subsequent prosecution for prison breach arising out of the same facts.

Decision

The Lord Chief Justice summarised the appellants' contention as being that the prison breach was in effect escaping by force; in other words, a simple escape with aggravation. It followed that if a man was already convicted for simple escape, then a charge cannot be brought against him subsequently for an aggravated offence if the offences in both cases arose on exactly the same matter. His lordship dealt with the appellant's argument by holding:

> "The court, however, feels that the principle…is meant to apply and can only apply to the decisions of courts of competent jurisdiction. Though not strictly a case of autrefois convict it is very much on those lines."

Appeals dismissed

Principle

The defendant can be in peril of conviction only when the magistrate sits at a hearing for the purpose of determining whether the defendant is guilty; that can be the first hearing when the plea is put, but is more likely to be the date fixed for the summary trial.

Court of Appeal

R v J (JF)

[2014] QB 561

Facts

The defendant was charged with common assault and pleaded not guilty at the magistrates' court. Before the matter could come to trial, the prosecution received medical evidence which showed that the alleged victim had received far more serious injuries than had at first been apparent, and therefore decided to add a charge of assault occasioning actual bodily harm.

At the next hearing in the magistrates' court the charge of assault occasioning actual bodily harm was put to the defendant and he entered a plea of not guilty. The justices adjourned the matter for committal. The prosecution offered no evidence on the common assault charge and the charge of common assault was dismissed.

The defendant was later committed to the Crown Court on the charge of assault occasioning actual bodily harm. In the Crown Court, the point was taken on behalf of the defendant that the dismissal of the common assault charge gave rise to a plea of autrefois acquit and that the Crown Court should enter a verdict of not guilty on the indictment charging him with assault occasioning actual bodily harm. The judge stayed the indictment, considering himself bound by Court of Appeal authority to do so. The prosecution appealed against that ruling.

Decision

Sir John Thomas P firstly reiterated the fundamental principle that a person is not to be harassed or prosecuted twice for a crime. Thus if a person has been convicted of a crime previously, he cannot be tried again (autrefois convict); similarly, if he has been acquitted of a crime, he cannot be tried again for the crime (autrefois acquit). His lordship further reasoned that the present case provided compelling illustration as to the need to confine the plea of autrefois to a narrow basis.

His lordship held:

> "...In any case where the narrow application of the principle would result in unfairness or injustice to a defendant amounting to oppression, the remedy lies in the power of the court to stay the proceedings."

The learned judge stated that a crucial issue was whether JFJ was in peril given (1) the fact that the charge of common assault was dismissed as part of a reorganisation of the prosecution case to which the defendant did not object and (2) the stage of the proceedings at which the justices dismissed the charge. He held in this regard:

> "No submission has been made, nor could it be made, that in the present case, the Crown's conduct in seeking to have JFJ tried on a greater charge when he has technically been acquitted on the lesser charge is in any way unfair or unjust, let alone abusive or oppressive."

The learned judge further held:

> "The application of these principles to the present case turns in our view on two questions: (i) Was the defendant in peril if the charge was dismissed in the context of a simple reorganisation of the prosecution case in a manner to which the defendant did not object? (ii) Was the dismissal of the charge of common assault done at a stage in the proceedings when the defendant could not realistically be said to be in peril?"

The learned judge concluded that since all that was done amounted to the Crown reorganising its case and no objection was taken, then the defendant could not be in peril in such circumstances. This was so even in spite of the fact that the record stated that there was an acquittal on the charge of common assault. The formality of the court record made no difference to the reality.

On the issue of when a defendant could be said to be in peril, his lordship distilled the following principles:

1. In the Crown Court, the defendant is in peril when he is put in charge of the jury.

2. If the court sets a date for trial, the defendant attends and the prosecutor unsuccessfully applies for an adjournment of the trial, then the justices are entitled to proceed with the trial. In this case the defendant is in peril. If the prosecution then has no evidence to call, then an acquittal by the justices would be at a time when the defendant is in peril for the purpose of autrefois.

3. It does not mean that the trial always commences when the information is put and the plea made. There is no reason for treating the position in the magistrates' courts as being different. The defendant can be in peril only when the justices or district judge are at a hearing for the purpose of determining whether the defendant is guilty; that can be the first hearing when the plea is put, but in recent times it is more likely to be the date fixed for the summary trial.

Sir John Thomas P held on the facts of the instant case:

> "In the present case, at the time that no evidence was offered, JFJ had been charged with assault occasioning actual bodily harm, the magistrates' court had determined that the case should be committed to the Crown Court and the court had adjourned the proceedings under that charge for committal. No objection was taken to that course. In our view, JFJ was not in peril at the time the prosecutor subsequently offered no evidence and the charge was dismissed by the justices. That was both because the defence had not objected to the

reorganisation of the way in which the prosecution was to put its case and because in any event a stage in the proceedings had not yet been reached where he could be in peril."

Appeal allowed

CHAPTER NINE

IMPORTANT ASPECTS OF SUMMARY PROCEDURE

Summary trials are conducted in the magistrates' court. The magistrate presides over these trials and sits as a tribunal of fact and law. The magistrate also passes sentence on a defendant found guilty after a summary trial or who has entered a plea of guilty. The procedure in summary courts is governed by summary procedure legislation and the relevant rules of court (where applicable).

THE DEFENDANT'S RIGHT TO BE HEARD

Principle

An accused person has the right to be represented by counsel at his trial and to have his witnesses give evidence. A denial of these rights is a denial of natural justice.

Court of Appeal of the Windward and Leeward islands

Allette v Chief of Police

(1965) 10 WIR 243

Facts

The appellant was arrested on 3 August 1965, at 12.45 pm and charged with a traffic offence. He was released on bail at 4.30 pm on the same day. The next morning the appellant appeared in court to answer the charge, and requested an adjournment to brief counsel and summon witnesses. The magistrate refused his request for an adjournment and proceeded to hear the charge. The appellant refused to cross-examine the witnesses for the prosecution, did not give evidence on his own behalf or call any witnesses. He was convicted and appealed.

Decision

Field CJ affirmed that an accused person has the right to be represented by counsel at his trial and to have his witnesses give evidence, and to deny him the opportunity to retain and instruct counsel or secure the attendance of any witnesses to be called on his behalf was a clear denial of natural justice.

Field CJ held:

> "When a person is arrested and brought before a court within hours after his arrest, the ends of justice would best be met by an adjournment for such time as the magistrate considers reasonable to enable him to retain counsel having regard to the nature of the charge and the time needed to retain counsel to prepare the defence."

Appeal allowed. Case remitted for hearing de novo.

ADJOURNMENTS

Principle

Whether or not an adjournment should be granted in any particular circumstances is a matter in the discretion of court.

Divisional Court of Barbados

Green v Springer

(1976) 28 WIR 9

Facts

The respondent was charged and appeared before a magistrate with two offences. When the matter was called for hearing the appellant, the Comptroller of Customs, appeared in person and unsuccessfully sought an adjournment to enable him to be represented. The magistrate gave reasons for refusing the request for an adjournment. The case proceeded.

At the commencement of the afternoon session, counsel entered appearance for the appellant and unsuccessfully sought an adjournment to enable him to study the evidence. The magistrate gave reasons for refusing the application. The magistrate dismissed both charges and the Comptroller of Customs appealed on the ground that the refusal of the magistrate to grant the adjournment requested by him was unreasonable, in breach of the rules of natural justice.

Decision

Williams J affirmed the principle that an appellate court does not seek to usurp the functions of an inferior court. Thus should a magistrate exercise a discretion judicially, the Divisional Court would not seek to substitute its own discretion. The learned judge cited Allette v Chief of Police and approved of the principle expressed therein that requests for adjournments for the purpose of obtaining counsel or to call witnesses should be considered on their merits and that reasons should be supplied for refusing such requests.

On the facts of the instant case his lordship held that the magistrate did deliberately exercise a discretion and that his reasons for so doing disclosed the considerations which he took into account in refusing to grant the adjournment requested.

Williams J concluded:

> "We are unable to say that he took into account matter that was irrelevant or that he proceeded on any wrong principle."

Appeal dismissed.

EX PARTE HEARINGS

Principles

a) Magistrates are entitled to presume that practitioners who appear on behalf of clients are properly authorized.

b) Where a defendant is afforded an opportunity to be heard but no use is made of it, a conviction after a hearing ex parte would only be set aside if there had been no culpable neglect on the part of the defendant.

Court of Appeal of Trinidad and Tobago

Bharath v Cambridge

(1972) 20 WIR 450

Facts

The appellant was convicted, in his absence, of using obscene language to the annoyance of persons contrary to s 54 of the Summary Offences Ordinance. He appealed. The appellant contended that the hearing of the summons against him was adjourned in his absence and in the absence of any counsel or solicitor retained by him, that no notice of the date of the adjourned hearing had been served on him and that the court should not have proceeded with the matter *ex parte* on the adjourned hearing because all the prerequisites of such a hearing had not been fulfilled.

Decision

Georges JA (Ag) recounted the facts and noted that the appellant admitted that he was duly served with a summons to appear on 23 June 1971, and stated that he did not appear on that day because he was unwell. He further stated that he had 'made arrangements' with Mr Misir 'to obtain an adjournment of the said complaint' on the ground of his illness. The appellant later argued that if someone did appear on 20 July on behalf of the appellant, this person was not authorised to do so and it could not be said that the hearing had been adjourned in the presence and hearing of the appellant or his counsel or solicitor as required by s 63.

His lordship held that the appellant was submitting that a magistrate would have to satisfy himself that a legal practitioner who stated that he appeared for a defendant who was absent was indeed authorised to do so. Otherwise the magistrate would have to ensure that the defendant was informed of the adjourned date by issuing a fresh notice in any such case. His lordship held that this submission was untenable since it would place far too heavy a burden on the courts.

Georges JA held:

> "Magistrates are entitled to presume that practitioners who appear on behalf of clients are properly authorised to do so."

In disposing of the appeal his lordship stated:

> "In our judgment, even if the counsel who appeared on behalf of the appellant was not authorised to do so, he would be his counsel or solicitor within the meaning of s 63 of the Ordinance, so that on 20 July the case would have been adjourned in the presence of the appellant's counsel. All the

prerequisites prescribed by the Ordinance were therefore fulfilled and we find that the conviction was regularly obtained."

Appeal dismissed.

Principle

Where a defendant who is given a reasonable opportunity of being heard, through his own culpable neglect, fails to take advantage of that opportunity, the court will be entitled to proceed ex parte.

Supreme Court of Trinidad and Tobago Appellate Jurisdiction

Spencer v Bramble

Decision of the Court of Appeal of Trinidad and Tobago, 19th March 1960

Facts

The appellant was charged before a magistrate in two complaints alleging the commission of traffic offences. He pleaded not guilty to both and the magistrate in the hearing and presence of the appellant and his solicitor adjourned the cases to a fixed date for trial. On the day so fixed the appellant failed to appear.

No explanation for his absence was forthcoming, and no application for any further adjournment was submitted on his behalf. The magistrate in pursuance of the powers conferred upon him by s 63 (4) of the Summary Courts Ordinance, Cap 3, No 4 [T], proceeded to hear the two complaints, and finding them proved, convicted and fined the appellant. The appellant appealed against both convictions stating as his ground of appeal on each, "I was mistaken as to the date of hearing", and the charge was heard *ex parte*.

Decision

Blagden J stated that the issue to be decided was that even if the appellant was genuinely mistaken as to the date to which the hearing of his case was adjourned, whether the case could be re-opened before the magistrate and leave granted to adduce evidence.

His lordship held:

> "The critical question to consider here is whether the defendant was given a reasonable opportunity of putting forward his case or, to put it another way, whether he was given an opportunity of being heard. It is clear that he was given due notice of the complaints against him and in pursuance thereof he appeared in court and pleaded not guilty to them. On the application of his solicitor and in his presence the cases were adjourned to 3 April 1959. Through an error on his part he did not appear on that date, and thus, by his own culpable neglect, he deprived himself of the opportunity of putting forward his case in answer to the complaints against him."

Blagden J concluded that persons summoned before magistrates' courts were expected properly and diligently to acquaint themselves with simple procedural details as the time when and the place where their cases will be heard. Permission to re-open cases would only be granted on the strongest grounds where it was manifest that otherwise gross injustice would result, otherwise the process of the magistrates' courts might be subject to grave abuse.

Appeals dismissed.

Principle

Where it has been proved on oath that the absent defendant was served with a summons, the magistrate is entitled to proceed ex parte to hear the complaint. Following the hearing, the court is functus officio and has no jurisdiction to re-hear the complaint.

High Court of St Lucia West Indies Associated States

Agdoma v Tomy

(1968) 12 WIR 296

Facts

Section 1075 (1) (a) of the Criminal Code, Cap 250 [St Lucia], reads:

"1075. (1) If the defendant against whom a summons is issued does not appear before the court at the time mentioned therein, and it is proved upon oath, to the satisfaction of the court, that the summons was duly served within the time appointed for appearing to the same or that the defendant wilfully avoids service, the court may, in its discretion, either–

(a) proceed *ex parte* to the hearing of the complaint and adjudicate thereon as fully and effectually to all intents and purposes as if the defendant had personally appeared before it in obedience to the summons...."

The defendant was summoned to appear before a magistrate to answer two offences with which he was charged but failed to appear at the time of hearing mentioned in the summonses. The court heard evidence on oath proving service upon the defendant and thereby adjudicated upon the matters and convicted the defendant on both complaints. Later at about 2.45 pm the same day, the defendant appeared in court with his counsel who submitted a medical certificate on his behalf and explained that his absence from court that morning was due to illness.

The magistrate decided the convictions and sentences should not stand and he set them aside and arranged to re-hear the cases on a later date. On this date when the cases came up for re-hearing, the magistrate announced in open court that he would instead refer the cases to the High Court for an opinion on a case stated, and he submitted for the opinion of the High Court the question:

"Whether on the above statement of facts the District Court came to a correct decision in point of law in setting aside the convictions and sentences and acceding to a re-hearing of the cases?"

Decision

Bishop J held that the court had effectually and fully disposed of the matter when he heard it *ex parte* on the morning of 17 June. In these circumstances, the magistrate had no authority to set aside the convictions and to decide to re-hear the cases, even considering that a medical certificate was submitted by the defendant which explained that his absence from court that morning was due to illness.

Reference answered in the negative.

DISMISSAL FOR NON-APPEARANCE OF COMPLAINANT

Principle

A magistrate's discretion to dismiss a complaint for non-appearance of the complainant must be exercised reasonably and judicially and not in an ad hoc and arbitrary manner.

Court of Appeal of Trinidad and Tobago

WPC Burgess v Silverton

Mag. Appeal No. 98 of 2008

Facts

The respondent was charged with summary offences, which were dismissed by the court for non-appearance of the appellant/complainant. The matters had been called 14 times. The respondent was not ready to proceed on 9 occasions while the appellant/complainant was absent on 4 occasions with no explanation being offered for her absence. The prosecution appealed the dismissal.

Decision

S John JA held that while magistrates have a discretion to dismiss a complaint for non-appearance of the complainant that discretion had to be exercised reasonably and judicially and not in an *ad hoc* and arbitrary manner. Before proceeding to dismiss a matter for non-appearance of the complainant, the court should first stand the matter down to ascertain from the prosecutor the reason for the non-appearance. The learned judge stated that on the facts, the magistrate erred when he dismissed the complaint since there was no indorsement that the matter was fixed for trial on that date.

John JA held:

> "In our view on the facts of this case the magistrate had the jurisdiction to show his disapproval of the absence of the complainant by referring the matter to the court prosecutor for transmission to the head of the Court and Process Branch for such action if any as he deemed necessary. This he failed to do."

BIAS OF JUDICIAL OFFICERS

Principle

There is a presumption of impartiality when a judicial officer hears a second case involving the trial of a litigant who had been previously tried by the same judicial officer.

Court of Appeal of Jamaica

R v Gordon (Ruel)

Decision of the Court of Appeal of Jamaica, 28th March 1969

Facts

The appellant was summoned to appear at a resident magistrate's court to answer two charges. The resident magistrate proceeded to hear one of the charges and found the appellant guilty thereon. He then proceeded to hear the other charge on which he also found the appellant guilty. On appeal against the conviction on the second charge, it was contended that the resident magistrate had acted contrary to the principles of natural justice as the circumstances indicated a real likelihood that he would have had a bias.

Decision

Henriques P held that in certain circumstances prudence might dictate that a further case against the same defendant be presided over by another magistrate. He went on to add that:

> "The learned resident magistrate, who is a trained lawyer, must be taken to have disabused his mind of any knowledge he may have gained from the previous trial, and must be taken to have applied himself to the issues presented to him in the case of the second information.

The learned judge concluded:

> "We are unable to say that there was a real likelihood of bias on the part of the learned resident magistrate."

Principles

1. *A judicial officer should recuse himself from hearing a case where there is either direct or indirect bias.*

2. *Where a judge is shown to have any direct pecuniary or proprietary interest (or even a limited class of non-financial interest) in the subject-matter of a case, it operates as an automatic disqualification.*

3. *A party may waive his right to object to a judge hearing or continuing to hear a case but any waiver must be clear and unequivocal, and made with full knowledge of all the facts relevant to the decision whether to waive or not.*

4. *The test of apparent bias is whether there is a real danger or possibility of bias.*

Court of Appeal

Locabail (UK) Ltd v Bayfield Properties Ltd and Another

[2000] QB 451

Facts

Five applications for permission to appeal were listed and heard together since they raised common questions concerning disqualification of judges on grounds of bias.

Decision

Lord Bingham of Cornhill CJ, Lord Woolf MR and Sir Richard Scott V-C

Their lordships held that in determination of litigants' rights and liabilities, civil or criminal everyone was entitled to a fair hearing by an impartial tribunal. All legal arbiters are bound to apply the law without partiality or prejudice. Any judge who allows any judicial decision to be influenced by partiality or prejudice deprives the litigant of the right to a fair hearing.

Their lordships further held:

> "There is, however, one situation in which, on proof of the requisite facts, the existence of bias is effectively presumed, and in such cases it gives rise to what has been called 'automatic disqualification.' That is where the judge is shown to have an interest in the outcome of the case which he is to decide or has decided. The principle was briefly and authoritatively stated by Lord Campbell in Dimes v Proprietors of Grand Junction Canal when orders and decrees made by and on behalf of the Lord Chancellor were set aside on the ground that he had had at the relevant times a substantial shareholding in the respondent company…"

Their lordships stated that in any case giving rise to automatic disqualification the judge should recuse himself from the case before any objection was raised. The same course should be followed if, the judge felt personally embarrassed in hearing the case. In either event it was highly desirable, in order to avoid extra cost, delay and inconvenience that the judge should stand down at the earliest possible stage of the proceedings. Where a judge became aware of any matter which could arguably be said to give rise to a real danger of bias, it was generally desirable that disclosure should be made to the parties in advance of the hearing. If objection was then made, the judge had a duty to consider the objection and rule thereon.

The court noted that a party to a case could waive his right to object to a judge hearing or continuing to hear a case. Such waiver however had to be clear and unequivocal, and made with full knowledge of all the facts relevant to the decision whether to waive or not.

Their lordships in deciding what factors could give rise to a real danger of bias held:

> "It would be dangerous and futile to attempt to define or list the factors which may or may not give rise to a real danger of bias. Everything will depend on the facts, which may include the nature of the issue to be decided. We cannot, however, conceive of circumstances in which an objection could be soundly based on the religion, ethnic or national origin, gender, age, class, means or sexual orientation of the judge.

Nor, at any rate ordinarily, could an objection be soundly based on the judge's social or educational or service or employment background or history, nor that of any member of the judge's family; or previous political associations; or membership of social or sporting or charitable bodies; or Masonic associations; or previous judicial decisions; or extra-curricular utterances (whether in textbooks, lectures, speeches, articles, interviews, reports or responses to consultation papers); or previous receipt of instructions to act for or against any party, solicitor or advocate engaged in a case before him; or membership of the same Inn, circuit, local Law Society or chambers."

The court stated that a real danger of bias may well arise in the following instances:

1. If there was personal friendship or animosity between the judge and any member of the public involved in the case

2. If the judge was closely acquainted with any member of the public involved in the case, particularly if the credibility of that individual could possibly be significant in the decision of the case

3. If on any question at issue in the proceedings before him the judge had expressed views, during the hearing, in such extreme and

unbalanced terms as to throw doubt on his ability to try the issue with an objective judicial mind.

However, the mere fact that a judge, earlier in the same case or in a previous case, had commented adversely on a party or witness, or found the evidence of a party or witness to be unreliable, would not without more found an objection based on bias.

Principle

Where there is an allegation of perceived or apparent bias there must be cogent evidence that gives rise to the apprehension of bias before leave to apply for judicial review is granted.

Supreme Court of Trinidad and Tobago

Baksh and Kuei Tung v Her Worship the Senior Magistrate Ejenny Espinet and The DPP

CV2009-00868

Facts

The Claimants and other high-profile persons and corporations were charged with corrupt practices in relation to the construction of a new Airport Terminal. The charges were laid indictably and the Claimants alleged that the ongoing Preliminary Inquiry should be quashed for *inter alia*, the appearance of bias in the Defendant conducting the Preliminary Inquiry. The Claimants alleged that it had come to their attention that the Defendant was a trustee of a charitable Non-Governmental Organization (NGO) known as the Morris Marshall Foundation.

The Claimants alleged that the Foundation was closely affiliated to the P.N.M. and that the P.N.M. used the Foundation to garner support for itself and to further the influence of the P.N.M. in the

Laventille area, a traditional P.N.M. seat of power. The Claimants further discovered that the Defendant's father was a cabinet minister and Member of Parliament under a former P.N.M. administration.

Decision

G. Smith J noted that the case was founded upon the perception of bias from the Defendant being a trustee of the Foundation and by her being the daughter of a former official of the P.N.M. The learned judge summarised the relevant legal principles touching direct and apparent bias. He noted that where a judicial officer had a direct interest in the proceedings or in its outcome, disqualification was automatic. Secondly, where the judicial officer did not have a direct interest in the case, but in some other way, his associations or conduct could give rise to a suspicion that he was not impartial, the disqualification was not automatic.

His lordship held that in the present case:

> "The present matter is concerned with the second type of bias, namely apparent bias. The test for apparent bias is now established by the case Porter v Magill [2002] 2 A.C. 359 (H.L.) Per Lord Hope at page 494. *'The question is whether a fair-minded and informed observer having considered the facts would conclude that there was a real possibility that the tribunal was biased'*. …"

Smith J noted however that there was no suggestion, that the Defendant had espoused any political cause or even adopted the views of any employee or of the other persons who attended the Foundation. Furthermore there was no suggestion that by word or deed, the Defendant had affiliated herself to the P.N.M. The learned judge held further that in the present matter, there was nothing to suggest that the Foundation itself was such an extremist organization so that to associate with it necessarily implied hostility or antipathy to the U.N.C. In fact the expressed purposes of the Foundation were charitable and positive.

In relation to the Defendant's connection to her father Smith J held:

> "The Claimant's case for presumed bias here is even weaker than the failed case with respect to the Defendant's connection to the Foundation. There is no evidence whatever that the Defendant has any type of relationship with her father. There is nothing to found an apprehension of bias on the part of a fair minded and informed observer. The Claimants have failed to make out a case with any realistic prospect of success based on this allegation."

> "Further the reasoning from Helow's case as applied in paragraph 23 above is also relevant here; namely, there is no evidence that the Defendant has by word or deed adopted or espoused any ideology or acts of her father or of the P.N.M…"

Application for leave refused.

THE OATH

Principle

A witness should be allowed to take the oath in a form binding on his conscience.

Court of Appeal of Jamaica

R v Hines and King

Decision of the Court of Appeal of Jamaica, 24th September 1971

Facts

H was a member of the Rastafarian sect. The members of that sect regard the Emperor of Ethiopia (referred to by the sect as Rastafari) as their living God, the returned Messiah and representative of God the Father on earth, and they do so despite the fact that the Emperor has not been known to claim any divine powers. When Hines elected to give evidence on oath, he declined to take the oath in the form usually administered to witnesses "I swear by Al-mighty God that..." but instead wished to take the oath in the form" I swear by Almighty God, King Rastafari..." As transpired later the trial judge seemed to think that an oath could only be taken lawfully by a witness in the form, namely, "I swear by Almighty God that..." prescribed by s 3 of the Oaths Law, Cap 264, as substituted by s 2 of the Oaths (Amendment) Law, 1954 (No 43 of 1954).

The trial judge thereupon ascertained from H that he would not take the oath in the "prescribed" form and would not affirm and that the only form of oath he would take "bearing on my conscience" would be by reference to "I God" Rastafari. The trial judge, thus apprised of the fact that Hines did believe in a Deity albeit one in human form, declined to permit Hines to take the oath in the form in which Hines wished to do so, adding that as far as he was aware that form of oath was not lawful.

Decision

Luckhoo JA stated that Hines's professed belief as a member of the Rastafarian sect was that the Emperor of Ethiopia was a Divine Being. The learned judge held that in such circumstances:

> "The form in which Hines wished to take the oath was consistent with that professed belief and declared by him to be binding on his conscience..."

Appeal of Hines allowed.

THE PROSECUTION'S RIGHT TO BE HEARD

Principle

The prosecution has a right to be heard. Should the court dismiss a case without affording the prosecution the opportunity to call witnesses who were present, this will amount to a breach of natural justice rendering the dismissal a nullity.

House of Lords

Harrington v Roots

[1984] AC 473

Facts

On the date fixed for the hearing of charges, the defendant appeared in the magistrates' court. At the start of the hearing the prosecutor applied for an adjournment because the virtual complainant was on vacation. The defence raised no objection to an adjournment. The magistrates decided to adjourn the case to a certain date but the defence then asked for an adjournment to another date.

The magistrates refused to allocate another date for the hearing of the case and instead, without asking the prosecution if they were in a position to proceed forthwith, decided to dismiss the charges. The prosecutor applied for judicial review of the magistrates' decision by way of orders of *certiorari* to quash the decision to dismiss the informations and mandamus to direct the magistrates to hear the evidence against the defendant.

Decision

Lord Roskill pointed out that at no time did the prosecution tell the justices that he could not proceed with the case. In fact, the prosecution had available another witness to the offence. The prosecutor had also informed the justices that if they had refused the adjournment sought by the prosecution it was their duty to inform the prosecution of that fact and then let the prosecution decide whether to proceed on the available evidence or to offer no evidence.

Lord Roskill concluded:

> "...My Lords, no explanation has been vouchsafed of the reasons for what can only be regarded as this remarkable action by the justices. No doubt they were not obliged to give any explanation or to reveal what advice they had been given if they did not wish to do so. But, in the absence of some explanation (none is readily apparent), it is clear that their action was both wrong and unjudicial. As I have already stated it was conceded below that the rules of natural justice had not been complied with and indeed that phrase is used in the certificate which I have already quoted."

His lordship stated further that what happened in the instant case was, "no trial at all." The dismissal of the informations was without jurisdiction and was a nullity.

Appeal allowed.

CHAPTER TEN

SUMMARY APPEALS

Summary Procedure legislation in most instances allows the prosecution and defence to appeal the magistrate's verdict in a summary trial. Appeals lie to the Court of Appeal (or the Full Court in Guyana for certain matters).

VALIDITY OF THE NOTICE OF APPEAL

Principle

In order to be valid a notice of appeal must be in writing and signed.

Court of Appeal of Trinidad and Tobago

Stanley v Andrews

Decision of the Court of Appeal of Trinidad and Tobago, 8th February 1963

Facts

The appellant was convicted by a magistrate in Port of Spain on 19 March 1962, for the offence of housebreaking and larceny and remanded for sentence to the next day when he was ordered to be imprisoned with hard labour for 12 months. He thereupon gave verbal notice of appeal which was reduced to writing the same day but the appellant did not sign it until 19 September 1962.

Decision

Wooding CJ held that the relevant statutory provision required that for an appeal to be commenced, the appellant had to give to the Clerk of the Peace notice of his appeal. If verbal notice had been given, it had to be forthwith reduced to writing by the clerk and signed by the appellant. His lordship held that the purpose of requiring the appellant's signature was to authenticate the notice of appeal.

Wooding CJ acknowledged that in some cases, the requirement that the notice be signed could cause hardship to an appellant who gave verbal notice and who was not required by the clerk to sign the formal notice, or whose verbal notice the clerk failed to reduce to writing. The learned judge emphasised that in cases where verbal notice of appeal was given by anyone convicted by a magistrate, as a condition for its efficacy, the notice had to be reduced to writing on the correct form and signed by the appellant 'forthwith.'

The learned judge concluded:

> "As a consequence of the conclusions which we have reached, it follows that this "appeal" in the circumstances in which it is now before us is really not an appeal. The proceedings so far are really a nullity. There is nothing, therefore, for us either to confirm or to set aside.

> *Appeal struck out.*

TIME LIMIT TO FILE APPEAL AND EXTENSIONS OF TIME

Extensions of time to file the notice of appeal may be provided by statute. The court must consider each case on the merits in deciding whether to grant leave to extend the time.

Principle

Where a defendant who applies for an extension of time to appeal has absented himself from the jurisdiction of the court without permission, this voluntary absence is a relevant factor for the court to take into consideration when exercising its discretion whether to grant an extension of time.

Court of Appeal of Guyana

Partin v D'Oliveira

Decision of the Court of Appeal of Guyana – 26th October 1976, 21st January 1977

Facts

Following the hearing in the Magistrates' Court, the applicant, through an oversight by those in authority, did not renew his bail when entering his recognisances for appeal to the Full Court, and that court for some unknown reason, did not give its decision dismissing the appeal until some 4½ years after the hearing began. Meanwhile, the applicant had left Guyana illegally, without informing either the Full Court or the police authorities of his intended departure. While still out of jurisdiction, the applicant requested an extension of time to appeal the decision of the Full Court to the Guyana Court of Appeal.

Decision

Crane JA noted that the applicant had chosen to remain out of jurisdiction when making an application for an extension of time to prosecute his appeal. If the applicant won the appeal, his precious stones and platinum would be returned to him. On the other hand, if he lost, since he was out of the jurisdiction, he would be immune from any legal penalty. His lordship concluded that the applicant would not be allowed to conduct from afar an appeal in which his presence was absolutely necessary.

Crane JA held:

> "...For my part, I cannot see the cause of justice being advanced by the exercise of our discretion permitting an applicant who is desirous of applying for an extension of time within which to appeal, to stay out of jurisdiction and to contest his appeal from Manaus in Brazil. It might have been an entirely different matter if he were now appearing before us, for then we ourselves could impose such conditions as bail to ensure the judgment of this court will not be frustrated..."

Application refused.

Principle

The Court of Appeal may grant an extension of time to serve a notice of reasons for appeal.

Supreme Court of Trinidad and Tobago Appellate Jurisdiction

Spencer v Bramble

Decision of the Court of Appeal of Trinidad and Tobago, 19th March 1960

Facts

The appellant was charged before a magistrate in two complaints alleging the commission of traffic offences. He was convicted and appealed.

By s 141 of the Summary Courts Ordinance, Cap 3, No 4 [T]:

"On the hearing, it shall not be competent for the appellant to go into, or to give evidence of, any other reason for appeal than those set forth in his notice of reasons for appeal: Provided that where, in the opinion of the Court, other reasons for appeal than those set forth in the notice of reasons for appeals should have been given, or the statement of reasons is defective, the Court, in its discretion, may allow such amendments of the notice of reasons for appeal upon such conditions as to service upon the respondent and as to costs as it my think fit."

In addition, s 140 of the Summary Courts Ordinance, Cap 3, No 4 [T], includes a provision giving the Supreme Court a discretion to "extend the time for service of notice of reasons for appeal upon such conditions as it may think fit."

Decision

Blagden J held that s 131 of the Ordinance expressly confined an appellant to all or any of the reasons stated in that section and prohibited him from giving any other reasons. Where a notice was defective because it did not conform to the section, this was not the end of the matter.

His lordship held:

> "In order, however, to settle the practice and procedure in matters of this nature, the court in the exercise of its discretion under s 140 of the Ordinance, allowed that defect to be cured by extending the time for service of notice of reasons for appeal, and granting leave to the appellant to give as his reason for appeal the statutory ground of 'not guilty'."

Principle

Leave will be granted to extend time to file the notice of appeal where there are substantial grounds for the delay in filing the notice. This would include a case where the applicant had formed an early intention to appeal, pursued that intention with due diligence and the appeal was arguable.

Court of Appeal of Trinidad and Tobago

Vyse v Cpl Warwick

Case No. 11582/08, POS Magisterial Appeal No. 14 of 2009

Facts

The appellant, an American citizen, pleaded guilty to an offence triable either way on August 6th 2008 and was convicted and fined. He subsequently applied for leave to extend the time to file a notice of appeal against conviction and sentence. He claimed *inter alia* that he was pressured to plead guilty and that he was represented by an attorney not of his choosing. He also claimed that he was forced to leave the jurisdiction on the same date as his conviction and sentence but he took immediate steps to initiate the process to file an appeal upon his arrival home.

Decision

Soo Hon JA found the following undisputed facts to be relevant to the application:

1. The appellant was convicted and sentenced on August 06 2008. He returned to North Carolina on August 07 2008. On August 09 2008 he retained the services of attorneys in North Carolina to launch his appeal against both conviction and sentence.

2. Between August and September 26 2008 the services of an investigator were engaged. Telephone calls were made to the authorities in Trinidad including a DEA agent. Mr. Chatoor, attorney-at-law, was contacted and the applicant's attorneys had several conversations with him. Mr Chatoor promised to contact them but

did not. Further efforts were made to retain a local attorney and contacts were made with the applicant's Congressman, the American Immigration Department, Lawyers Association and the United States Embassy in Trinidad.

3. Towards the end of October 2008 the applicant's attorneys were able to contact an attorney in Trinidad through an international listing of attorneys. He was referred to both Ms. Seetahal and Mr. G Petersen. Ms. Seetahal's office was contacted but she was ill at the time. On November 2008 Mr. Petersen was contacted and he agreed to look into the matter. For 3 weeks thereafter attempts were made to contact Mr. Petersen but to no avail. After speaking with Mr. Petersen the applicant decided to pursue more affordable options. Ms. Seetahal was contacted again on December 15 and retained. After several conference calls and the Christmas and New Year holidays this application was eventually filed on February 17 2009.

The learned judge then held that:

> "Before exercising its power to extend time the Court must be satisfied that there are substantial grounds for the delay. ...
>
> "It is the court's view that the applicant had formed an early intention to appeal and that he pursued that intention with due diligence...This applicant displayed an earnest effort to follow through such intention at earliest opportunity upon his return to the USA...The evidence presented by the applicant was therefore sufficient in substance to enable the Court to find that he had formed an intention to appeal in a timely basis and that the explanation for the delay was reasonable. ..."

Soo Hon JA concluded that in all the circumstances the voluntariness of the applicant's plea was a serious issue which needed to be fully ventilated. The appellant had therefore established that he had an arguable appeal and not a frivolous one. The learned judge went on to hold that the applicant, who was a young man whose future lay ahead of him was convicted of a very serious offence, especially considering that it was likely that such conviction would impact on any future application for employment.

Leave granted to extend time for the filing of the notice of appeal

ORDERS MADE BY THE COURT OF APPEAL AT THE HEARING OF THE APPEAL

The Court of Appeal hearing the summary appeal exercises statutory powers in giving judgment. The Court may for example dismiss the appeal and affirm the magistrate's decision or it may even modify or amend a decision in whole or in part.

Principle

The Court of Appeal has the power to enter a conviction supported by the evidence and thereafter to remit the matter to the adjudicating magistrate for sentence.

Court of Appeal of Trinidad and Tobago

Paynter v Lewis

Decision of the Court of Appeal of Trinidad and Tobago, 12th April 1965

Facts

The magistrate convicted the respondent but he later recalled the conviction and entered an acquittal. The prosecution appealed.

Decision

Wooding CJ held that the issue raised by the appeal was whether the magistrate had any power to recall the conviction. The learned judge on this issue held:

> "...Once a magistrate has accepted a plea of guilty or has adjudicated and found a defendant guilty or not guilty, he is *functus officio* as regards the commission or noncommission of the offence and accordingly he has no power to alter the conviction or acquittal as the case may be."

The learned judge concluded that the magistrate was right when at first he convicted the respondent and that his powers were thereupon spent as regards rendering any verdict.

Wooding CJ thereafter dealt with the appeal by holding:

> "...The appeal is accordingly allowed and a conviction must be entered against the respondent. And we order that the matter be remitted for the magistrate to pass such sentence upon her as the justice of the case requires."

Appeal allowed.

Principle

The Court of Appeal may allow an appeal and set aside a conviction. In such cases, instead of allowing the appellant to go free a trial de novo may be ordered.

High Court of Justice Grenada

Lewis v Commissioner of Police

Decision of the High Court of Grenada, 5th March 1969

Decision

Facts

The appellant was charged with assaulting a member of the police force in the execution of his duty and pleaded guilty. After the facts had been stated by the prosecution, the appellant gave his version of the facts which in effect amounted to a plea of not guilty, but the magistrate nevertheless convicted him on his plea as entered.

Decision

St. Bernard J reviewed the salient facts:

> "The facts were given to the court by the prosecuting officer and then the appellant said:
>
> 'I did not insult detective constable Bain. I was upstairs the canteen and he told me to go outside. I did not go out the same time. He asked me again to go outside and he started to chuck me out. When he chucked me I stumbled and my hand touched him'."

The learned judge concluded that the explanation given by the appellant amounted to a plea of not guilty and the magistrate should have entered such a plea and proceeded to try the case. It was therefore erroneous for the magistrate to say that he believed the facts stated by the prosecuting officer, and then proceed to convict and sentence the appellant.

The appeal was accordingly allowed and the case remitted to the magistrate for trial *de novo*.

Appeal allowed. Conviction and sentence set aside. New trial ordered

REASONS FOR DECISION

In certain jurisdictions, statute mandates the supplying of the magistrate's reasons for the decision. In the absence of such statutory provisions, the court insists on the magistrate's reasons being supplied especially where the individual's liberty is at stake.

Principle

The failure of the magistrate to state his reasons may result in the decision being quashed.

Judicial Committee of the Privy Council

Forbes v Maharaj

[1998] UKPC 13

Facts

The petitioner was convicted of an offence and appealed to the Court of Appeal. The magistrate failed to state his reasons even though it was a statutory requirement that he do so. The Court of Appeal reviewed the magistrate's decision to see whether there had been sufficient evidence on which he could have arrived at the decision which he reached.

The court dismissed his appeal against conviction for the possession of cannabis, but varied his sentence. The petitioner was granted special leave to appeal to the Judicial Committee.

Decision

Lord Clyde held that it was of fundamental importance that a magistrate furnished reasons for his decision, particularly in circumstances where the deprivation of liberty was at stake. The learned judge further held in this regard that without the statement of reasons it would usually be impossible to know whether the magistrate has misdirected himself on the law or misunderstood or misapplied the evidence. The absence of reasons could therefore enable an appellant to argue from a strong position that there could not have been a sound reason for the court's decision.

Lord Clyde concluded:

> "....In the absence of reasons in the present case it may be unsafe to draw conclusions merely from the decision itself and it may be dangerous to speculate on what may or may not have been the factual conclusions which the magistrate drew from the conflicting evidence before him. It is in the light of these circumstances in the present case that their lordships decided to grant special leave, to allow the appeal and quash the conviction."

Advice that the conviction be quashed.

Principle

A magistrate's written decision may suffice (where the pertinent factual and legal issues have been properly identified and analysed) where no reasons for decision have been provided.

Full Court of the High Court of Guyana

D'Aguiar v PC Maurice Cox

(1971) 18 WIR 44

Facts

The appellants were charged in the magistrates' court with entering an Amerindian district otherwise than in accordance with the permission in writing of the Chief Interior Development Officer, and without lawful excuse. The appellants pleaded not guilty before a magistrate of the G Judicial District, whereupon the case was transferred to the E Judicial District to be heard by a magistrate there. The latter proceeded to hear evidence without taking the pleas of the appellants, and convicted them. The appellant argued that the magistrate failed to comply with s 8 of the Summary Jurisdiction (Appeals) Ord, Cap 17 [G], in that he did not draw up a statement of his reasons for the decision appealed against.

Decision

Bollers CJ cited the case of Ressouvenir Estates Ltd v Dhanraj where the magistrate had delivered his decision in writing. This was a very short decision and failed to analyse the evidence led at the trial. The Court of Appeal in this case held that such a brief memorandum could not be considered a statement of the magistrate's reasons for his decision and accordingly held that there was a non-compliance with s 8.

On the facts of the instant case his lordship held that the magistrate had delivered a written decision in which he considered and examined at length all the points and submissions made by counsel and solicitor who appeared. This was a very comprehensive statement of his reasons for his decision.

Appeal dismissed

THE COURT RECORD

The Court of Appeal refers to the court record to ascertain both the evidence recorded during the trial as well as any matters of procedure, such as adjournments and the grant of bail.

Principle

The court record prevails over the magistrate's reasons.

Court of Appeal of Trinidad and Tobago

Roberts (Sheldon) v PC William Nurse

Mag. App. 31 of 2002

Facts

The appellant was convicted of certain summary offences and appealed. The appellant submitted *inter alia* that the Magistrate erred in law in admitting illegal evidence of one "C" who was a child at the time of giving evidence. The appellant further submitted that since the only evidence of C's age was that given by her grandfather who stated that she was 15 years old, she was not a child (by virtue of the Children's Act) and there was no need for an enquiry. The Magistrate stated in her reasons that C's evidence was unsworn. Furthermore, the record of the notes of proceedings showed that the Magistrate held an enquiry pursuant to section 19 of the Children's Act before taking the evidence.

Decision

Jones JA noted that although the Magistrate had held an enquiry before taking the virtual complainant's evidence, the reason for so doing was unknown since the evidence of the virtual complainant was sworn.

His lordship concluded:

> "...It is evident that the statement in the Magistrate's reasons contradicts the record, both as to the age of the witness and

the manner in which her evidence was taken. In our view the record must prevail."

APPEARANCE AT THE APPEAL

Principle

An appellant who wishes to prosecute his appeal must appear personally at the Court of Appeal when his appeal comes on to be heard.

Court of Appeal of Trinidad and Tobago

Bach v Ferreira

(1965) 9 WIR 282

Facts

B was convicted by a magistrate of dangerous driving. He appealed against the conviction and sentence. Upon the appeal coming on for hearing, counsel asked the court to hear and determine the appeal in the absence of the appellant. Section 139 of the Summary Courts Ordinance, Cap 3, No 4, provides:

"139. (1) If, on the day of hearing or at any adjournment of the case, the appellant does not appear, the case shall be struck out and the decision shall be affirmed, unless the Supreme Court thinks fit, for sufficient cause, to order otherwise.

"(2) If in any such case the respondent appears, the judgment shall be with costs of the appeal against the appellant, unless the Supreme Court expressly orders otherwise; but if the respondent does not appear, the costs of the appeal shall be in the discretion of the court."

Decision

Fraser JA disagreed with counsel's submission that the power of the court 'to order otherwise' included the power to adjourn the hearing and the power to hear and determine the appeal in the absence of the appellant. His lordship ruled that the power created by s 139 was a limited one. It followed that if the appellant failed to appear on any day fixed for the hearing of the appeal the court was enjoined to strike out the appeal and affirm the decision of the magistrate.

His lordship elaborated further on the issue:

> "In any case in which the court thinks that sufficient cause is shown, however, the court may elect not to strike out the appeal. In such a case the appeal remains on the list and can be heard on any day fixed by the court in the exercise of its inherent power to adjourn the hearing of any cause or matter to a convenient time or date."

By way of illustration his lordship stated that if on the day of hearing the appellant did not appear and the court was informed by counsel representing him of the reason for his non-appearance, e.g., illness or accident or unforeseen circumstances, and the court was also informed of the likelihood of the appellant's appearance on another day, the court in such a case could order that the appeal be not struck out and could then adjourn the hearing to a day upon which the appellant was able to appear.

Fraser JA concluded that under the Summary Courts Ordinance, an appellant was required to be present in person at the hearing of an appeal. He held:

> "...This appears manifestly to be the position contemplated by the Ordinance. To express it another way, an appellant who wishes to prosecute his appeal must appear personally

at the Court of Appeal when his appeal comes on to be heard. Having so appeared, he may then prosecute his appeal by representation through counsel."

Appeal dismissed.

CHAPTER ELEVEN

TRIABLE EITHER WAY OFFENCES

These are indictable offences which may be tried summarily where the court thinks that this mode of trial is suitable and where the defendant consents (where applicable) to be tried summarily.

PROCEDURE FOR TRIABLE EITHER WAY OFFENCES

Principle

Magistrates must strictly follow the statutory procedure for trying either way offences. Failure to do so will mean that the court had acted without jurisdiction.

Queen's Bench Division

R v Kent Justices Ex parte Machin

[1952] 2 QB 355

Facts

The applicant, having consented to be dealt with summarily, was convicted by a court of summary jurisdiction and he was committed to quarter sessions for sentence under s 29(1) of the Criminal Justice Act, 1948. The court failed to explain to the applicant that he might be so committed, as is required by the relevant statute. He made an application for an order of *certiorari*.

Decision

Lord Goddard CJ stated that the correct statutory procedure was that a person, who was charged with an indictable offence which could be dealt with summarily, had to be informed of his right to be tried by a jury and that his consent was also needed for the case to be dealt with summarily. Furthermore it must be explained to him that, if he was convicted by the justices, he could be committed to quarter sessions for sentence.

Lord Goddard noted:

> "...In the present case the procedure prescribed by the earlier Acts was followed, but the applicant was not told of his liability to be committed under s 29. There is no question of any advantage having been taken of the applicant. The offences charged against him were undoubtedly offences with which the justices could deal with his consent. He was represented by a solicitor who told the justices that he desired to be dealt with by them. Clearly he consented, but the jurisdiction of justices to deal with cases which are *prima facie* indictable is purely statutory and the provisions of these statutes are peremptory."

His lordship concluded that the convictions had to be quashed since the justices had decided to try the cases summarily without a strict compliance with all the statutory provisions which allowed an indictable offence to be dealt with summarily.

Order for certiorari

ELECTION OF SUMMARY TRIAL

Principle

Where an accused person who was charged with an offence triable either way has elected summary trial, the magistrate has a discretion to allow the appellant to change his election.

Court of Appeal of Trinidad and Tobago

Chadee v Santana

(1987) 42 WIR 365

Facts

The appellant was represented by an attorney-at-law when the prosecution recommended, and the appellant elected, summary trial and pleaded not guilty. The matter was adjourned further on the application of both sides. The appellant was subsequently advised that he should require the matter to be tried on indictment and not to consent to summary trial.

That advice was accepted and the court informed accordingly. No reason was given for the change of election and none was sought by the court. The magistrate stated that he would try the case himself since the appellant had already elected summary trial and pleaded on a previous occasion before another magistrate, and he proceeded to try the case.

The appellant was convicted and appealed.

Decision

McMillan JA held that a magistrate has a discretion whether or not to allow a defendant to withdraw his consent previously given to summary trial; but that a magistrate would be entitled to refuse to allow it if the withdrawal amounted to a sharp practice.

His lordship noted that the facts showed that the magistrate did not attempt to ascertain the reason for the withdrawal of consent to summary trial. In those circumstances, the court had failed to exercise its discretion properly, and the appeal would be allowed.

Appeal allowed. Order for re-hearing granted.

Principles

1. *If a defendant elects summary trial and pleads guilty he is not precluded from re-visiting his election.*

2. *Where the accused elects summary trial and pleads guilty but then applies to re-elect trial on indictment the test whether he should be allowed to re-elect was whether he had properly understood the nature and significance of the choice which he had made when he elected summary trial. The magistrates' view that the case was more suitable for summary trial is irrelevant to the application to re-elect as to the mode of trial.*

Queen's Bench Division

R v Birmingham Justices, ex parte Hodgson and another

[1985] QB 1131

Facts

The applicants were charged in a magistrates' court with an offence which was triable either way. On their first appearance in court neither applicant was represented, and believing that they had no defence to the charge, both applicants intended to plead guilty. The applicants were put to their election as to the mode of trial, in accordance with ss 18 to 20a of the Magistrates' Courts Act 1980, and both elected summary trial.

They then pleaded guilty but indicated in mitigation that they had a defence. The magistrates then directed that not guilty pleas be entered and after advising the applicants to take legal advice adjourned the case. Having received legal advice that they had a defence the applicants applied to the magistrates to be allowed to elect for jury trial but the magistrates refused the application without reasons. The applicants applied for judicial review of the magistrates' refusal.

Decision

McCullough J stated that the applicants' principal submission was that no bench of justices acting reasonably could have refused an application to re-elect. Since the applicants were mistaken about their plea then this must have affected their election and, once the justices had accepted that this mistake vitiated their plea, they should have recognised that it vitiated their election.

His lordship went on to state that when justices were faced with an application to re-elect, attention had to be paid to the state of mind of the accused at the time he made his election. Did he properly understand the nature and significance of the choice which was put to him? The learned judge stated that one of the most important factors in the mind of the accused himself, deciding which court he would like to deal with his case, was whether or not he believed he had any defence. A justice should look favourably upon an application to re-elect made by a defendant who when unrepresented elected summary trial and pleaded guilty and at a later stage said that a solicitor had told him that he had a defence and should plead not guilty.

McCullough J concluded:

> "Thus, in the decided cases I find nothing to prevent me from saying that in my opinion the broad justice of the situation in the case before us demanded that the accused be allowed to re-elect. No other conclusion was reasonable. They had pleaded guilty under the misapprehension that they had no defence. They had elected summary trial under the misapprehension that they would not be tried, but merely sentenced. When they took advice from their solicitor the reality of their situation for the first time became apparent."

The court allowed the application, quashed the refusals to allow the applicants to re-elect, and the case was remitted the case for reconsideration by a fresh bench.

Certiorari granted

Principle

Once a magistrate allowed an accused to elect summary trial of an offence which was triable either way and the accused's plea of guilty was accepted, the court could not thereafter exercise its power to discontinue the summary trial and act as examining magistrate in committal proceedings for the trial of the accused on indictment.

House of Lords

Chief Constable of West Midlands Police v Gillard

[1985] 3 All ER 634

Facts

On 6 February 1984 the respondent appeared before the Dudley Magistrates' Court charged jointly with one Thompson with an offence of assault occasioning actual bodily harm. The offence being triable either way, the court heard representations, pursuant to s 19 of the Magistrates' Courts Act 1980, whether the case was more suitable for summary trial or for trial on indictment.

The prosecutor argued for trial on indictment, while the respondent's solicitor requested summary trial. Thompson's solicitor, at this stage, said nothing. The court considered the case more suitable for summary trial and accordingly, having given the explanations required by s 20(2) of the 1980 Act, put each of the accused to his election. The respondent elected to be tried summarily and thereupon pleaded guilty.

One week later they were brought up again before a differently constituted bench. The prosecutor, differently represented, argued that, notwithstanding the course followed on 6 February leading to the respondent's election of summary trial and plea of guilty, the court should discontinue the summary trial of the respondent and proceed to deal with the matter in relation to both accused as examining justices with a view to committing them both for trial on indictment. Having heard argument to the contrary for the respondent, the court indicated that they proposed to take the course urged on them by the prosecutor in purported exercise of the power conferred by s 25(2) of the 1980 Act.

The respondent applied to the Divisional Court for judicial review, seeking orders of prohibition to restrain the magistrates' court from committing him for trial and mandamus to require them to continue his summary trial, i.e. to proceed to pass sentence on him. The Divisional Court granted orders of prohibition restraining the magistrates from committing the respondent for trial in the Crown

Court and mandamus requiring them to proceed with the summary hearing. The prosecutor appealed to the House of Lords.

Decision

Lord Bridge of Harwich held that an accused would justifiably feel aggrieved in a situation where having been told by the justices that they were prepared to try him summarily, and who had elected to be so tried and promptly pleaded guilty was subsequently informed by the court that the matter would be dealt with indictably. This is because an accused who had entered the guilty plea in the circumstances outlined above was entitled to take comfort from the knowledge that he had chosen a course which limited the punishment to which he was liable.

Appeal dismissed.

TRIAL OF LIKE KIND OFFENCES

In some jurisdictions, the magistrate who has embarked upon committal proceedings may elect to discontinue these proceedings and proceed instead to try summarily a like kind offence, provided that such an offence is available on the evidence.

Principle

In order to allow a magistrate to proceed to try a summary offence of a like kind the substantive indictable charge must contain such an offence.

Court of Appeal of Trinidad and Tobago

George v Francois

(1969) 15 WIR 394

Facts

After conducting a preliminary inquiry, a magistrate committed the appellant for trial at the Criminal Assizes for the offence of assault with intent to rape. The depositions were in due course forwarded to the Attorney-General who directed the magistrate to hear the matter summarily. Without obtaining the consent of the appellant to be tried summarily, the magistrate heard the case, convicted the appellant and sentenced him to two years' imprisonment. The appellant appealed his conviction.

Decision

Fraser JA held that the magistrate was required to ascertain whether the evidence appeared likely to 'establish the commission of a summary offence of a like kind to the offence charged, and inform the appellant accordingly'. It followed that if there was a summary offence akin to assault with intent to rape, the magistrate was entitled to inform the appellant that he intended to deal with the case summarily and proceed to do so without the consent of the appellant.

His lordship noted however that there was no summary offence akin to the indictable offence of assault with intent to commit rape. The only offences of a like kind were the indictable offences of indecent assault and attempt to commit indecent assault.

Fraser JA held:

> "It therefore follows that the provisions of s 91 could not be invoked to authorise dealing with the case summarily without the consent of the appellant."

Appeal allowed.

Principle

If the essential constituents of one offence are in substance the same as of another, the two qualify to be classified as being of a 'like kind.'

Court of Appeal of Trinidad and Tobago

Robbles v Glanville

Decision of the Court of Appeal of Trinidad and Tobago, 5th June 1964

Facts

The appellant was charged indictably with the offence of unlawful and malicious wounding. At the commencement of the preliminary inquiry before a magistrate and again at the end of the prosecution evidence but before the case against him was formally closed, he was offered summary trial as provided by s 97 of the Summary Courts Ordinance, Cap 3, No 4 [T], but he refused to consent.

The evidence showed that the offence was not of a serious character and could be adequately dealt with by the magistrate in his summary jurisdiction. In these circumstances the magistrate intimated that he was of opinion that the evidence established or appeared likely to establish the commission of a summary offence of a like kind to wit, assault occasioning a wound, and called upon the appellant to answer a charge therefor.

His counsel objected and advised him not to plead. Accordingly, a plea of not guilty was recorded and, as the appellant maintained his refusal to answer the charge, he was convicted. On appeal it was argued, *inter alia*, that the offence of assault occasioning a wound was not of a like kind to unlawful wounding and consequently the magistrate acted outside his jurisdiction in taking the course which he did.

Decision

Wooding CJ held that 'like kind' offences were offences which had essential features in common. If the essential constituents of one offence were in substance the same as of another, then the two qualified to be classified as being of a like kind. His lordship concluded that upon an application of this test the offence of an assault occasioning a wound was an offence of a 'like kind' to unlawful wounding.

Appeal dismissed.

CHANGING MODE OF TRIAL FROM SUMMARY TO INDICTABLE

Principle

The court must have a good reason before deciding to switch from summary to indictable proceedings.

Queen's Bench Division

R v West Norfolk Justices, ex parte McMullen

(1993) 157 JP 461

Facts

The applicant was charged together with two co-defendants. He failed to attend court when his co-accused elected trial by jury and were later committed to trial. When the applicant was arrested and brought before the court, the justices decided that the case was suitable for summary trial.

Section 25(2) of the Magistrates' Courts Act 1980 reads:

"Where the court has (otherwise than in pursuance of s 22(2) above) begun to try the information summarily, the court may, at any time before the conclusion of the evidence for the prosecution, discontinue the summary trial and proceed to inquire into the information as examining justices and, on doing so, may adjourn the hearing without remanding the accused."

The applicant consented to summary trial and pleaded not guilty. At the subsequent hearing the prosecutor invited the court to discontinue the summary proceedings and sit as examining justices on the ground that it was preferable that all three co-accused should be tried by the same court. The justices agreed and adjourned the case. On application for judicial review:

Decision

Mc Cowan LJ held that subs (2) gave the justices an unfettered discretion to discontinue the summary trial and to proceed to inquire into the information as examining justices, subject to Wednesbury principles. It followed that if a good reason was demonstrated for justices to switch to being examining justices, they could do so.

On the facts of the instant case his lordship held:

> "It is obvious to me, however, that he planned to use subs (2) to get round both the difficulty posed for the prosecution by the decision in Nicholls and the decision of the first bench of justices. I would hold that the decision of the justices to accept his arguments was irrational. I would, therefore, grant the relief sought."

Application granted.

ELECTION BY JOINTLY CHARGED PERSONS

Principle

Where more than one defendant is jointly charged with an offence which is triable either on indictment or summarily, the right of election as to the mode of trial given to the accused is given to each accused individually and not to all the accused collectively. Accordingly, where one accused has elected summary trial but a co-accused has elected trial on indictment the court should proceed to try summarily the accused who elected summary trial and should proceed with committal proceedings in respect of the accused who elected trial on indictment.

House of Lords

Nicholls v Brentwood Justices

[1992] 1 AC 1

Facts

The appellant was charged along with two others, C and W, with the offence of affray which was a triable either way offence. The appellant and C elected summary trial but W elected to be tried on indictment. The prosecutor then invited the magistrates to reconsider the mode of trial who subsequently decided to proceed indictably. The appellant applied for judicial review, seeking an order requiring the justices to try him summarily.

Decision

Lord Keith of Kinkel held that the effect of s 20(3) was that the right of election was given to each accused individually, and that this was supposed to be unaffected by a different election made by any of his co-accused. The learned judge stated that where justices were told in advance that one of two co-accused intended, if given the opportunity, to accept summary trial and plead guilty but that the other accused would elect to be tried on indictment, this situation could not amount to a reason for committing both for trial.

Appeal allowed.

THE DPP'S POWER TO ORDER A MAGISTRATE TO CHANGE THE MODE OF TRIAL FROM SUMMARY TO INDICTABLE

Principle

In accordance with section 34 of the Summary Jurisdiction (Procedure) Act (Guyana) the DPP may, in writing, direct the magistrate to stay a summary trial and to conduct a preliminary inquiry instead.

Full Court of the High Court of Guyana

Director of Public Prosecutions v Sullivan and Others

(1996) 54 WIR 256

Facts

A police officer swore an information charging the defendants with an offence triable either way. When the case came before a magistrate, State Counsel representing the police applied to have the case tried summarily; the defendants consented and the magistrate agreed to deal with the matter summarily. About a year later counsel for the police applied to the magistrate to change the mode of trial. The defendants objected to the application and the magistrate declined to make the order applied for. Shortly thereafter the Director of Public Prosecutions wrote to the court intimating, in accordance with section 34 of the Summary Jurisdiction (Procedure) Act that he believed that the case ought to be tried on indictment.

Section 34 of the Summary Jurisdiction (Procedure) Act provides:

"If, on the hearing of a complaint it appears to the court that the cause ought to be tried as an indictable offence before the High Court or if the Director of Public Prosecutions intimates to the court his opinion in writing to that effect, all further proceedings in the cause as for a summary conviction offence shall be stayed, and depositions shall be taken and the cause shall in all other respects be dealt with as if the charge had been originally one for an indictable offence."

The magistrate declined to follow the written direction from the director and the director moved the court to order the magistrate to show cause why he should not cause further proceedings in the case to be conducted before him as a preliminary inquiry.

Decision

Kennard CJ noted that the DPP must have decided that the matter should proceed indictably after taking into account, among other things, the large sum of money involved. His lordship stated that there was nothing to suggest that in exercising his power the director had acted in bad faith.

The learned Chief Justice held:

> "In my view section 34 of the Summary Jurisdiction (Procedure) Act, as it relates to the instant matter, is mandatory as the word used is 'shall'. It seems to me, therefore, that the magistrate was bound to comply with the direction of the Director of Public Prosecutions."

The matter was finally disposed of by the court ordering the magistrate to stay the summary trial and to proceed with the matter as an indictable one by conducting a preliminary inquiry with a view to committing the defendants to the High Court for trial.

Order accordingly.

HYBRID OFFENCES

Principle

Hybrid offences are those for which statute creating the offence will stipulate different penalties depending on whether there was either a summary conviction or a conviction on indictment. Whether an offence fell to be classified as indictable or summary depends the nature and quality of the offence when committed.

Court of Appeal

Hastings and Folkestone Glassworks Ltd v Kalson

[1949] 1 K.B. 214

Facts

A company's articles provided that a director "convicted of an indictable offence" should vacate his office. The defendant, a director of the company, pleaded guilty before a court of summary jurisdiction to and was convicted and fined. It was alleged that the director was in breach of regulations which provided for particular penalties depending on whether there had been a summary conviction or a conviction on indictment. The company claimed a declaration that the defendant was disqualified from acting as a director.

Decision

Tucker LJ reasoned that the issue which arose in the appeal was whether the defendant was 'convicted of an indictable offence.' On this issue his lordship held:

> "On the other hand, the test contended for by the plaintiff company depends on the nature and quality of the offence when committed, irrespective of the procedural manner in which it may subsequently be dealt with. I have come to the conclusion that the contention of the plaintiff company is to be preferred to that of the defendant…"

Asquith L.J. held:

> "In my view, the material time is the time when the offence was committed, and before the prosecution has elected to proceed summarily or secured a conviction on that basis."

Appeal allowed with costs. Declaration in the terms asked for.

CHAPTER TWELVE

COMMITTAL PROCEEDINGS

The primary purpose of committal proceedings/sufficiency hearings is to facilitate disclosure of the prosecution's case. No plea is entered. Evidence is recorded on depositions (or witness statements where applicable). Evidence is taken from witnesses in the absence of other witnesses in the case. At the close of the prosecution's case the magistrate administers the statutory caution (where applicable). The accused may make a no-case submission at this time. The court's function is to determine if a *prima facie* case is made out. The accused is discharged if no *prima facie* case is made out on deposition. The accused may be committed for any indictable offence disclosed by the depositions.

FRESH EVIDENCE ADMITTED AT COMMITTAL PROCEEDINGS

Principle

If evidence which was available at the time of the preliminary inquiry was not led, it does not ipso facto become inadmissible. It is a matter for the court's discretion whether or not the evidence will be admitted.

Court of Appeal of Guyana

Abdool Salim Yaseen and Thomas v The State

Decision of the Court of Appeal of Guyana, 11th May 1990

Facts

In the course of a trial the prosecution sought to introduce evidence from a police officer whose evidence had not been given at the preliminary inquiry. Notice had been given to the appellants some seven days before the trial of the intention to call him as a witness. Objection was taken to the admission of the evidence. The evidence significantly strengthened the case for the prosecution. The judge satisfied himself that the defence was not taken by surprise and admitted the evidence. The appellants were convicted of the offence and appealed to the Court of Appeal.

Decision

George C. noted that the objection was taken based on the technical ground that the witness had not been called at the preliminary inquiry and no explanation had been proffered for his failure to be so called. The appellants also submitted that this had been the ruling of the court in R v Gomes, whose facts were similar to the instant case. The learned judge further noted that the said witness had given a written statement as to the part he had played in the police investigations since 30 March 1987, i.e. some four days after the appellants had been charged, and that he was at all times available to give evidence at the preliminary inquiry. This witness' evidence was important because in every material particular it accorded with that of Asst Supt Barran who had given evidence at the preliminary inquiry. It therefore must have significantly strengthened the case for the prosecution.

The learned judge held that as a matter of practice it would be expected that ordinarily all available and relevant evidence would be presented at the preliminary inquiry. He also admitted that except for Gomes' case, the court was unable to find any other authority to support the existence of a rule which barred the reception of additional evidence that was not given on deposition before a justice so long as adequate notice of an intention to do so and the contents of such evidence were given.

His lordship further elaborated upon this point:

> "I do not think that any of these cases intended to lay down that if the evidence was available at the time of the preliminary inquiry and was not led it ipso facto and as a matter of law became inadmissible. Indeed except in certain limited circumstances (an involuntary confession or admission is one of them), all relevant evidence is *prima facie* admissible in a criminal case…There could be several good or excusable reasons for the omission to lead a certain witness at the preliminary inquiry.

George C. proceeded to give examples of why evidence of a witness would not be led at committal proceedings. One such case would be where there was sufficient other evidence led on a particular issue as not to require the testimony of yet another witness; but then at the trial the evidence led at the preliminary inquiry may become unavailable due to the death or absence of the witness who testified at the inquiry.

Another example would be where the evidence omitted may only have become relevant during the course of the trial, or in yet another case the evidence may have been omitted through inadvertence due to the large volume of evidence that had to be presented.

The learned judge also stated that in reality prosecutors in the magistrates' court who are police officers sometimes lacked the required skill and experience to lead all the necessary evidence. In such instances, an accused person should not be allowed to benefit from the prosecutor's failure to lead important evidence. If, however, there was evidence that the omission to call an important witness or to lead an important piece of evidence at the preliminary inquiry was deliberate and not otherwise excusable, then this may well amount to such unfairness, even if adequate notice was given, as to justify a judge in exercising his discretion to exclude the evidence.

Appeal allowed. Order for retrial.

DISCLOSURE AT COMMITTAL PROCEEDINGS

Principle

The prosecution's duty of disclosure whether at committal proceedings or at trial extends to a case where he knows of a credible witness who can speak to material facts which tend to show the prisoner to be innocent, he must either call that witness himself or make his statement available to the defence.

Court of Appeal of Trinidad and Tobago

John v R

Decision of the Court of Appeal of Trinidad and Tobago, 16th March 1965

Facts

The prosecution had failed in its duty to make available to the defence at the trial statements taken by the police in the course of investigations from two persons who were present on the scene when the appellant inflicted the injuries which caused the death of the deceased.

It was admitted that these statements contained an account of the incident which pointed to the innocence of the appellant. The authors of these statements were friends of and available to the appellant as witnesses but he chose not to call them. The prosecution also did not call them as witnesses.

Decision

Wooding CJ held that it was the duty of prosecuting counsel to make the statements available to the defence. His lordship approved of dicta in the case of Dallison v Caffery which stated that the duty of a prosecuting counsel who knows of a credible witness who can speak to material facts which tend to show the prisoner to be innocent, must either call that witness himself or make his statement available to the defence. It would be highly reprehensible to conceal from the court the evidence which such a witness can give. If this prosecuting counsel knows of a witness whom he does not accept as credible, he should tell the defence about him so that they can call him if they wish.

Appeal dismissed.

Principle

A magistrate's function as examining magistrate does not include a determination of whether the prosecution has provided adequate disclosure.

Court of Appeal of Trinidad and Tobago

Director of Public Prosecutions v Chief Magistrate (No 2)

C.A.CIV. 2/2003

Facts

A magistrate, sitting as an examining magistrate in committal proceedings, required the prosecution (which had already made extensive disclosure to the defence) to provide a list of the materials in its possession to the defence and to the court. The Director of Public Prosecutions (the applicant) applied for an order setting aside or varying the ruling or order made in committal proceedings by the Chief Magistrate which required the State to provide to the accused and the court a list of all documents and other similar materials in its possession relating to the informations which were the subject of the committal proceedings.

Decision

Warner JA noted the order made by the Chief Magistrate, which was as follows:

"That the State provide to the accused and the court a comprehensive list of all the documentation and other material of a similar nature which is or has been in its possession which relates to the several informations under inquiry and that on that list the prosecution should indicate which items they have already disclosed and to which accused and in respect of which charge. Further, from that list the prosecution should indicate which items they refuse to disclose giving their reasons for declining to disclose.' ..."

The learned judge held:

> "In this jurisdiction there is no express or implied right to disclosure under the Constitution... I am of the view that the function of the Chief Magistrate when inquiring into a charge laid indictably is limited to determining whether a *prima facie* case has been made out. It does not include a determination whether the State has provided adequate disclosure. This proposition has been established and applied by a number of cases in England and I shall also refer to one such authority from the Canadian jurisdiction. Secondly, while a magistrate exercising summary jurisdiction may be

entitled to determine contentious issues of disclosure, this is not so when he is inquiring into a charge laid indictably. ..."

Warner JA stated that while it was always preferable that full disclosure be made before the preliminary inquiry this could not always be achieved in complex cases. However, full disclosure should be made in sufficient time before the trial. Ideally, matters of disclosure ought to be resolved by reasonable discussions between counsel, in good faith and in a practical manner so that the matter could proceed without further delay.

Her ladyship concluded on the facts of the instant case, the Chief Magistrate had exceeded the limits of his function when he made his ruling or order. She held further in this regard:

> "...In the interest of all parties, I think it would be appropriate to give the following direction in relation to the material which the prosecution has disclosed up to the present time, in terms of the undertaking given by counsel for the Director of Public Prosecutions:

"That on or before 14 June 2003, the Director of Public Prosecutions do serve on the relevant attorneys at law for the interveners, in relation to each charge a list of all relevant documents disclosed."

Remitted to the Chief Magistrate

CRITERIA FOR ADMISSION OF A DEPOSITION INTO EVIDENCE

On occasion, a witness who testified at the committal proceedings may be unable to testify at the trial. This situation may arise in circumstances such as the death of the witness or the fact that the witness is out of the jurisdiction and cannot be found.

Principle

In admitting a deposition into evidence, the magistrate's certificate proving the deposition does not need to be proved separately.

Court of Appeal of Trinidad and Tobago

La Vende v The State

Decision of the Court of Appeal of Trinidad and Tobago, 26th November 1979

Facts

The appellant filed grounds of appeal following his conviction one of which was that the trial judge wrongly admitted in evidence the deposition of a doctor taken at the preliminary enquiry in which he stated the results of a post-mortem examination performed on the body of the deceased and the cause of death. By s 38(1)(*a*) of the Indictable Offences (Preliminary Enquiry) Ordinance ('the Ordinance') it is provided:

"Where any person has been committed for trial for any offence, the deposition of any person taken before a magistrate may, if the conditions hereafter set out are satisfied, without further proof be read as evidence on the trial of that person, whether for that offence or for any other offence arising out of the same transaction or set of circumstances as that offence.

'The conditions hereinbefore referred to are the following:-

...(*b*) It must be proved at the trial, either by a certificate purporting to be signed by the magistrate before whom the deposition purports to have been taken or by the oath of a credible witness, that the deposition was taken in the presence of the accused person or the prosecutor, as the case may be, and that he or his legal adviser had full opportunity of cross-examining the deponent.

(c) The deposition must purport to be signed by the magistrate before whom it purports to have been taken.'"

Decision

Sir Issac Hyatali CJ held that when the trial judge decided that it was proved that Dr. Edwards was absent at the relevant time, he admitted the deposition in evidence, to which was attached the certificate referred to in s 38(1)(*b*) and which contained a statement that the witness was not cross-examined by the appellant. It followed that the certificate and the deposition were admitted in evidence together. His lordship decided that this satisfied the conditions of the section.

His lordship held:

> "Counsel's submission is accordingly well taken and we uphold it as sound. We do not agree with him, however, that before the deposition could have been properly admitted in evidence it was necessary to prove separately and independently the certificate referred to in s 38(1) (*a*) and (*b*) of the Ordinance..."

Appeal dismissed.

Principle

In order to be valid a deposition must conform to statutory requirements.

Court of Appeal for the Windward Islands and the Leeward islands- Criminal Appellate jurisdiction

Bramble v R

(1959) 1 WIR 473

Facts

The only evidence connecting the appellant with the alleged crime was a deposition taken from the deceased in hospital shortly before his death. The appellant was present when the deposition was taken and cross-examined the deponent. The main question for determination by the Court of Appeal was whether the evidence of the deceased on deposition was properly admitted. The appellant submitted that the deposition of George Blake was wrongly admitted in evidence in that it was not in the form of a deposition within the meaning of s 60 of the Magistrate's Code of Procedure Act, Cap 61 [LIs], which required the evidence of a witness at a preliminary inquiry, after the taking thereof, to be read over to, and be signed by, the witness.

Decision

Henriques CJ held that before a deposition could be admitted in evidence under the provisions of s 206, evidence had to be given that the evidence of the witness was read over to, and signed by, or at least, assented to, by the witness. It was conceded that there was no evidence in the court below that this had been done, and on the deposition itself, there was no record to that effect, and accordingly the deposition was not properly admissible.

Appeal allowed.

THE DEFENDANT'S RIGHT TO BE HEARD AT COMMITTAL PROCEEDINGS

Principle

The defendant at committal proceedings is entitled to call evidence even following the magistrate's rejection of a no-case submission.

Queen's Bench Division

R v Horseferry Road Magistrates' Court, ex parte Adams

[1978] 1 All ER 373

Facts

Following a no-case submission at committal proceedings, the magistrate ruled that there was a *prima facie* case against the applicant. Counsel for the applicant then sought to call the applicant as a witness. The magistrate refused to allow the applicant to be called on the ground that it was not part of his function as an examining magistrate to assess the applicant's credibility, that being a matter for the jury at the trial. Accordingly, he committed the applicant for trial. The applicant applied for an order of *certiorari* to quash the committal order. He submitted that the magistrate erred in law in refusing to hear the applicant before he finally made up his mind whether the case should be committed or not.

Decision

Lord Widgery CJ noted that the general rule at a criminal trial that the defendant had a right to call evidence, even though he had unsuccessfully made a submission of no case to answer also applied to committal proceedings.

His lordship held:

> "I do not see any objection to the defendant having, as it was put, two bites of the cherry. It seems to me perfectly logical that, if the submission at the close of the prosecution case fails, the defendant should be able to call his own evidence and then make another effort to get the magistrate to refuse to commit later on."

> *Application granted; committal quashed.*

COMMITTAL PROCEEDINGS IN ANTIGUA

Principle

Antiguan committal proceedings satisfy the constitutional right to a fair hearing even though there is no right to cross-examine or call or give oral evidence. This is because these proceedings are conducted by an independent magistrate to whom both sides may submit evidence and make submissions. The restriction to written evidence also applies to both prosecution and defence.

Judicial Committee of the Privy Council

Humphreys v Attorney General of Antigua and Barbuda

[2009] 4 LRC 405

Facts

The Parliament of Antigua and Barbuda passed the Magistrate's Code of Procedure Amendment Act, No 13 of 2004, which abolished the preliminary inquiry. It substituted committal proceedings which differed from the preliminary inquiry in that there was no right to cross-examine or call or give oral evidence. The appellant commenced judicial review proceedings claiming that the abolition of the preliminary inquiry had infringed his constitutional rights by retrospectively depriving him of the procedural protection to which he had been entitled at the time he had been charged, and secondly by depriving him of the right to a fair trial.

The appellant appealed against the decision of the Court of Appeal allowing the appeal of the respondent, the Attorney General of Antigua and Barbuda, from the decision of Thomas J in the High Court that the appellant's constitutional rights had been infringed.

Decision

Lord Hoffman noted that the right to a fair hearing was guaranteed by section 15(1) of the Constitution:, which stated:

'If any person is charged with a criminal offence then, unless the charge is withdrawn, he shall be afforded a fair hearing within a reasonable time by an independent and impartial court established by law'

His Lordship stated that the issue in the case was whether the new system of committal proceedings and trial, taken as a whole, satisfied the requirements of section 15(1). In this regard the learned judge stated that committal proceedings are not determinative of guilt but filtered out cases in which there was insufficient evidence to justify a trial. These proceedings are conducted by an independent magistrate to whom both sides may submit evidence and make submissions. Furthermore, the restriction to written evidence applied to both prosecution and defence.

Lord Hoffman concluded:

> "The specific requirements of section 15(2) of the Constitution are all satisfied by the composite procedure of charge, committal proceedings, indictment and trial. In particular, the accused is entitled at the trial to cross-examine the prosecution witnesses and give oral evidence in accordance with section 15(2) (e)."

Appeal dismissed

THE VOLUNTARY BILL OF INDICTMENT AND COMMITTAL PROCEEDINGS

Principle

In preferring a voluntary bill of indictment the Jamaican DPP may seek the direction and consent of a judge.

Judicial Committee of the Privy Council

Brooks v Director of Public Prosecutions of Jamaica and another

[1994] 1 AC 568; [1994] UKPC 1

Facts

A resident magistrate in Jamaica dismissed an information charging the appellant. The Director of Public Prosecutions (the DPP) disagreed with that decision and on his application by summons under s 2(2)a of the Criminal Justice (Administration) Act, a Supreme Court judge ordered that a voluntary bill of indictment be preferred against the appellant for the same offence and that a warrant be issued for his arrest. The appellant applied to the Full Court for redress under s 25 of the Constitution of Jamaica on the grounds (i) that, since s 2(2) conferred exclusively on the DPP the power to prefer an indictment and since by virtue of s 94(6)b of the Constitution the power to institute or continue criminal proceedings was vested in the DPP to the exclusion "of any other person or authority", the DPP should not have sought an order from the judge to do that which he could lawfully have done without an order.

Decision

Lord Woolf stated that s 2(2) conferred upon the DPP an unfettered discretion, to seek the directions or consent of a judge as to whether an indictment should be preferred. His lordship stated that the DPP was empowered to seek the judge's approval since preferring a bill of indictment without relying on any additional evidence, after a resident magistrate had concluded that there was no *prima facie* case, was an exceptional course to adopt.

Lord Woolf held:

> "By seeking that approval, the doctrine of separation of powers was not offended in any way….If he had not adopted the course of seeking the authority of a judge for the initiation of the proceedings, but had initiated the proceedings himself, the proceedings would become subject to the control of the court in due course, and in the event that they were held to constitute an abuse they would be dismissed."

His lordship concluded that the only difference, which would have resulted from the DPP initiating the proceedings himself, without going to a judge, was that the court's control would be exercised at a later stage of the proceedings.

Appeal dismissed.

SUBSEQUENT COMMITTAL PROCEEDINGS FOLLOWING DISCHARGE AT THE ORIGINAL PROCEEDINGS

Principle

Where available prosecution evidence is not led at committal proceedings in which the defendant was discharged then, should further committal proceedings be conducted for the same offence, this evidence will not be allowed.

Court of Appeal of Trinidad and Tobago

Cadogan v R

(1963) 6 WIR 292

Facts

A magistrate discharged the appellant after conducting a preliminary inquiry into a charge of murder against him. In consequence of another information laid against him for the same offence a further inquiry was held and at the end thereof the magistrate committed the appellant to stand his trial. The appellant was thereafter indicted, tried and convicted for murder.

On appeal, it was shown that additional evidence of a material nature was led and received at the second inquiry but that, though available to the prosecution at the first, it was not tendered or called thereat. It was contended on behalf of the appellant that the evidence of the witnesses was available to the prosecution at the time of the first preliminary inquiry, that it did not "become available" thereafter within the meaning of s 23 (6) of the Indictable Offences (Preliminary Inquiry) Ordinance, Cap 4, No 1 [T], and that accordingly, the second inquiry, the committal for trial of the appellant thereon, and all subsequent proceedings were a nullity, as being contrary to the provisions of s 23 (6) of the Ordinance which states:

'Where an accused person has not been put upon his trial for any offence disclosed by the evidence taken at a preliminary inquiry and additional evidence of a material nature in support of any such offence becomes available, a further inquiry may be held in the like manner and with the like consequences as if it were an original preliminary inquiry.'

Decision

Phillips JA stated that the main issue to be decided was whether it could be said that the prosecution had called at the second preliminary inquiry any additional evidence of a material nature in support of the charge that became available within the meaning of s 23 (6) of the Ordinance. His lordship held in relation to this issue that in order to satisfy the required test the evidence must not have been available at the time of the first inquiry and must have become available only after its termination.

His lordship concluded:

> "In these circumstances we are of the opinion that the prosecution must be held to have known that Dr McShine's evidence was material to the case, and it is clear that it was open to them to call him at the first inquiry. For these reasons we hold that Dr McShine's evidence was available at the time of the first inquiry."

Appeal allowed.

Principle

Where the defendant at committal proceedings has been discharged due to the prosecution's inability to proceed, then unless the delay is exceptional the prosecution is free to relay a fresh information for the same charge.

Queen's Bench Division

R v Grays Justices, ex parte Graham

[1982] QB 1239

Facts

There was a long delay in holding committal proceedings. On the date fixed for the proceedings the prosecution were unprepared to proceed and the magistrates refused to adjourn proceedings. The prosecution offered no evidence and the Defendant was discharged. The prosecution subsequently commenced fresh proceedings in respect of the same offence. The applicant applied for judicial review.

The issue before the court was whether the delay on the part of prosecution rendered fresh proceedings vexatious and an abuse of the court's process.

Decision

May LJ summarised the appellant's grounds which were that because of the delay of two years since the alleged offences, the continued prosecution of the applicant was in the circumstances vexatious and an abuse of the process of the court, the delay being in no way due to any fault on the part of the applicant herself, and that in all the circumstances of the case such continued prosecution was contrary to natural justice. His lordship affirmed the principle that delay of itself, if sufficiently prolonged, could in some cases be such as to render criminal proceedings both vexatious and an abuse of the court's process.

His lordship held:

> "Clearly, as a matter of policy, prosecutions should be brought and heard as quickly as practicable. We think that in the majority of cases excessive delay is likely to prejudice the prosecution just as much as, if not more than, the defence... Although we appreciate that it will not be easy for the Crown to present its case or for the applicant to meet it, in these proceedings because of the delay that there has been, there has been no instance of mala fides on the prosecution's part."

May LJ concluded that in all the circumstances it was not vexatious to require the applicant to stand trial.

Application dismissed.

Principle

Where a defendant has been discharged on committal proceedings, the examining magistrate has jurisdiction to hear fresh committal proceedings in respect of the same offence. The risk that there might be repeated committal proceedings in respect of the same offence is overcome by the discretion of the court to ensure that repeated committal proceedings were not vexatious or an abuse of the process of the court.

Queen's Bench Division

R v Manchester City Stipendiary Magistrate, ex parte Snelson

[1978] 2 All ER 62

Facts

The applicant applied for an order of prohibition to prohibit the stipendiary magistrate from enquiring further as examining justices into offences

The ground on which relief was sought was, *inter alia*, that the stipendiary magistrate had been wrong in law in holding that he could conduct another enquiry as examining justice when the applicant had already been discharged after previous enquiry into the same offences alleged against him.

Decision

Lord Widgery CJ held that although the usual course in such cases as the instant one was to seek a voluntary bill it was incorrect to argue that the justices had no power to hear the second committal proceedings. His lordship then considered the issue of whether there would be a risk that a defendant might be prejudiced by repeated committal proceedings. He concluded on this issue:

"I am satisfied that that particular difficulty is overcome, as counsel for the prosecution suggested, by saying that this court has a discretionary power to see that the use of repeated committal proceedings is not allowed to become vexatious or an abuse of the process of the court."

Application refused.

Principle

Where earlier proceedings were a nullity the court may later conduct committal proceedings for the same charge.

Court of Criminal Appeal

R v West

[1962] 2 All ER 624

Facts

The appellant was charged with an either way offence. The magistrates (who summarily tried the charge at the request of the prosecutor with the consent of the appellant) dismissed the charge. A second information for the same charge was sworn.

The magistrates in their capacity as examining justices heard the evidence supporting the charge and committed the appellant for trial. He was convicted at the trial and appealed.

Decision

Streatfield JA held that in purporting to hear and determine and try the first summons the justices had acted beyond their jurisdiction, and those proceedings were therefore a nullity. It followed that although the matter had ended in an acquittal, it was an acquittal by a court which had acted without competent jurisdiction.

As regards the subsequent committal proceedings his lordship held:

> "The justices had not exhausted their jurisdiction by assuming jurisdiction which they had never had, and they certainly had not debarred themselves from acting in their other capacity as examining justices, and committing for trial."

Appeal dismissed.

DPP'S POWER IN GUYANA TO DIRECT A MAGISTRATE TO RE-OPEN COMMITAL PROCEEDINGS AND COMMIT

Principle

The DPP in Guyana under the Criminal Law Procedure Act may direct a magistrate to re-open an inquiry and commit the accused for trial. The magistrate must however ensure compliance with the same statute by allowing the accused the right to be heard.

Supreme Court of British Guyana-Full Court

R v Hussain Ex Parte Director of Public Prosecutions

Decision of the Supreme Court of British Guiana, 12th February 1965

Facts

The accused together with other persons were charged with the offence of murder. The preliminary inquiry into the charge was held by a magistrate who took the view, upon a submission being made at the close of the evidence for the prosecution, that a *prima facie* case had not been made out against any of the accused persons; and he discharged them. After an examination of the depositions, the Director of Public Prosecutions, purporting to act in pursuance of the powers conferred upon him by s 72 of the Criminal Law (Procedure) Ordinance, Cap 11 [BG], referred the matter back to the magistrate with directions to commit the accused and the other persons for trial for the offence of murder.

Section 65 provides:

"(1) After the examination of the witnesses called on the part of the prosecutor has been completed, and after the depositions have been signed as aforesaid, the magistrate shall, unless he discharges the accused person, address him in these words, or to the like effect..."

Section 66 provides:

"(1) After the proceedings required by the preceding section are completed, the magistrate shall ask the accused person if he wishes to call any witnesses.

(2) Every witness called by the accused person who testifies to any fact relevant to the case shall be heard, and his deposition shall be taken, signed, and authenticated in the same manner as the deposition of a witness for the prosecution."

Section 69 provides:

"When all the witnesses on the part of the prosecutor and of the accused person, if any, have been heard, the magistrate shall, if, upon the whole of the evidence, he is of opinion that no sufficient case is made out to put the accused person upon his trial, for any indictable offence, discharge him; and in that case any recognisance taken in respect of the charge shall become void."

Section 72 provides:

"(1) In any case where the magistrate discharges an accused person, the Attorney-General may require the magistrate to send to him the depositions taken in the case or a copy thereof, and any other documents or things connected with the case which he thinks fit.

(2) If, after the receipt of those documents and things, the Attorney-General is of opinion that the accused person should have been committed for trial, the Attorney-General may, if he thinks fit, remit them to the magistrate, with directions to deal with the matter accordingly, and with any other directions he thinks proper.

(3) Any directions given by the Attorney-General under this section shall be in writing signed by him, and shall be followed by the magistrate, who shall have all necessary power for that purpose.

(4) The Attorney-General may at any time add to, alter, or revoke any of his directions."

Upon the matter being called before the magistrate, counsel for the accused submitted that the direction given by the Director of Public Prosecutions was a nullity, in that it was not competent for him to direct the magistrate as he purported to do. The magistrate held the view that he was bound by the decision of Chung J, in R v Lall (1964) unreported (referred to in the judgment of Luckhoo CJ), and he refused to comply with the directions.

Decision

Luckhoo CJ held that the provisions of s 72 of Cap 11 [BG] allowed the Director of Public Prosecutions to require the magistrate to send him the evidence or a copy thereof together with any other documents and things in respect of any case when the magistrate discharged an accused person. This would include not only a case where the discharge was effected at the close of the evidence of witnesses for the prosecutor but also a case where the magistrate discharged an accused person either on his own motion for want of prosecution or for want of jurisdiction or on the motion of the prosecutor even before any evidence was taken.

His lordship stated that the Director of Public Prosecutions could not give the directions contemplated by that sub-section where the discharge was on motion of the magistrate for want of prosecution or lack of jurisdiction or on the motion of the prosecutor. In these cases there was obviously no material upon which the Director can form the opinion that the accused person should have been committed for trial and he therefore cannot give any directions to the magistrate under the sub-section.

Luckhoo CJ held further:

> "A magistrate can only lawfully commit an accused person for trial prior to sending the depositions to the Director of Public Prosecutions if he had regard to the whole of the evidence. In that context the whole of the evidence includes the evidence for the accused person (if any) tendered before the magistrate."

His lordship concluded that in the circumstances of the present case the magistrate could not have committed the accused persons until due compliance had been made with the provisions of ss. 65 and 66 of the Ordinance, Cap 11 [BG]. The Director of Public Prosecutions was therefore not competent to give the relevant directions he purported to or indeed any directions at all pursuant to the provisions of s 72 (2) of Cap 11 [BG]. It followed that the learned magistrate was not in error in refusing to comply with those directions.

Motion dismissed.

CHAPTER THIRTEEN

EXTRADITION

Extradition is a legal procedure whereby a person who is accused or convicted of an offence (an extraditable offence) is returned to the State that wishes to try the person or to ensure that the person serves his sentence. The conduct of extradition proceedings is governed by statute, and the statutory procedures must be strictly complied with.

THE REMEDY OF HABEAS CORPUS

Principle

The remedy of habeas corpus is available to a person even though that person is on bail.

Queen's Bench Division

R v Secretary of State for the Home Department Ex parte Launder (No. 2); Launder v Governor of Brixton Prison and another

[1998] QB 994

Facts

The applicant applied for judicial review by way of an order for *certiorari* to quash the decision of the Secretary of State for the Home Department on 31 July 1995 to order the applicant's return to Hong Kong under section 12(1) of the Extradition Act 1989 despite the applicant's submissions of 23 December and 31 December 1997 that his detention was unlawful. The applicant also sought a writ of *habeas corpus* directed to the Governor of Brixton Prison to show cause why he should not be released immediately.

Decision

Simon Brown LJ affirmed that it was well recognised in the context of *habeas corpus* proceedings that an applicant on bail was to be treated as if in custody.

Mance J similarly held that in the context of extradition it was clear that *habeas corpus* would lie, although the person being sought to be extradited has been committed on bail, rather than in custody.

His lordship also noted:

> "In other contexts, too, as Simon Brown L.J. has pointed out, there is authority that the bailing of a person seeking *habeas corpus* is no bar to the issue of the writ…"

Principle

The Supreme Court has jurisdiction to grant an application for habeas corpus on the ground of abuse of the court's process.

Judicial Committee of the Privy Council

Fuller *v* The Attorney General of Belize

[2011] UKPC 23

Facts

Following the extradition hearing the Chief Magistrate ordered the appellant's extradition. The appellant was granted leave to apply for a writ of *habeas corpus*. The application was refused by the Chief Justice, and the Court of Appeal dismissed the appellant's appeal.

He appealed to the Privy Council. The major issue raised by the appeal related to the extent of the jurisdiction of the Supreme Court of Belize on an application for *habeas corpus* in an extradition case. It was the appellant's contention that the application for extradition was an abuse of process.

Decision

Lord Phillips noted that in the instant matter, the allegation of abuse of process was largely based on delay that had occurred. His lordship stated that the court possessed the jurisdiction to grant the application for *habeas corpus* on the ground that it was contrary to justice that the court's process should be used in such circumstances as existed.

On the issue of delay his lordship held:

> "The relevant delay so far as an allegation of abuse of process is concerned is not the delay in commencing the extradition proceedings, but the delay in pursuing them. Inordinate delay in pursuing extradition proceedings is capable of amounting to an abuse of process justifying the discharge of the person whose extradition is sought."

His lordship also considered the issue of whether the fugitive could have a fair trial in the United States. He held in this regard that Extradition proceeded on the basis that the person whose extradition is sought would receive a fair trial in the requesting State. If it was plain that a fair trial would not be possible, it would obviously be unjust and oppressive to return the person. Furthermore, if it was alleged that the delay that had occurred, or any other matter, had rendered a fair trial in Dade County impossible, the appropriate remedy was to apply to the court there for relief.

Lord Phillips stated that although there was a period of inertia of nearly 6 years after the filing of the appellant's notice of appeal, it was significant that the appellant's appeal against the judgment of the Supreme Court was also delayed. Had the appellant wished to progress his appeal he could and should have made representations to the Registry. The fact that he did not do so indicated that, he was only too happy that the hearing of his appeal should be delayed.

His lordship concluded that in the circumstances justice did not demand that the extradition proceedings should be abandoned due to the delay

Advice that appeal be dismissed

Principles

1. ***The court should be wary of paying excessive heed to "hardship to the accused resulting from changes in his circumstances" following upon the accused's move to another country when equivalent hardship is likely to have occurred even had he remained in his country of origin.***

2. ***In considering whether it would be unjust to return a fugitive for trial, the court is entitled to have regard to whatever safeguards may exist in the domestic law of the requesting State to ensure that the accused would not be subjected to an unjust trial there.***

3. ***There can be no cut-off point beyond which extradition must inevitably be regarded as unjust or oppressive.***

High Court of Justice Queen's Bench Division

Woodcock v The Government of New Zealand

[2003] EWHC 2668

Facts

The applicant applied for *habeas corpus* alleging that to extradite him would be unjust and oppressive pursuant to s11(3)(b) of the 1989Act, which, so far as material, provides:

"(3) Without prejudice to any jurisdiction of the High Court apart from this section, the court shall order the applicant's discharge if it appears to the court in relation to the offence, or each of the offences, in respect of which the applicant's return is sought, that—

...(b) by reason of the passage of time since he is alleged to have committed it ... it would, having regard to all the circumstances, be unjust or oppressive to return him."

Decision

Lord Justice Simon Brown noted the relevant authorities on point. His lordship cited Kakis -v- Government of the Republic of Cyprus which held (by reference to s 8(3)(b) of the Fugitive Offenders' Act 1967, the materially identical predecessor provision) that 'unjust' in the statute was 'directed primarily to the risk of prejudice to the accused in the conduct of the trial itself', 'oppressive' was 'directed to hardship to the accused resulting from changes in his circumstances that have occurred during the period to be taken into consideration [from the date of the offence(s) to the present date]', but there was room for overlapping, and between them they would cover all cases where to return [the accused] would not be fair.

His lordship noted that the main thrust of the applicant's argument was directed to the impossibility of having a fair trial of the charges so long after the offences were said to have taken place, on average some 20 years ago. His lordship also noted that the charges were based solely on accusations, unsupported by any documentary or 'forensic' (meaning scientific) evidence. In such a case the applicant had submitted that it was inevitable that he would be severely impeded in establishing his defence.

Lord Justice Simon Brown held:

> "Section 11(3) (b) in terms requires this court's decision not upon whether, having regard to the passage of time, it would be unjust to *try* the accused, but rather whether it would be unjust to *return* him (albeit, of course, return him for trial). To my mind that entitles, indeed requires, this court to have regard to whatever safeguards may exist in the domestic law of the requesting state to ensure that the accused would not be subjected to an unjust trial there. There are, it should be borne in mind, clear advantages in having the question whether or not a fair trial is now possible decided in the domestic court rather than by us. That court will have an altogether clearer picture than we have of precisely what evidence is available and the issues likely to arise."

His lordship emphasised that if the court concluded that the domestic court in the requesting state would be *bound* to hold that a fair trial of the accused was now impossible, then the court in the requested state would regard it as unjust (and/or oppressive) to return the applicant. A similar result would occur where the court was not persuaded that the courts of the requesting state had a satisfactory abuse of process jurisdiction.

In this regard, his lordship concluded:

> "Here, however, it seems to me plain, for the reasons already indicated, first that the New Zealand courts have satisfactory procedures for guarding against an unjust trial and, secondly, that, under those procedures, they would certainly not be bound to find a fair trial impossible."

The learned judge then turned to another submission advanced which was that it would now be oppressive to return the applicant to New Zealand since firstly, the applicant had left New Zealand freely in 1987 and had ever since lived with no complaint about his conduct abroad, initially in Ireland, and since 1990 in England. Secondly, the applicant had heard nothing more about the matter until 2002, notwithstanding that two of the complainants had already made their complaints to the police.

His lordship dealt with this submission as follows:

> "These considerations, I have to say, to my mind fall far short of what is necessary to establish a case of oppressiveness. It must also be recognised that the charges here related to grave offences: sexual offences mostly against minors involving a serious abuse of the applicant's position of trust as priest and teacher. The gravity of the offences, as Lord Diplock observed in Kakis is relevant to the question of oppressiveness."

His lordship stated that someone should not be able to improve their chances of escaping trial by travelling abroad and then changing their circumstances in their new country of residence. In other words, why should an Australian who has committed a series of frauds in Sydney, be better placed to escape trial (through it being found oppressive to extradite him) if he moved to England than if he moved to Darwin?

On the subject of hardship his lordship held:

> "The court should to my mind be wary of paying excessive heed to 'hardship to the accused resulting from changes in his circumstances' following upon the accused's move to another country when equivalent hardship is likely to have occurred even had he remained in his country of origin."

The learned judge held that there was nothing in the applicant's circumstances to make it oppressive to return him to New Zealand to stand trial and similarly, taking both limbs of s11(3)(b) together, there was nothing that 'would not be fair' in returning the applicant. The court also stated that there could be no cut-off point beyond which extradition must inevitably be regarded as unjust or oppressive although trial after 20 years or more was far from ideal.

Application dismissed

Principle

Delay in the commencement or conduct of extradition proceedings which is brought about by the accused himself by fleeing the country, concealing his whereabouts or evading arrest cannot be relied on (save in the most exceptional circumstances) as a ground for holding it to be either unjust or oppressive to return him to the Requesting State.

House of Lords

Gomes v Government of Trinidad and Tobago; Goodyer v Government of Trinidad and Tobago

[2009] 3 All ER 549

Facts

A and B were wanted by the government of Trinidad and Tobago for trial on charges of possession of cocaine for the purposes of trafficking. Each had fled Trinidad, breaching bail conditions.

They had each argued that extradition would be unjust or oppressive by reason of the passage of time. Each was arrested in the United Kingdom following an extradition request by Trinidad. The extradition of each was ordered by the Secretary of State and each appealed. The Divisional Court allowed their appeals and remitted their cases to the district judge for redetermination. The district judge redetermined the issue on the passage of time in the same way, relying on a subsequent decision of a differently constituted Divisional Court. The Divisional Court then certified a question for the House of Lords as to the correct approach to the barring of extradition by reason of the passage of time.

Decision

Lord Brown of Eaton-under-Heywood held that the decision in Kakis v Government of Republic of Cyprus lay at the very heart of the appeal. The facts in that case were that Kakis's extradition was sought by Cyprus in relation to an EOKA (Ethniki Organosis Kyprion Agoniston - National Organisation of Cypriot Fighters) killing in April 1973. Although a warrant for Kakis's arrest had been issued that very night, he had escaped into the mountains and remained hidden for 15 months.

Subsequently, Kakis settled in England with the apparent approval of the Cyprus government and so too did a Mr Alexandrou, Kakis's only alibi witness, who swore that he would not return to give evidence in Cyprus. It was these two circumstances, the first going to oppression, the second to injustice, that ultimately led the House to allow Kakis's appeal against the Divisional Court's refusal to discharge him under s 8(3) of the Fugitive Offenders Act 1967 (a provision materially indistinguishable from s 82:

'... the High Court ... may ... order the person committed to be discharged from custody if it appears to the court that ... (b) by reason of the passage of time since he is alleged to have committed [the offence] ... it would, having regard to all the circumstances, be unjust or oppressive to return him.'

His lordship cited dicta from Kakis which stated that 'unjust' was directed primarily to the risk of prejudice to the accused in the conduct of the trial itself, while 'oppressive' was directed to hardship to the accused resulting from changes in his circumstances that had occurred during the period to be taken into consideration; but there was room for overlapping, and between them they would cover all cases where to return the applicant would not be fair.

Further dicta from Kakis stated that delay in the commencement or conduct of extradition proceedings which was brought about by the accused himself by fleeing the country, concealing his whereabouts or evading arrest cannot be relied on as a ground for holding it to be either unjust or oppressive to return him.

His lordship also cited dicta from Kakis which dealt with delay which was not brought about by the acts of the accused himself. It was stated in Kakis that the question of where responsibility lies for the delay is not generally relevant. What matters is not so much the cause of such delay as its effect; or, rather, the effects of those events which would not have happened before the trial of the accused if it had taken place with ordinary promptitude.

His lordship concluded that neither appellant, as a 'classic fugitive', could invoke the passage of time, lengthy though it was, since their respective alleged offences. In any event there could be no question of regarding their extradition as either unjust or oppressive.

Appeals dismissed

Principles

1. ***In deciding whether there is sufficient cause to conclude that it is unjust or oppressive to return an applicant to the requesting state it will not normally be sufficient to allege unfairness or oppression in the trial process of the Requesting State.***

2. ***Weighing the evidence or assessing credibility is not part of the extradition magistrate's jurisdiction.***

3. ***On an application for a writ of habeas corpus, a court may look at the evidence that was before the magistrate.***

High Court of Justice of Trinidad and Tobago

Kadir and Kareem Ibrahim v The Commissioner of Prisons

CV 2007-2063

Facts

The applicants were charged in the United States of America with being involved in a plot to blow up fuel tanks and pipelines at the JFK international airport in New York City. Provisional warrants were issued for their arrest in Trinidad and Tobago and they were arrested and brought before the Chief Magistrate. The applicants applied for writs of *Habeas Corpus* pursuant to the Extradition Act Chap. 12:04 S. 13. They contended *inter alia* that it would be unjust and oppressive to extradite them.

Decision

Bereaux J noted that the applicants had claimed that it was unjust and oppressive to extradite them. This was based on the following:

1. To extradite the applicants to the United States would likely result in their being tried by military commissions as enemy combatants pursuant to the Military Commissions Act 2006 ("The MCA").By the use of such military commissions the United States government sought to circumvent the various protections stipulated by international law and the Geneva Convention.

2. In addition to removing *habeas corpus* jurisdiction, the MCA contained a number of related objectionable features. It applied to alien or non -American unlawful enemy combatants which term has been given a wide interpretation. Such an approach could very well result in any person being labelled an unlawful enemy combatant and subjected to indefinite executive control.

3. The USA had not given any assurances to the Government of Trinidad and Tobago that the applicants would not become subject to the MCA.

4. The alleged offences were given massive coverage in the United States media as a result of which the applicants faced a substantial risk of a prejudicial trial in the United States of America.

5. It was likely that the applicants if convicted would be sentenced to a super max prison where inmates were confined to single cells for twenty-three hours a day in sterile isolation and permanent lock down. These posed a risk to the mental health of the applicants.

This was especially so in the case of Abdul Kareem Ibrahim whose health had rapidly deteriorated since he was remanded into custody.

His lordship noted in this regard:

> "The affidavit of Sunita Harrikissoon attaches a diplomatic note which provides an assurance from the Embassy of the USA to the Government of Trinidad and Tobago that 'upon extradition to the United States Kareem Ibrahim, Abdul Kadir and Abdul Nur will be prosecuted before a Federal Court in accordance with the full panoply of rights and protections that would otherwise be provided to a defendant facing similar charges.' The note assures that the applicants 'will not be prosecuted before a military commission as enabled by the Military Commissions Act 2006 nor will they be treated as enemy combatants.' This is a direct response to Mr. Abdus Salaam's contention that there had been no assurances given to the Trinidad and Tobago Government by the USA that the applicants would not be tried by a Military Commission."

His Lordship further held that Ibrahim's medical report did not show that Mr. Ibrahim's medical and psychiatric condition were such as to amount to sufficient cause to conclude that it was unjust or oppressive to extradite him to the United States. The learned judge added that in any event Ibrahim's complaints both physical and mental could be more than adequately dealt with in the United States.

On the issue of whether the United States had satisfactory procedures which guarded against an unfair trial his lordship stated that the legal system in the United States was common law with pre-trial common law mechanisms to deal with adverse publicity questions.

Bereaux J then considered the complaint that there was a paucity of evidence upon which to commit and that the Record of Case was woefully incomplete. His lordship cited the decision in United States v Yang in which it was held that in determining whether there was a *prima facie* case whether at the preliminary inquiry or trial stage, the judge is not to consider the quality of the admissible evidence. The learned judge also cited United Sates v Schulman where it was held that weighing the evidence or assessing credibility was not part of the extradition judge's jurisdiction.

His lordship concluded on this issue:

> "Both these submissions raise the ordinary *habeas corpus* jurisdiction. That jurisdiction is of course supervisory and not by way of appeal. It is sufficient for the purposes of my review that there was evidence in the Record of Case upon which the Chief Magistrate could have concluded there were *prima facie* cases against both applicants."

Applications dismissed

Principle

Where the Requesting State is allowed leave to re-open the prosecution case, in order that supplemental evidence may be

adduced, this would not amount to a breach of the state's duty of candour.

High Court of Trinidad and Tobago

Pierre v The Commissioner of Prisons

Claim No. CV 2011-01865

Facts

Pierre applied for a writ of *habeas corpus ad subjiciendum* challenging the committal order made against him by the Chief Magistrate pursuant to the Extradition (Commonwealth and Foreign Territories) Act Chapter 12:04 ('the Extradition Act'). On 11 November 2010 the Office of the Attorney General of Trinidad and Tobago received a bundle of documents from the Government of the United States of America requesting the extradition of the applicant to stand trial in Boston, Massachusetts. He was alleged to have murdered three persons and attempted to murder a fourth person. The allegations of fact were contained in the Record of the Case dated 4 November 2010 and the Supplemental Record of the case dated 4 February 2011.

The Record of the Case and the Supplemental Record of the Case set out the evidence proposed to be led against the applicant at the proposed criminal trial in Boston. They contained summaries of the evidence of nine witnesses. On 12 January 2010 a grand jury sitting in Suffolk County, after examining the evidence of the witnesses, and being satisfied that there was probable cause to believe that crimes were committed and that the applicant had committed the crimes, returned and filed with the Commonwealth of Massachusetts an Indictment.

This Indictment charged the applicant with three counts of Murder in the First Degree in violation of Massachusetts General Laws, Chapter 265, Section 1; one count of Armed Assault with intent to murder in violation of Massachusetts General Laws, Chapter 265, Section 18(b), and one count of possession of an unlicensed firearm in violation of Massachusetts General Laws, Chapter 269, Section 10(a).

On that same day a warrant for the arrest of the applicant was issued. The Record and the Supplemental Record of the case revealed that the Requesting State intended to rely on eyewitness and expert testimony, ballistic evidence and circumstantial evidence to prove that the applicant was guilty of the offences outlined in the Grand Jury Indictment. On the 15th November, 2010 the Attorney General issued an Authority to Proceed pursuant to Section 9 (1) of the Extradition Act. The applicant was arrested on 13 September 2010 in Trinidad and Tobago.

Decision

Mr Justice Aboud noted that the Record of the Case and the Supplemental Record of the case were not filed on the same day. The Supplemental Record was filed after the applicant's counsel had made a no-case submission, contesting, among other things, that there was no direct identification evidence from any of the witnesses in the Record of the Case that the applicant was the shooter. The State sought leave to re-open their case, for the purpose of tendering the Supplemental Record of the Case. The Chief Magistrate granted leave and the Permanent Secretary then tendered the Supplemental Record of the Case which supplied evidence from an additional witness, one of the applicant's friends. This evidence was intended to provide positive identification of the applicant as being the person who discharged his firearm into the cabin of the white Nissan Sentra.

His lordship considered the nature of *habeas corpus* proceedings. On this issue he stated that during the judicial phase of the proceedings, the magistrate examines the evidence to determine whether the offence is an extraditable offence and whether it would justify committal for trial in Trinidad and Tobago. If the magistrate so decides the committed person may apply to the High Court to be discharged on the grounds set out in section 13(3). In *habeas corpus* proceedings the High Court is not exercising an appellate function nor is it responsible for rehearing the case already concluded before the magistrate.

It is not the function of the High Court to substitute its own discretion for that of the magistrate. The final determination of the *habeas corpus* proceedings concludes the judicial oversight phase of the statutory process. The next phase is purely executive and the Attorney General may choose to order or not to order the return of the committed person in exercise of his statutory discretion.

The learned judge considered the duty of candour issue raised by the applicant. The argument raised was to the effect that when the defence counsel made his no-case submission and the matter was adjourned for the response of the prosecuting attorney, the Requesting State then improperly obtained the evidence (in the Supplemental Record of the Case) that 'plugged the holes' ostensibly exposed in the no-case submission. That original no-case submission basically attacked the quality of the identification evidence, which was described as circumstantial.

Aboud J held on this issue:

> "The narrative of the events at the magistrates court...however demonstrates that the Chief Magistrate duly considered the application to re-open the prosecution case, allowed the supplemental evidence to be adduced, and gave leave for the defence counsel to make another no-case submission."

His lordship further held:

> "I can find nothing in the evidence to suggest that the Requesting State has withheld any evidence that is inimical

to the evidence presented in the Record or the Supplemental Record. Certainly, the evidence in the Supplemental Record does not undermine the evidence in the Record. It strengthens it. And there is no proof that the Supplemental Record was obtained on the basis of anything that undermines its accuracy or efficacy at this stage. Of course, should the Attorney General sign the Warrant of Return, and should the applicant be extradited, all of the applicant's rights to test the veracity of the evidence in the trial in Boston are preserved."

His lordship concluded that the sequence in which the evidence was presented did not raise any disclosure issues. The Chief Magistrate in allowing the prosecution to re-open the case and lead further evidence was lawfully exercising powers akin to those in a preliminary enquiry. Furthermore the applicant was not denied the opportunity to cross examine the witness who adduced the Supplemental Record and to make a further no-case submission. In these circumstances, the applicant failed to establish any breach of the duty of candour.

THE AUTHORITY TO PROCEED

Principles

1. *The Authority to proceed may be issued by the appropriate authority even in an instance where the relevant documents have not yet been properly authenticated.*

2. *Only properly authenticated documents can be considered by the magistrate in an extradition hearing when exercising his powers of committal or discharge.*

Queen's Bench Division

R v Governor of Brixton Prison and Another Ex parte Cuoghi

[1998] 1 WLR 1513

Facts

The applicant was arrested pursuant to a provisional extradition warrant issued on behalf of the Government of Switzerland. The Home Secretary gave authority to proceed under section 7(4) of the Extradition Act 1989. Subsequently, at the commencement of the committal proceedings, it was submitted by counsel on behalf of the applicant that the papers served in support of the extradition request had not been authenticated in accordance with section 26(1) of the Act of 1989 and the reservation to article 12 in Schedule 4 to the European Convention on Extradition Order 1990

The magistrate held that authenticated documents were necessary before he was able to commit and granted an adjournment. At the resumed committal hearing on 2 June 1995, the magistrate proceeded to make a committal order on the basis of the re-authenticated bundle of documents. The applicant applied for *habeas corpus*. The applicant submitted that the Secretary of State should have refused to grant authority to proceed because he should have perceived that at the committal proceedings, the magistrate would be unable to commit without authenticated documents.

Decision

Kennedy LJ held that the Secretary of State would have been entitled to grant an authority to proceed even in the absence of documents duly authenticated since the necessary authentication would be forthcoming before the end of the committal proceedings in the magistrates' court. His lordship also held that the magistrate had acted correctly when he concluded that he needed authenticated documents in order to proceed

The learned judge further held on this latter issue:

> "In order to discharge his function the magistrate needs to know what the person in question is alleged to have done so

that he can reach a conclusion as to whether it would constitute an offence punishable by 12 months' imprisonment or more if done in the United Kingdom. He also may need to know what the punishment could be under the foreign law...In order to obtain that information it seems to me that the magistrate must have resort not only to the extradition request and the authority to proceed but also, to some extent at least, to the material which was furnished with (or subsequently to) the extradition request namely (1) the particulars of the conduct which constitute an offence in the requesting state, (2) the particulars of the law of the requesting state under which the conduct is punishable and (3) the warrant of arrest inserted by the requesting state. If those foreign documents are going to be consulted they need to be authenticated in accordance with section 26 and paragraph (4) of the reservation to article 12."

His lordship finally concluded that the magistrate was entitled to commit when he did.

Application dismissed.

BAIL IN EXTRADITION HEARINGS

Principle

Bail in extradition cases should be granted only in exceptional cases in the case of serious offences in respect of which severe sentences are likely in the event of a conviction and where there may be a prospect of the persons concerned fleeing the jurisdiction.

Judicial Committee of the Privy Council

Knowles (Austin) and Others v Superintendent of Fox Hill Prison and Others

[2005] UKPC 17

Facts

The Appellants appealed to the Judicial Committee of the Privy Council asking the Board to *inter alia* set aside the order of the Court of Appeal revoking the grant of bail by Thompson J to the appellants.

Decision

Lord Slynn of Hadley noted the various grounds relied upon by the judge in deciding to grant bail, namely:

1. The appellants had strong connections with the Bahamas since they were resident in the Bahamas and had no ties with any other country. They had also worked there and apart from one appellant (N Knowles) they had children there.

2. One was a member of the Bahamas police (Bethel) and two had interests in family businesses (N Knowles and A Knowles). She said that although international criminals had been able to flee and live in other countries in the past

3. Affidavits were filed on behalf of the appellants alleging inhuman and degrading treatment in prison and setting out personal details relating to the individuals as to why they should be released on bail. The judge had also paid a personal visit to the prison where the appellants were detained, and found that the conditions constituted inhuman and cruel treatment. She criticised the affidavit of the Superintendent of Prisons which dealt with this matter on the basis that the affidavit could not have been made from his personal knowledge and he did not give information concerning the source or sources of his knowledge.

Lord Slynn further noted the respondent's objections to bail:

> "They also say that the connections relied on by the appellants are those which are normally relied on in extradition cases

without there being any special reason to grant bail. Mere residence and having a family in the country do not necessarily lead to the conclusion that there will be no attempt to flee the jurisdiction, particularly in a case where it is possible that substantial sums of money may be available from drug smuggling. Moreover it is not accepted that the only way out of the Bahamas would be to the USA to which the appellants could not safely go without risk of being arrested there."

The Board concluded that the judge did not give sufficient weight either to the nature of the crimes alleged or to the risk of, and the advantage of, their fleeing. It was only in exceptional cases that bail as a matter of discretion was granted.

THE DUTY OF DISCLOSURE IN EXTRADITION PROCEEDINGS

Principles

1. *A Requesting State is not under any general duty of disclosure similar to that imposed on a prosecutor in English criminal proceedings. It does, however, owe the court of the Requested State a duty of candour and good faith.*

2. *On an application for habeas corpus in extradition proceedings the court is not confined to reviewing the formal validity of an order for detention but may also enquire into its substantial merits.*

Judicial Committee of the Privy Council

Knowles Jr *v* (1) The Government of the United States of America (2) The Superintendent of Prisons of the Commonwealth of the Bahamas

[2006] UKPC 38

Facts

Following a committal hearing the magistrate committed the appellant to await extradition to the United States. The appellant applied to the Supreme Court for an order of *habeas corpus*. The Government submitted that the role of the Supreme Court on an application for *habeas corpus* in criminal proceedings (such as extradition) is to review the formal validity of an order for detention and not enquire into its substantial merits.

Decision

Lord Bingham of Cornhill held on the issue of the *habeas corpus* application:

> "This proposition cannot be accepted, for three compelling reasons. First, it is contrary to sound Bahamian authority: see R v Superintendent at Her Majesty's Prison Fox Hill, Ex p Darville (No 1) [1989-90] 1 LRB 128; R v Superintendent at Her Majesty's Prison Fox Hill, Ex p Bain [1989-90] 1 LRB 156. Secondly, it is contrary to English authority of high standing: Armah v Government of Ghana [1968] AC 192.
>
> Thirdly, it is irreconcilable with sections 7 and 11 of the 1994 Act which expressly authorise the Supreme Court to enquire into specified aspects of the merits of the detention order which is challenged."

On the issue of disclosure his lordship held that a requesting state is not under any general duty of disclosure similar to that imposed on a prosecutor in English criminal proceedings. The requesting state does, however, owe the court of the requested state a duty of candour and good faith. While it is for the requesting state to decide what evidence it will rely on to seek a committal, it must in pursuance of that duty disclose evidence which destroys or very severely undermines the evidence on which it relies.

THE COTRONI DECISION

Principle

Where conduct can or is being charged locally, the Attorney General must make a Cotroni decision before an extradition order can be made.

High Court of Justice of Trinidad and Tobago

Ferguson, Galbaransingh v The Attorney General of Trinidad and Tobago

CV 2010 – 04144

Facts

Both claimants (citizens of Trinidad and Tobago) and their companies, benefitted from the award of contracts related to the construction and outfitting of a new airport in Trinidad and Tobago. From 2002, the claimants and their companies, along with other persons were charged with crimes related to the award of contracts in the construction of the airport. Among the persons charged were business colleagues, government officials and persons who were Cabinet Ministers at the time. The United States government, through the Department of Justice, began investigations and later charged persons including the claimants and other persons, some of whom were citizens of the United States. In 2006, the United States made an extradition request for the claimants.

The claimants asserted that they did not wish to be extradited to the United States, but they wished to be tried in Trinidad and Tobago where they had been prosecuted for many years and where they had invested significant personal and financial resources to defend themselves. The Attorney General, in exercise of the powers given by section 16 of the Extradition Act Chap. 12:04, decided to order the claimants return to the United States. The claimants applied for judicial review of this decision of the Attorney General.

Decision

Mr Justice Ronnie Boodoosingh noted that few extradition cases would be the same and that the weight to be given to relevant factors will differ from case to case. Furthermore, other factors, not present in Cotroni, could feature prominently in other cases. The learned judge summarised the Cotroni factors as follows:

- Where was the impact of the offence felt or likely to be felt?
- Which jurisdiction has the greater interest in prosecuting the offence?
- Which police force played a major role in the development of the case?
- Which jurisdiction has laid charges?
- Which jurisdiction has the most comprehensive case?
- Which jurisdiction is ready to proceed to trial?
- Where is the evidence located?
- Is the evidence mobile?
- The number of accused involved and whether they can be gathered together in one place for a trial.
- In which jurisdiction were most of the acts in furtherance of the crime committed.
- The nationality and residence of the accused.
- The severity of sentence the accused is likely to receive in each jurisdiction.

His lordship stated that in examining the Attorney General's decision, the court was entitled to give significant weight to his decision and to the reasons given. This, however, did not pre-empt an analysis of the facts as related to the factors considered.

Boodoosingh J considered the facts of the instant case and applied the relevant factors. He found that a comparison of the US charges and the local charges and the possible indictments that could be filed, clearly showed that when conduct was considered, the local charges were more comprehensive. He also found that the core conduct was aimed at Trinidad and Tobago. The underlying scheme was one to defraud the government of Trinidad and Tobago and the true loss was a loss to the citizens of this country.

The Trinidad and Tobago police led the investigations which then helped the United States investigation. This was supported by the Harrikissoon affidavit which noted that 3 CDs containing 121,459 documents were provided to her by the Director of Public Prosecutions in Piarco and that all of these documents were obtained by the investigating authorities of Trinidad and Tobago.

The learned judge further held that the domestic charges were clearly inter-related, comprehensive and significantly wider than the scope of the United States charges. Furthermore, the defence of the local charges undoubtedly involved the application of significant resources on the part of both claimants.

Boodoosingh J held on the issues of location of evidence and mobility:

> "At 32 vi of Ms Harrikissoon's affidavit, the statement was made that the United States authorities have certain witnesses who are not available in this jurisdiction, but nothing further is added. Who are these witnesses and why can't they be made available? In the year 2011, it is difficult to conceive that the prosecution could have difficulty in moving its evidence from one jurisdiction to another. The witnesses can be moved

through the cooperation of the prosecuting authorities. In the case of the bid rigging or conspiracy to defraud allegations, such evidence would be available in Trinidad and Tobago since it is here that the bulk of the conduct took place. These are the foundational charges. The money laundering and wire transfer allegations may largely be based in the United States but it would not be impossible for that evidence to be brought here."

The learned judge further held:

"What may be more difficult is for the claimants' witnesses, if any, to be available to them in the United States. There would be no way to compel them to travel to the United States to give evidence. While arrangements could possibly be made to receive their evidence by video and audio link, any potential prejudice would fall on the claimants only. These factors are of less significance but they still too weigh in favour of Trinidad and Tobago regarding the foundational charges."

His lordship held, on the issue of where the acts were committed that the majority of conduct related to the bid rigging or conspiracy to defraud allegations took place in Trinidad and Tobago. The moneys which formed the basis of the wire transfer and money laundering allegations ultimately came from local institutions and was put into United States financial institutions.

On the issue of nationality and residence of the accused the learned judge noted that both claimants were nationals of Trinidad and Tobago who resided there with their families. They also worked in Trinidad and Tobago. For much of the time they had been prosecuted they were confined to Trinidad and Tobago either on bail or in custody.

In furtherance of this issue his Lordship held:

"In this case there have been proceedings against the claimants for several years. There have been complex proceedings. They have taken place over hundreds of court days. No doubt the proceedings would have occupied the attention of the claimants for many, many other days researching records, giving instructions to attorneys and preparing for court. The local proceedings would have impacted on their social, domestic and business lives. They have made several challenges in court, which the rule of law in this jurisdiction permits. To suddenly abandon these proceedings – but not fully – in favour of foreign proceedings regarding matters (the conspiracy conduct) which have already been proceeded with here, does suggest unfairness and oppression. ..."

His lordship concluded that the decision of the Attorney General to order the return of the claimants had to be quashed. He also stated that the appropriate forum to try the claimants for the charges resulting from the Piarco Airport investigations was Trinidad and Tobago, and that it would be unjust and oppressive to extradite them.

THE RECORD OF CASE

Principle

The record of case must be properly certified.

High Court of Trinidad and Tobago

Jagmohan v The Commissioner of Prisons and the AG

CV 2013-04131

Facts

The applicant was arrested in Trinidad pursuant to a provisional warrant issued under Section 10(1) (b) of the Extradition

(Commonwealth and Foreign Territories) Act, 1985 as amended ("Extradition Act"). The Chief Magistrate failed to fix a date by which the Attorney General should issue an Authority to Proceed in respect of the Applicant and the Applicant filed *habeas corpus* proceedings. At these proceedings it was ordered that the Applicant be brought before the Chief Magistrate before 4:00 p.m. on that same day failing which the Applicant's continued detention would be unlawful. The Applicant was brought before the Chief Magistrate as per the Order of Rahim J and on that day the Authority to Proceed was read to the Applicant. At the hearing, a record of case was tendered into evidence.

Following the close of the case for the Requesting State, Counsel for the Applicant made a submission of no case to answer. He stated *inter alia* that the Record of Case did not conform to section 19A (5) of the Extradition Act. The gravamen of the submission was that the Record of Case was incorrectly certified.

It was certified by one K. Shammugam, Minister for Law of the Republic of Singapore, who did not qualify as a judicial or prosecuting authority as required by provisions of the amended Act of 2004. Instead of responding to the no case submission of Counsel for the Applicant, Counsel for the Requesting State sought leave to re-open their case. The Chief Magistrate granted leave to do so.

The Permanent Secretary tendered into evidence a Supplemental Record of Case dated July 25, 2013, which was certified instead by Mr. TAN Ken Hwee, who on the face of the certificate was designated the prosecuting authority. The Applicant was committed to await the warrant of the Attorney General. Counsel for the Requesting State relied on both the record of case and supplemental record of case for committal. The Applicant later filed an application for a writ of *habeas corpus* pursuant to Section 13 of the Extradition Act.

Decision

Madam Justice C. Gobin held that the issue of certification was fundamental in this case since its absence thereof, in accordance with the Act rendered the record of the case inadmissible. It followed that a Magistrate cannot lawfully make an order for the return of a person on the basis of an inadmissible record of the case.

The learned judge also held that the issuance of the ATP was null and void and of no effect and the committal was therefore unlawful. She stated that Section 9 (7) imposed a statutory prohibition on the issuance of the ATP unless the Attorney General applied his mind to compliance with the statute, and before he invoked the judicial process. This, by implication, imposed a duty on the part of the Attorney General to consider the matter of the admissibility of evidence on the face of the record of the case.

Gobin J held:

> "A Magistrate cannot lawfully order the return of the requested person on the basis of an inadmissible record of case. The Act imposes the duty on the Attorney General to protect the judicial process as well as the right of the person whose release is sought in precisely these circumstances where the issuance of an ATP raises the risk of illegality in the contemplated proceedings."

THE PRINCIPLE OF DOUBLE CRMINALITY

Principle

The offences for which the accused is charged in the Requesting State need not be named, defined and characterized in identical terms under local law. What is relevant is that the conduct of the accused constitutes an offence against the law of the Requested state.

Court of Appeal of Trinidad and Tobago

Nurse and De Four and De Merieux and Clarke v The Commissioner of Prisons and The AG of Trinidad and Tobago

CA Nos. 49, 50, 52, 53 of 2007

Facts

The Appellants, all citizens of Trinidad and Tobago, were indicted by a Grand Jury in the United States of America (US) in connection with the kidnapping and death of BM and the conspiracy to kidnap DM. They were charged under Title 18, United States Code section 1203 with the offences of conspiracy to commit hostage taking resulting in death and hostage taking resulting in death and aiding and abetting and causing an act to be done.

Following the Grand Jury indictment the Attorney General received a formal request from the US for the Appellants' extradition to that country to stand trial for the offences for which they were charged. The Attorney General issued the authority to proceed in respect of each of the Appellants pursuant to section 9 of the Extradition Act. The authority to proceed identified as the corresponding local offences, offences contrary to section 3 of the Taking of Hostages Act. The matters were heard before the Chief Magistrate who committed the Appellants to custody pursuant to section 12 of the Extradition Act.

The Appellants subsequently applied to the High Court for a writ of *habeas corpus*. Dean-Armorer J. dismissed the Appellants' applications. The Appellants appealed to the Court of Appeal.

Decision

Mendonca JA held on the issue of disclosure that different principles of disclosure applied in extradition proceedings from those that applied in domestic criminal trials. The learned judge cited with approval Ralston Wellington v The Governor of HMP Belmarsh [2004] EWHC 418 (Admin.) where the issue of disclosure in extradition proceedings was considered and the following principles established:

1. It is for the requesting state to determine the evidence upon which it relies to seek a committal.

2. The requesting state is not under any general duty of disclosure similar to that imposed on the prosecution at any stage in criminal domestic proceedings.
3. The Magistrates' Court has the right to protect its process from abuse.
4. The requesting state has a duty not to abuse that process. That is no different from saying that the requesting state must fulfil the duty which it has always had of candour in making applications for extradition. In fulfilment of that duty, the requesting state must disclose any evidence which would render worthless the evidence on which it relies to seek committal.
5. It is for the person subject to the extradition process to establish that the requesting state is abusing the process.
6. The requesting state may be given power to request further evidence under the relevant Order in Council but, in the absence of evidence of abuse, the court is entitled to, and should generally, refuse to request the UK authorities to exercise that power or to adjourn to permit it to be exercised.

On the issue of disclosure his lordship held:

> "In this matter there is no material to suggest that the requesting state is in possession of evidence that destroys or undermines the evidence on which it relies. The only thing the Appellants can point to is the evidence which shows that BM was born in Trinidad and Tobago. This, as has already been discussed, does not in any way severely undermine or destroy the evidence on which the requesting state relies. There is therefore no merit in these grounds of appeal."

The learned judge next considered the submission that there was no 'double criminality between the offences' contained in the US indictment and those identified under local law in the authority to proceed. Counsel submitted that the offences under US law had to be named, defined and characterized in identical terms as the offences under local law and in this case they had not. The US charges were all qualified by the words 'if the death of any person results shall be punished by death' whereas these words did not occur in section 3 of the Taking of Hostages Act which it was alleged contained the corresponding offences.

His lordship held on this issue:

> "The premise on which Counsel's submission is made is however misconceived. The offences for which the accused is charged in the requesting State need not be named, defined and characterized in identical terms under local law. What is relevant is that the conduct of the accused constitutes an offence against the law of Trinidad and Tobago. This is made clear by several sections of the Extradition Act. The first is section 6 (1) (b) which refers to conduct in defining what is an extraditable offence…"

His lordship also held:

> "Section 6 (3) underlines that the label attached to the conduct is not relevant. This section provides as follows:

'(3) For greater certainty, it is not relevant whether the conduct referred to in subsection (1) is named, defined or characterised by the declared Commonwealth territory, or the declared foreign territory, in the same way as it is in Trinidad and Tobago.'

Mendonca JA concluded that what was relevant was not that the foreign offence of which the accused was charged carried the same name or label as the offence in the requested state but that the conduct of which he was accused would constitute an offence against the law of Trinidad and Tobago. There was no dispute that the alleged conduct of the Appellants described in the records of the case would amount to offences under section 3 of the Taking of Hostages Act.

Appeals dismissed

CHAPTER FOURTEEN

HIGH COURT TRIALS

High Court trials are conducted before a judge and jury. The judge is the tribunal of law while the jury sits as the tribunal of fact. The charges or counts alleged against the defendant are contained in the indictment.

THE INDICTMENT

The indictment is prepared by the Director of Public Prosecutions and contains counts or charges against the accused.

Principle

The accused must be served with the indictment in accordance with the relevant statutory provisions.

Court of Appeal of Trinidad and Tobago

Lester (Kurt) v The State

C.A. CRIM.21/1992

Facts

The accused was not served with an indictment on a charge of shooting with intent. The accused was convicted and appealed to the Court of Appeal. The indictment was indorsed and signed by a police officer who was not identified and whose signature was illegible. The indorsement read:

'A copy of this indictment was served by the undersigned by sticking same on the door of the [applicant] at the given address at 10.00 a.m. on Monday, 7th June 1988.'

Decision

de la Bastide CJ noted that there was no indication of what the given address was or where or to whom it was given. More crucially, the court was previously informed that there had been no service on the applicant.

The learned Chief Justice noted rule 14(4) of the Indictment Rules which constitutes the First Schedule to the Criminal Law Procedure Act which reads:

'If upon the arraignment of any accused person, it appears to the court that such copy [i.e. of the indictment] was not served according to this Act, such accused person shall, on an application by himself or on his behalf, be entitled as of right to have the trial of the indictment postponed to the next criminal Session held in the place in which he is arraigned.'

His lordship concluded that the appellant was never served with a copy of the indictment at all, and had no notice that he would be tried on the charge until 12 February, the day on which he was called upon to plead and on which a jury was empanelled.

Appeal allowed; conviction quashed.

Principle

The indictment must be signed by the proper officer of the court. Failure to do so will result in the indictment being invalid.

Court of Appeal Criminal Division

R v Morais

[1988] 3 All ER 161

Facts

The appellant appealed against conviction on the ground that, the bill of indictment not having been signed by the proper officer was invalid. The Administration of Justice (Miscellaneous Provisions) Act 1933 s. 2 provided:

"Subject as hereinafter provided no bill of indictment charging any person with an indictable offence shall be preferred unless either— *(a)* the person charged has been committed for trial for the offence; or *(b)* the bill is preferred ... by the direction or with the consent of a judge of the High Court ..."

Decision

Lord Lane CJ held that the 1933 Act was intended to fill the gap which was left by the abolition of the grand jury. It was intended to ensure not only that the proper requirements had been fulfilled before a trial proper could start, but that also there should be a certification by way of the signature of the proper officer to indicate that he had inquired into the situation and satisfied himself that the requirements of the subsection had properly been complied with.

His lordship concluded that the appending of the proper officer's signature was not merely a comparatively meaningless formality but it was a necessary condition precedent to the existence of a proper indictment. It followed that in the present case there was no valid indictment, there was no valid trial, no valid verdict and no valid sentence.

JOINDER OF CHARGES ON THE INDICTMENT

Principle

In order that charges be properly joined in the same indictment, the test is whether the charges have a common factual origin.

Court of Appeal

R. v Barrell (Victor Sidney), R. v. Victor Sidney Barrell, R. v. Alan Henry Wilson

(1979) 69 Cr. App. R. 250

Facts

At a trial in the High Court, applications were made to the trial judge to sever the indictment on the ground that the inclusion of count 3 was a misjoinder in that the joinder was not within the ambit of section 4 of the Indictments Act 1915 since it lay outside the scope of rule 9 of the Indictments Rules 1971. The judge overruled that submission. On appeal, it was submitted, *inter alia*, that count 3, so far from being founded on the same facts as count 1, derived from a new and different set of facts which was not only different in its nature but also separated by a substantial interval of time from the set of facts which gave rise to counts 1 and 2.

Decision

Shaw L.J held that the phrase 'founded on the same facts' did not mean that for charges to be properly joined in the same indictment the facts in relation to the respective charges must be identical in substance or virtually contemporaneous. His lordship held that the correct test was whether the charges had a common factual origin. On the instant facts, If the charge described as the subsidiary charge was one that could not have been alleged but for the facts which gave rise to what was called the primary charge, then it was true to say for the purposes of rule 9 that those charges were founded on the same facts and could legitimately be joined in the same indictment.

Appeals dismissed.

Principle

The prosecution should avoid overloading the indictment since this would prejudice the defendant's right to a fair trial.

Court of Appeal

R. v Novac (Andrew),

(1977) 65 Cr. App. R. 107

Facts

An indictment contained 19 counts (out of an original of 38) against four defendants. This led to a long and complex trial occupying in all 47 working days, and which put an immense burden on judge and jury.

Decision

Bridge L.J held that if multiplicity of defendants and charges threatened undue length and complexity of trial then a heavy responsibility rested on the prosecution to consider whether joinder was essential in the interests of justice or whether the case could reasonably be sub-divided or otherwise abbreviated and simplified. In jury trial brevity and simplicity were the hand-maidens of justice, while length and complexity were its enemies.

His lordship stated that most of the difficulties which bedevilled the trial, and which ultimately led to the quashing of all convictions except on the conspiracy and related counts, arose directly out of the overloading of the indictment. The learned judge further stated that even in its reduced form of an indictment containing 19 counts against four defendants there resulted a trial of quite unnecessary length and complexity.

Bridge L.J in assessing the disadvantages of a long trial stated that such a trial placed an immense burden on both judge and jury. In the course of a four or five day summing-up the most careful and conscientious judge could also easily overlook some essential matter. Even if the summing-up was faultless, it was doubtful whether the average juror could be expected to take it all in and apply all the directions given.

His lordship concluded that while some criminal prosecutions involved consideration of matters so plainly inextricable and indivisible that a long and complex trial was an ineluctable necessity, nothing short of the criterion of absolute necessity could justify the imposition of the burdens of a very long trial on the Court.

SEPARATE TRIALS

Where accused persons are lawfully joined in a count in an indictment the trial judge may still make an order for separate trials.

Principle

Separate trial of persons who are alleged to have acted pursuant to a joint enterprise should only be ordered in exceptional circumstances.

Court of Appeal

R. v Moghal (Mohammed Ilias)

(1977) 65 Cr. App. R. 56

Facts

One R was murdered in circumstances in which only the appellant or his mistress or both of them could have killed him. They were jointly charged with R.'s murder. The mistress applied to the judge for separate trials, and he acceded to her application. She was tried first and acquitted, the defence being that the appellant alone was the cause of R.'s death (the "cut-throat" defence). The appellant's defence was similar—that his mistress alone had murdered R. The Crown conceded at his trial that the act of killing was that of the mistress, who had previously threatened to kill R. The appellant appealed on the ground that the trial judge should not have ordered separate trials and a miscarriage of justice had occurred.

Decision

Scarman L.J. held that *prima facie* where the essence of the case is that the prisoners were engaged on a common enterprise, it was obviously right and proper that they should be jointly indicted and jointly tried, and in some cases it would be as much in the interest of the accused as of the prosecution that they should be. His lordship added that only in very exceptional cases was it wise to order separate trials when two or more persons were jointly charged with participation in one criminal offence.

His lordship detailed one instance where separate trials would not be suitable:

> "Suppose, for instance, that the defence of one was that he or she was acting under the positive duress of the other. It would be obviously right that they should be tried by the same jury, who might see in one prisoner a harmless or nervous looking little man or woman and in the other a savage brute whom they might deem capable of forcing his co-prisoner against his will into assisting in a crime."

Principle

It is desirable that the same verdict and the same treatment should be returned against all those concerned with the same offence. It follows that joint offences should be tried jointly. This should be so even in cases where inadmissible evidence is put before the jury and possible prejudice which may result from such non-severence.

Court of Appeal

R. v. Lake

(1977) 64 Cr. App. R. 172

Facts

B and D were the accused's co-conspirators. At some stage they had signed written statements which not only admitted their own participation in this burglary but also said that the appellant had set it up for them. Those statements were not admissible as against the appellant L. L applied for a separate trial, and the basis of his application was that the statements by B and D would go before the jury alleging that L had set up the burglary. It was submitted that, whatever direction the judge gave to the jury about the inadmissibility of that evidence, in fact it was bound to be prejudicial to the appellant. The judge declined to order separate trials and the appellant was convicted. He appealed the conviction.

Decision

The Lord Chief Justice noted that it was long accepted English practice that there were powerful public reasons why joint offences should be tried jointly. The importance was not merely one of saving time and money, but it also affected the desirability that the same verdict and the same treatment should be returned against all those concerned in the same offence. If joint offences were widely to be tried as separate offences, all sorts of inconsistencies could arise.

The learned judge held:

> "The judge declined to order separate trials and we think that he was right. Accordingly it is accepted practice, from which we certainly should not depart in this Court today, that a joint offence can properly be tried jointly, even though this will involve inadmissible evidence being given before the jury and the possible prejudice which may result from that."

His lordship cautioned that in such cases the trial judge should warn the jury against considering any of the evidence that was not admissible.

Appeal dismissed.

ENTERING THE PLEA

When the indictment is read the accused is called upon to enter a plea. This is known as the arraignment.

Principle

Where an indictment contains multiple counts the defendant must plead separately to each count.

Court of Criminal Appeal

R v Boyle

[1954] 2 QB 292

Facts

The appellant was charged on an indictment containing four counts. After all four counts were read to him, he was asked to plead to the whole indictment. He made one plea to the whole indictment. He was convicted and appealed against conviction.

Decision

Lord Goddard CJ affirmed that the correct practice was that each count in an indictment where there was more than one count should be put to the prisoner separately and he should be asked to plead to each separate count. His lordship also noted that every count in an indictment is equivalent to a separate indictment; the prisoner can be tried on one or on all the counts. Where there are multiple counts, the verdicts have to be taken separately.

The learned judge further held:

> "…What I have said is to be taken as applying, not only to counts which are of a different nature, but even where there are alternative counts. For instance, in counts for stealing and receiving it is better that the two counts should be put. The count for stealing should be put to the prisoner, and, if he pleads guilty to that, there is no need to put the count for receiving. But, if he pleads not guilty, then the count for receiving should be put as a separate count and a plea taken on it."

Principle

Where the defendant fails to formally enter a plea of not guilty (although that was his intention) but the trial proceeds on the basis of a not guilty plea then the proceedings would still be valid.

Court of Appeal Criminal Division

R v Williams (Roy)

[1978] QB 373

Facts

The appellant appeared before the Crown Court to stand trial and was not called on to plead. The clerk then read out the indictment to the jury and informed them that the appellant had pleaded not guilty to it. The appellant did not demur. The trial proceeded in the normal way, as if the appellant had been arraigned and had pleaded. The appellant was convicted. He appealed, contending that the proceedings were a nullity since he had not been called on to plead, and had not pleaded, to the indictment.

Decision

Shaw LJ held that it was difficult to conceive what possible prejudice could be caused to an accused person in a case where a plea of not guilty was vicariously offered or tacitly conveyed. His lordship cited with approval the 'Corpus Juris Secundum' from the United States of America which stated that the plea may be waived in criminal cases. Waiver in such cases may be express or by conduct, as where the accused, without objection, and with the intention of entering a not guilty plea, proceeds to trial as if he had been duly arraigned.

His lordship concluded:

> "In the judgment of this court, while the omission of a formal arraignment was unfortunate and regrettable, it did not, in the peculiar circumstances of this case, have the result of vitiating the trial as such. It follows that counsel for the appellant's submission fails and that the appeal is dismissed."

PREPARATION OF THE INDICTMENT

Principle

The DPP may indict for any offence founded on facts disclosed in the legally admissible evidence adduced at the preliminary inquiry.

Supreme Court of British Guyana

R v Manning

Decision of the Supreme Court of British Guiana, Demerara Assizes, 11th December 1959

Facts

Before the accused pleaded to the indictment it was submitted on his behalf that all of the counts except the sixth count of the indictment should be quashed because the Attorney-General (DPP) had no power to include in the indictment counts charging the commission of offences alleging wrongful acts or omissions other than the wrongful act or omission alleged in the information.

Section 113 of Cap 11 states:

"On receipt of the documents relating to the preliminary inquiry, the Attorney-General, if he sees fit to do so, shall institute those criminal proceedings in the court against the accused person which to him seem legal and proper."

Decision

Date J noted that at the preliminary inquiry before the magistrate, only one offence was mentioned in the information, and that was in respect of the alleged falsification of accounts of 11 July 1958, which now forms the subject-matter of the sixth count of the indictment, but evidence had been led regarding all the acts or omissions contained in the indictment.

His lordship held:

> "...In my opinion s 113 of Cap 11 clearly empowers the Attorney-General to include in the indictment, either in substitution for or in addition to a count charging the offence for which the accused was committed, any counts for related offences founded on facts disclosed in the legally admissible evidence adduced at the preliminary inquiry."

Motion dismissed.

DEFECTS IN THE INDICTMENT

Where an indictment is defective it may be amended depending on the defect, otherwise it will be null and void and liable to be quashed.

Principle

An indictment will be merely defective and not a nullity where a count in the indictment fails to state the statute which the accused is alleged to have contravened.

Court of Appeal

R. v. Nelson

(1977) 65 Cr. App. R. 119

Facts

The appellant was charged, *inter alia* with possessing an offensive weapon. The "Statement of Offence" in respect of that count in the indictment failed to state the statute which the appellant was alleged to have contravened [*i.e.* section 1 (1) of the Prevention of Crime Act 1952]. At the end of his trial, counsel for the appellant moved to arrest judgment on the ground that the indictment on that count was defective. The trial judge did not allow an amendment but proceeded forthwith to sentence the appellant. The appellant appealed contending that the defect made the indictment a nullity.

Decision

Lawton L.J held that whereas there was a defect in the indictment the trial judge was entitled to amend the indictment. On the issue of whether the defect in the indictment made it a nullity, his lordship held that the fact that the judge could have amended the indictment meant that the indictment was not a nullity but was merely defective.

The learned judge held:

> "Accordingly, though we are dismissing the appeal on the merits, in the circumstances of this case we would not have quashed the proceedings on the ground that they had been a nullity."

THE ORDER OF THE EVIDENCE

The prosecution leads evidence first, followed by the defence. In certain circumstances, the court may on application of either side change this order of evidence.

Principle

Trial judges are given wide discretion to re-open the case for the prosecution or defence. In exercising that discretion, the court must always protect the accused's right to a fair trial.

Court of Appeal of Trinidad and Tobago

Briggs v The State

Cr. App. No. T-013 of 2014

Facts

The appellant was charged with the murder of KG. At the close of the evidence, the judge, on her own motion, raised an issue with prosecutor and defence counsel. After discussions, and with the consent of trial counsel for the appellant, the judge permitted the prosecution to reopen its case. The purpose and effect of so doing was to admit into evidence part of one of the statements of the appellant, which had previously been edited out.

The judge stated that her reason for doing so was to show the history and context of the fatal encounter, so as to assist the jury in their deliberation on the issue of provocation. The appellant was convicted and appealed.

One of the grounds was that the judge wrongly exercised her discretion when she allowed the prosecution to reopen its case. The appellant submitted that on the authority of R v Francis, a trial judge has a discretion to allow the prosecution to call further evidence after the close of its case, the discretion not being confined to cases in which the evidence was in rebuttal of a matter which had arisen *ex improviso* or where the evidence omitted was a mere formality and not central to the case. The respondent contended that the judge had correctly exercised her discretion and that the lately-admitted evidence was allowed in order to adequately and contextually present the appellant's defence of provocation for the jury's consideration.

Decision

P. Weekes, JA affirmed that a judge has a wider discretion than that stated in R v Francis but although the limits of that discretion should not be precisely defined, only rarely should it be exercised outside the two established exceptions to the rule.

The learned judge also noted that the judge's decision to put the disputed part of the statement in evidence did not cause prejudice to the appellant but rather, was of benefit to him by ensuring that the issue of provocation, raised on the prosecution case, and relied on by the appellant, was not starved of relevant evidence. The jury therefore had before it all of the available evidence to allow them to fairly consider the issue.

The learned judge held:

> "It is the responsibility of a trial judge in a criminal matter to ensure that the accused enjoys a fair trial. This responsibility imposes upon the trial judge a duty to be constantly vigilant as the trial takes its course to see whether any decision previously made by the court needs to be revisited. In order to accomplish the desired end, trial judges are given wide discretion, the discretion to re-open the case for the prosecution or defence included.
>
> In the instant matter, having ruled a part of the appellant's statement to be inadmissible as being irrelevant, and possibly unfairly prejudicial, the judge, on reassessing the case from the perspective of all the evidence, saw the previously omitted evidence in a different light. In her view, provocation arose as a live issue on the prosecution case and the previously omitted evidence served to bolster that contention. It was additional or further evidence that the jury could consider in favour of

the accused as they grappled with the issue of whether he was provoked to do as he did."

Weekes JA concluded that defence counsel's acquiescence to the evidence being admitted was correct. This was because the issue of provocation was squarely before the jury and the newly admitted evidence had the potential to support the case for the appellant. While the evidence did introduce the question of the appellant having acted in revenge on Saturday 22nd September 2007, it also introduced the concept of a course of action to be considered on the issue of provocation, i.e., that the acts of provocation were continual, having begun on the Thursday evening and culminating on the Saturday. Trial counsel for the appellant, having exercised her professional judgment, balanced the advantage to be gained from the admission of the evidence against the possible disadvantage and elected to have the evidence admitted. The appellant could not enjoy the benefit without courting the detriment.

FAIRNESS OF THE TRIAL

Principle

It is the responsibility of the trial judge to ensure that the proceedings are conducted in an orderly and proper manner which is fair to both prosecution and defence.

Judicial Committee of the Privy Council

Randall (Barry) v R

[2002] UKPC 19

Facts

The appellant was convicted after a trial in the High Court and appealed. The primary ground of his appeal against conviction was that the trial was conducted in a manner which was grossly and fundamentally unfair. The source of this unfairness, was the conduct of prosecuting counsel, and also that the trial judge wrongly failed to restrain the conduct of prosecuting counsel and on occasion endorsed it.

Decision

Lord Bingham of Cornhill affirmed the following principles:

1. Evidence should ordinarily be given without interruption by counsel. If either counsel has cause to object to any evidence adduced or about to be adduced such objection should be made promptly and shortly and the judge should rule. If such an objection prompts any extended argument or seems likely to do so, and particularly if the argument bears on the substantial merits of the case, it should take place in the absence of the jury.

2. The procedure of the criminal courts provides opportunities for prosecuting and defence counsel to address the jury, usually before and after the calling of evidence. Counsel are not (save where the rules allow defence counsel to open the defence) permitted to address the jury at any other time, nor is it permissible under the guise of an interjection for counsel to make observations intended to influence the mind of the jury.

3. While the duty of counsel may require a strong and direct challenge to the evidence of a witness, and strong criticism may properly be made of a witness or a defendant so long as that criticism is based on evidence or the absence of evidence before the court, there can never be any justification for bullying, intimidation, personal

vilification or insult or for the exchange of insults between counsel. Any disparaging comment on a witness or a defendant should be reserved for a closing speech.

4. Reference should never be made to matters which may be prejudicial to a defendant but which are not before the jury.

5. Unless the judge seeks the assistance of counsel on a point of factual detail, or makes a factual misstatement which can be quickly and uncontroversially corrected, his summing-up should proceed without any interruption by counsel. If as not infrequently happens, prosecuting or defence counsel wish to bring some suggested misdirection or omission or inaccuracy to the attention of the judge, this should be done, preferably at the close of the summing-up or at some convenient interlude in the proceedings, and in the absence of the jury unless the point is one which can safely be discussed in their presence without risk of prejudice. It can never be proper for counsel to make any interjection prejudicial to the defendant when the judge is in the course of summing-up to the jury.

6. It is the responsibility of the judge to ensure that the proceedings are conducted in an orderly and proper manner which is fair to both prosecution and defence.

His lordship further held, on the role of the trial judge that the judge must neither be nor appear to be partisan. He should not disparage the defendant in the course of the evidence. Nor should he disparage defence counsel, since jurors inevitably tend to identify clients with their counsel. If the judge needs, in any serious or sustained manner, to criticise the conduct of the defence case or to criticise or rebuke defending counsel, it will usually be prudent for the judge to do so in the absence of the jury. Furthermore, he should ensure that his disapproval of or irritation with counsel does not affect the jury's judgment. If he chooses to express personal opinions in the course of the summing-up, he should do so in a restrained, moderate and balanced way.

On the facts of the instant case his lordship held:

> "The crucial issue in the present appeal is whether there were such departures from good practice in the course of the appellant's trial as to deny him the substance of a fair trial. The Board reluctantly concludes that there were. Prosecuting counsel conducted himself as no minister of justice should conduct himself. The trial judge failed to exert the authority vested in him to control the proceedings and enforce proper standards of behaviour. Regrettably, he allowed himself to be overborne and allowed his antipathy to both the appellant and his counsel to be only too manifest. While none of the appellant's complaints taken on its own would support a successful appeal, taken together they leave the Board with no choice but to quash the appellant's convictions."

Advice that appeal be allowed.

THE DUTY OF THE PROSECUTOR

Principle

The duty of prosecuting counsel is not to obtain a conviction at all costs, but to act as a minister of justice. It follows that misconduct by the prosecutor may violate the defendant's right to a fair trial.

Judicial Committee of the Privy Council

Benedetto v R

[2003] UKPC 27 (7 April 2003)

Facts

The appellant was convicted of murder and appealed. It was claimed on appeal that the prosecutor cross-examined certain witnesses in an oppressive manner. Furthermore, in his address to the jury the prosecutor used terms which were xenophobic and inflammatory, referred to inadmissible evidence and made improper attacks on the credibility of a witness.

Decision

Lord Hope of Craighead held that it was established in cases such as Randall v R that the duty of prosecuting counsel was not to obtain a conviction at all costs, but to act as a minister of justice. His lordship also cited Boucher v R with approval. In this case it was established that that the purpose of a criminal prosecution is not to obtain a conviction but rather it is to lay before a jury what the Crown considers to be credible evidence relevant to what is alleged to be a crime.

His lordship further held that the defendant has an absolute right to a fair trial and if the prosecutor's departure from good practice was so gross, or so persistent or so prejudicial as to be irremediable, an appellate court will have no choice but to hold that the trial was unfair and quash the conviction.

The learned judge concluded:

> "Their lordships have very much in mind the point which Satrohan Singh JA made (para [35] of the judgment of the Court of Appeal) that the principles which determine the proper role of the prosecutor have to be applied in the context of his own environment. He said that juries need to be spoken to in a language and style that they will understand, and there was nothing wrong with a prosecutor delivering a

robust but respectful speech. That is true. But there is an obvious difference between a robust speech and one which is xenophobic, inflammatory and seeks to make use of inadmissible and irrelevant material. Regrettably, some parts of Mr Guerra's speech fell plainly into the latter category."

Appeal allowed.

COMMON LAW DISCLOSURE

Principle

The prosecution at common law has a duty to disclose the previous convictions of prosecution witnesses to the defence. This duty entails making the necessary inquiries to ascertain whether its witnesses have any convictions. There is no corresponding duty on the part of the defence to make inquiries.

Court of Appeal of Trinidad and Tobago

Bishop (Glenroy) v The State

(2000) 60 WIR 370

Facts

The appellant was convicted in January 1996 of murder, but his conviction was set aside in April 1998 by the Court of Appeal and a retrial ordered. At his retrial in November 1998 he was again convicted, and his conviction was upheld by the Court of Appeal. The Judicial Committee of the Privy Council allowed his appeal and remitted the appeal to the Court of Appeal of Trinidad and Tobago to determine whether a third trial should be ordered.

Decision

Hamel-Smith JA noted that when the appellant's appeal was heard by the Privy Council the conviction was quashed. No reasons were furnished by the Privy Council but it seemed that it was quashed mainly on the ground that the prosecution had, at the trial, failed to disclose that the two main witnesses for the prosecution (Singh and Jacobs) had previous convictions.

His lordship held:

> "Counsel for the State submitted that the prosecutor at the trial was not aware of the previous convictions. That, in our view, does not absolve the State from its obligation to disclose them. It is certainly not sufficient for the prosecution to say that he or she did not know of the convictions.
>
> It is highly unlikely that generally he would be privy to such information. The prosecution nevertheless has a duty to disclose them and that duty entails making the necessary inquiries to ascertain whether its witnesses have any convictions. This it obviously did not do in this case. There is no corresponding duty on the part of the defence to make inquiries."

Retrial ordered.

ALLOWING INTO EVIDENCE THE DEPOSITION OF A WITNESS WHO IS UNABLE TO TESTIFY AT THE TRIAL

Principle

A trial judge, in the exercise of his duty to ensure a fair trial for the defendant has power at common law to refuse to allow the prosecution to adduce in evidence a deposition even though it was highly probative of the offence charged.

Judicial Committee of the Privy Council

Scott and another v R; Barnes and others v R

[1989] UKPC 10

Facts

The two appellants were charged with murdering a special constable in a bar. The only evidence of identification was that contained in the deposition of a witness who deposed that he had seen the appellants' faces as they ran from the bar and had subsequently pointed out the appellants to the police. The witness died before the trial.

The questions arose whether a trial judge in a criminal case had a discretion to refuse to admit the sworn deposition of a witness who had died before trial and, if so, in what circumstances that discretion should be exercised and what direction the judge should give on the issue of identification.

Decision

Lord Griffiths noted that the vital evidence of identification was contained in the sworn depositions of the deceased witnesses. Without the evidence in the depositions there would have been insufficient evidence to put any of the defendants on trial.

His lordship cited with approval the case of Barnes, Desquottes and Johnson which held that where the evidence in the deposition was relevant and admissible the trial judge had no discretion to exclude it from the trial. The learned judge concluded:

> "In the light of these authorities their Lordships are satisfied that the discretion of a judge to ensure a fair trial includes a power to exclude the admission of a deposition. It is, however, a power that should be exercised with great restraint. The mere fact that the deponent will not be available for cross-examination is obviously an insufficient ground for excluding the deposition, for that is a feature common to the admission of all depositions which must have been contemplated and accepted by the legislature when it gave statutory sanction to their admission in evidence."

Lord Griffiths stated that if the courts were too ready to exclude the deposition of a deceased witness, it could well place the lives of witnesses at risk particularly in a case where only one witness had been courageous enough to give evidence against the accused or only one witness had the opportunity to identify the accused. The learned judge cautioned that it would be necessary in every case to warn the jury that they had not had the benefit of hearing the evidence of the deponent tested in cross-examination and to take that into consideration when considering how far they could safely rely on the evidence in the deposition.

His lordship further elaborated on the judge's role in admitting such a deposition:

> "No doubt in many cases it will be appropriate for a judge to develop this warning by pointing out particular features of the evidence in the deposition which conflict with other evidence and which could have been explored in cross-examination but no rules can usefully be laid down to control the detail to which a judge should descend in the individual case. In an identification case it will, in addition, be necessary to give the appropriate warning of the danger of identification evidence.

> The deposition must of course be scrutinised by the judge to ensure that it does not contain inadmissible matters such as hearsay or matter that is prejudicial rather than probative and any such material should be excluded from the deposition before it is read to the jury."

His lordship held that neither the ability to cross-examine, nor the fact that the deposition contained the only evidence against the accused, nor the fact that it is identification evidence would of itself be sufficient to justify the exercise of the discretion. It was the quality of the evidence in the deposition that was the crucial factor that should determine the exercise of the discretion. The learned judge stated that by way of example, if the deposition contained evidence of identification that was so weak that a judge in the absence of corroborative evidence would withdraw the case from the jury, then, if there was no corroborative evidence, the judge should exercise his discretion to refuse to admit the deposition for it would be unsafe to allow the jury to convict on it.

Appeals allowed. Convictions quashed.

Principle

Under s 40(1)(b) of the Indictable Offences (Preliminary Enquiry) Act (Cap 12.01) of the Laws of Trinidad and Tobago, a deposition could be read as evidence in the trial if it was proved at trial that the deposition had been taken in the presence of the accused person and that he or his legal adviser had had full opportunity of cross-examining the deponent.

Judicial Committee of the Privy Council

Cauldero and another v The State

[2000] 4 LRC 33

Facts

The appellants appealed their convictions for murder to the Privy Council on a number of grounds, *inter alia*, that there were irregularities in the trial in that the judge had permitted the deposition of one AP a deceased witness to be read to the jury.

At the time of the trial AP had died and AS was not called as a witness so that the evidence implicating the appellants consisted of their two statements and, if it was admitted in evidence, the deposition made by AP at the proceedings in Port of Spain Magistrates Court. Counsel for the appellants objected to the deposition being read but the judge rejected their submissions and it was read to the jury.

Section 40(1) of the Indictable Offences (Preliminary Enquiry) Act, Ch 12.01 of the Laws of Trinidad and Tobago, permits a deposition taken before a magistrate to be read as evidence on the trial of a person if:

"(b) It is proved at the trial that the deposition was taken in the presence of the accused person and that he or his legal adviser had full opportunity of cross-examining the deponent."

Decision

Sir Roy Beldam noted that the prosecution had relied strongly on Francois' statement and Anderson Phillip's deposition to prove that the appellants had gone to Morvant with the intention to shoot and kill the deceased. He also noted the submission that the appellant Cauldero had no full opportunity to cross-examine Anderson Phillip because counsel who then appeared for him was not present.

His lordship held on this issue:

> "Their Lordships do not know why counsel was not present when Anderson Phillip gave his deposition but the Board

notes that on the preceding occasion the court recorded that counsel who appeared for Francois was 'holding for counsel for Cauldero' and that he, in fact, cross-examined Anderson Phillip when he gave his deposition. It seems to the Board that there was a full opportunity for cross-examination of the witness. The fact that Cauldero's counsel did not take advantage of the opportunity does not mean that he did not have the chance to do so. The Board is satisfied that the requirements for the admission of the deposition were met on this occasion."

Appeal allowed.

Principles

1. *The admissibility of depositions is not automatic. The exercise of a judicial discretion is required to see that no injustice inconsistent with a fair trial is likely to be produced.*
2. *Even where depositions are admitted, it is still necessary that suitable directions be given to the jury.*

Court of Appeal of Guyana

Sutherland v The State

Decision of the Court of Appeal of Guyana, 24th April 1970

Facts

The appellant was charged with the offence of manslaughter and was convicted. At the trial, the depositions of a witness who had given evidence at the preliminary investigation but who had since died were put in evidence.

Under s 95 (1):

"Where any person has been committed for trial for any offence, the deposition of any person taken before a magistrate may, if the conditions hereinafter set out are satisfied, without further proof be read as evidence on the trial of that person, whether for that offence or for any other offence arising out of the same transaction or set of circumstances as that offence."

The appellant submitted that the trial was unsatisfactory and resulted in a miscarriage of justice, because the learned trial judge exercised his discretion wrongly when he admitted in evidence the deposition of the witness Karim Khan under the provisions of s 95 (1) of the Evidence Ordinance, Cap 25, in that it was unfair to the accused and improperly prejudiced his case as the jury did not see and hear him in the witnessbox as they ought to have done, especially as his evidence related to a vital and material aspect of the case for the prosecution.

Alternatively, having admitted the evidence, the learned judge ought to have directed the jury:

(i) that in the circumstances Karim Khan's evidence could not be treated as carrying the same weight as if he had testified in court; and

(ii) that they should exercise proper caution in accepting his deposition as proved facts in the case.

Decision

Luckhoo C held that the admissibility of depositions under s 95 was not automatic. The exercise of a judicial discretion was required and this prohibited any whimsical or capricious approach. His lordship held further on this issue:

> "So that before ascertaining whether the statutory conditions necessary for the reception of the depositions exist, it is of importance that the nature of the evidence contained in the depositions should be first examined. When it is formal, no

problem arises. If it is irrelevant or extraneous, then obviously it must be excluded. But if material and relevant, this further precaution (subject to proof of compliance with the statutory conditions) must be taken, that is, the question must be asked and satisfactorily answered: 'Is the evidence sought to be tendered likely to produce injustice of a kind inconsistent with a fair trial?'"

The learned judge also stated that where the trial judge felt that the accused would be at considerable disadvantage if the deposition were to be admitted, then in the interest of justice he might deem it expedient to reject the evidence. In so deciding, he must first measure the degree of injustice. The greater the danger of possible injustice, the more urgent will be the necessity for the giving of suitable directions.

However where that danger is so great that it might not be easily counteracted even by specific warnings, then he should be wary in admitting what might unfairly prejudice the result of a trial, even though it be strictly admissible. In cases where the evidence was seriously disputed, the court should remind the jury that they did not have the benefit of assessing the demeanour of the deponent, and to warn them that caution should be exercised in accepting the evidence in the witness's absence.

Appeal dismissed.

PROCEEDING WITH THE TRIAL IN THE ACCUSED'S ABSENCE

Principle

Where the conduct of an accused during a trial was designed for the deliberate purpose of making it impossible to proceed with his

trial, the trial judge is entitled to proceed with the trial (including the sentence) in the accused's absence.

Court of Appeal of Trinidad and Tobago

Patrick and Small v R

C.A. Crim.70/1972 C.A. Crim.74/1972

Facts

On his arraignment before the jury S refused to plead and immediately sought to escape from the dock and generally behaved in such a violent and disorderly manner as to render it necessary for the trial judge to have him removed from the court. On more than one occasion he was requested to return but refused to do so, with the result that the trial proceeded and terminated with his being sentenced in his absence.

Decision

Phillips JA was of view that the appellant's behaviour was designed for the deliberate purpose of making it impossible for his trial to be conducted and thus rendered it imperative that he be sent out of court. His lordship concluded:

> "...it is clear to us that the applicant's conduct was 'due to caprice, malice [and] for the purpose of embarrassing the trial', which, as submitted by the learned SolicitorGeneral on behalf of the Crown, includes the sentence. In the result, we have come to the inescapable conclusion that the learned judge exercised his discretion properly in continuing with the trial in the applicant's absence. To hold otherwise would not merely be a means of encouraging accused persons to adopt the kind of behaviour adopted by the applicant in this case, but would have a direct tendency to render abortive the whole administration of justice in the criminal courts...".

Principle

The High Court may conduct a trial in the absence, from its commencement, of the defendant. The discretion to proceed with a trial in the absence, from the beginning, of the defendant is one to be exercised with extreme care and only in the rare case where, after full consideration of all relevant matters, including in particular the fairness of the trial.

House of Lords

R v Jones

[2002] UKHL 5

Facts

The defendant absconded prior to the start of his trial. The trial proceeded in his absence and he was convicted and sentenced. The defendant subsequently appealed against his conviction.

Decision

Lord Bingham of Cornhill held that whereas the presence of the defendant has been treated as a very important feature of an effective jury trial, the court has a discretion as to whether to continue the trial or to order that the jury be discharged with a view to a further trial being held at a later date. This discretion has to be exercised with great caution and with close regard to the overall fairness of the proceedings. A defendant afflicted by involuntary illness or incapacity will have much stronger grounds for resisting the continuance of the trial than one who has voluntarily chosen to abscond. His lordship added that it was hard to discern any principled distinction between continuing a trial in the absence, for whatever reason, of a defendant and beginning a trial which has not in law commenced.

The learned judge held on the issue of whether to commence a trial in the defendant's absence:

> "...In doing so I would stress, as the Court of Appeal did in that the discretion to commence a trial in the absence of a defendant should be exercised with the utmost care and caution...If the absence of the defendant is attributable to involuntary illness or incapacity it would very rarely, if ever, be right to exercise the discretion in favour of commencing the trial, at any rate unless the defendant is represented and asks that the trial should begin."

The learned judge also detailed the following principles pertinent to the exercise of the court's discretion:

1. The seriousness of the offence is not a matter relevant to the exercise of discretion. The judge's overriding concern will be to ensure that the trial, if conducted in the absence of the defendant, will be as fair as circumstances permit and lead to a just outcome. These objects are equally important, whether the offence charged be serious or relatively minor.

2. It is generally desirable that a defendant be represented even if he has voluntarily absconded. The task of representing at trial an absent defendant and who may well be out of touch, is of course rendered much more difficult and unsatisfactory, and there is no possible ground for criticising the legal representatives who withdrew from representing the appellant at trial in this case.

The presence throughout the trial of legal representatives, in receipt of instructions from the client at some earlier stage, and with no object other than to protect the interests of that client, provides a valuable safeguard against the possibility of error and oversight. For this reason trial judges should routinely ask counsel to continue to represent a defendant who has absconded during the trial, and counsel in practice should accede to such an invitation and defend their absent client as best they properly can in the circumstances.

Appeal dismissed.

CHAPTER FIFTEEN

THE JURY AND VERDICT

The jury sits as the tribunal of fact in High Court trials and is responsible for deliberating on the evidence and then returning a verdict of guilty or not guilty. The jury is obligated to accept any legal directions from the trial judge who sits as the tribunal of law.

THE VERDICT

Principle

The jury may correct its verdict before the jurors have left the jury box.

R v. Vodden

(1853) 169 ER 706

Facts

On the trial of an indictment for larceny, one of the jurors delivered a verdict of not guilty, and the prisoner was discharged out of the dock. Immediately after he was discharged, and before the jury had left the box, others members of the jury stated that the verdict was guilty. The prisoner was brought back to the dock, and the jury was again asked what their verdict was. They all answered guilty, and the person who delivered the first verdict said, that he had said guilty. The Chairman, thereupon, ordered a verdict of guilty to be recorded.

Pollock C. B. held that since the mistake that was made was corrected within a reasonable time, and on the very spot on which it was made, then no illegality had occurred.

His lordship added that:

> "We do not think the Court is called upon to say at what interval of time a correction should be made. All we do is to say that in the present case the interval was not too long."

Conviction affirmed.

Principle

When a verdict is delivered by the foreman of the jury in the sight and hearing of all the jurors without their protest, their assent to that verdict was conclusively to be inferred.

Court of Appeal of Belize

Sanker and Pitts v R

Criminal Appeals Nos. 11 and 12 of 1982 (Belize)

Facts

The appellants were tried jointly on a two count indictment and convicted of the alternative offence. The jury having returned the verdict were discharged and the trial judge adjourned the case to a later date for sentencing. One of the jurors, on the day following the adjournment, alleged that the verdict was not as had been stated by the foreman but that there was agreement in a proportion which did not allow a return of a verdict. The appellants appealed against conviction on the ground that the foreman had misrepresented the verdict.

Decision

Sir John Summerfield P distinguished the case of R v Vodden from the facts of the present case on the basis that in Vodden, the jury had not been discharged and also, on learning of the mistake, the jurors immediately resiled from it and made it clear that they were not acquiescing to the mistaken verdict. In the present case the jury had been discharged and the allegation made by the juror did not come to the notice of the trial judge until the next day.

His lordship concluded:

> "It is clear from these authorities that the juror ought not to have approached the deputy registrar with a complaint of something alleged to have happened in the jury room. It is contrary to public policy to inquire into such a matter. When the verdict is delivered by the foreman in the sight and hearing of all the jurors without their protest, their assent to that verdict is to be conclusively inferred. Accordingly, the appeal is dismissed."

DISCHARGING JURORS

A trial judge may exercise his discretion to discharge a juror/s in various instances such as where there has been unlawful communication with a juror or where inadmissible and seriously prejudicial evidence has been admitted.

Principle

Where unlawful communication involving jurors has occurred, once there was nothing about the communication which could prejudice the fair trial of the accused, the conviction will not be quashed.

Court of Criminal Appeal

R v Twiss

[1918] 2 K.B. 853

Facts

Before the summing-up by the judge, some members of the jury conversed with the alleged victim and other prosecution witnesses. Some of the members of the jury subsequently told the judge (to whom the incident had been reported) that the conversation had reference solely to the duration of the case and the length of a previous trial at which the jury had disagreed. The judge accepted the explanation. Another member of the jury stated that the nature of the conversation was such that it would tend to remove any bad impression the juryman might have formed of the accused. The accused was convicted and appealed.

Decision

Darling J held that it was not enough that the juror had spoken to someone who was a witness, although it was necessary to consider the matter more carefully if the person to whom the juror spoke was a witness.

His lordship concluded:

> "The matter was mentioned to Lord Coleridge J., who accepted the explanation given by the juryman that all that was said was that he asked one of the boy witnesses how long the case was likely to last. As to the conversation with Mrs. Hawkins.... If the juryman had formed a bad impression of the appellant, what she said would tend to remove it, because all she said was, 'I always found him a gentleman.' Therefore

there was nothing which in our opinion could prejudice the case of the appellant."

Appeal dismissed.

Principle

Where there had been an allegation of improper communication made to a juror, it would be correct for the judge to invite the jury to disregard what had happened and to also specifically inquire of each member of the jury whether they were capable of putting the incidents out of their minds and returning a fair verdict.

Court of Appeal of Trinidad and Tobago

Ramlogan (Arnold) v The State

C.A. Crim. 29/1999

Facts

After the trial had commenced the judge was informed that a member of the jury had spoken to relatives of the appellant's co-accused. The judge held an inquiry into what had happened and established that the juror had rebuffed the approaches made to him and had reported them at the first opportunity to the foreman of the jury; there had been no serious attempt to influence the juror and no inducement had been offered nor any threat made; the juror was emphatic that his ability to render a fair and impartial verdict had not been affected.

The foreman of the jury informed the judge that the other jurors had been told about the incidents, but the judge did not inquire of the other jurors what account of the incidents they had been given by the juror concerned. In open court the judge assured himself that each of the jurors individually was able to render a fair verdict before the trial was resumed. The appellant was convicted and appealed on the ground that the trial judge erred in law when he failed to discharge the jury and order a new trial after the inquiry had been conducted.

Decision

de la Bastide CJ noted that the judge specifically asked the juror if he was of the view that he could still render a fair verdict in the matter and the juror replied affirmatively. The judge then indicated that he was prepared to continue the trial. The judge's inquiry also showed: (a) that the juror rebuffed the approaches of the relatives and reported them at the first opportunity to the foreman of the jury; (b) there was no serious attempt by any of the relatives to influence the juror; no inducement or threat was offered, only an implied appeal for sympathy, and (c) the juror was quite emphatic that his ability to render a fair and impartial verdict had not been affected.

His lordship further stated:

> "The judge referred to the two incidents which had been reported to the jury. He explained that he had held an inquiry into them and gave them this warning:
>
> *'It is vital to the justice system that fairness be done and that you do not hold that incident either for the State or against the State or either for the accused or against the accused.'*
>
> He then proceeded to ask each one of the jurors starting with the foreman, whether they would be in a position to render a true and fair verdict. Each of them individually gave the assurance that he or she was in a position to do so."

His Lordship noted that the judge had embarked on a meticulous investigation of the nature and quality of the encounters with the juror, in order to ascertain whether those encounters contaminated the juror, whether the remaining jurors were contaminated, and whether in all the circumstances there was a real danger of bias.

The learned judge stated that in the present case the judge properly directed himself according to the 'real danger of bias test' laid down by the House of Lords in R v Gough. It was proper for the trial judge to investigate the relevant facts and circumstances by which to assess the risk of bias and to do so by means of an inquiry. The trial judge correctly invited the jury to disregard what had happened. He specifically inquired of each member of the jury whether he or she was capable of putting the incidents out of his or her mind and giving a fair verdict according to the juror's oath. He sought and received an assurance to this effect from each juror, a procedure which was approved in R v Thorpe and he directed them to report immediately to the marshal any approach that was thereafter made to them.

With regards to the issue of whether the trial judge ought to have inquired from the other jurors what account of the two incidents was given to them by the juror involved in them, his lordship stated that whether or not such an inquiry is necessary must depend on the circumstances of each case. His lordship concluded on this issue:

> "In these circumstances, we do not agree that it was necessary for the judge to inquire of each or any juror what account of these incidents he or she had been given. Certainly his failure to do so provides no basis for holding invalid the exercise by the trial judge of his discretion to proceed with the trial without discharging any of the jury."

Leave to appeal refused. Conviction and sentence affirmed.

Principle

If there is a realistic suspicion that one or more of the jurors might have been approached, tampered with or pressurised, it is the duty of the judge to investigate the matter. This could involve questioning the juror or jury. Moreover, the judge is entitled to question any member of the public or have the event investigated

by court officials and the police. Once the judge had completed his investigations, he could exercise his judicial discretion, as to whether the jury should be discharged. The test was whether there was a real danger of bias affecting the mind of the relevant juror.

Court of Appeal Criminal Division

R v Blackwell and others

[1995] 2 Cr App Rep 625

Facts

The appellant's counsel at a trial drew the judge's attention to a member of the public who had been paying more attention to the appellants than the evidence, coming and going at odd moments and who had stood for an hour outside the main building where the jurors and witnesses passed. The judge stated that he had no power to do anything on the available evidence.

The next day, one appellant thought that the man had hovered near people involved in the case to overhear conversations and the appellant's solicitor had seen the man talk to a juror and feared that evidence discussed in the absence of the jury was passed to the juror. The judge refused to conduct an investigation and cross-examine the jury, claiming that he could not exclude a member of the public due to apprehensions about the man's behaviour. The appellants were subsequently convicted, and appealed against conviction, *inter alia*, on the basis that the judge erred in the exercise of his discretion.

Decision

Morland J decided that if seemingly untoward events involving a member of the public occurred, the trial judge was entitled to question that member of the public. This inquiry must almost always be in the absence of the Jury. Further, the judge may have the event investigated by Court Officials or the Police.

His lordship further held:

> "If there is any realistic suspicion that the Jury or one or more members of it may have been approached or tampered with or pressurised, it is the duty of the Judge to investigate the matter and probably depending on the circumstances the investigation will include questioning of individual jurors or even the Jury as a whole. Any such questioning must be directed to the possibility of the Jury's independence having been compromised and not the Jury's deliberations on the issues in the case."

His lordship stated that at the conclusion of all the investigations, the Judge would be in a position to make an informed exercise of judicial discretion as to whether the trial should continue with all twelve jurors or whether an individual juror, or even the entire Jury would have to be discharged.

The learned judge concluded that on the facts of the instant case, the trial Judge's exercise of his discretion was not a proper exercise of discretion because he did not have the information required. The trial judge ought to have made inquiries into contamination or possible contamination, first of the one juror who was discharged, and secondly of the eleven jurors who remained.

Appeal allowed.

Principle

Failure to hold a Blackwell inquiry by the judge in a case where it is alleged that there was unlawful communication with the jury, is not necessarily fatal to a conviction.

Judicial Committee of the Privy Council

Lawrence v The Queen

[2014] UKPC 2

Facts

The appellant was convicted of murder and appealed. He claimed *inter alia* that the trial judge had failed to conduct a proper investigation when allegations of improper communication with jurors had been made during the trial. He submitted that this prejudiced his fair trial. It was alleged by the deceased's mother that four members of the jury had been communicating with relatives of the appellant and that the foreman of the jury had also spoken to members of the appellant's family before the jury was empanelled.

Junior counsel for the prosecution raised the issue in court in the presence of the jury on the morning of the third day of the trial, before the judge commenced his summing up. The judge did not send the jury out of the courtroom but had the mother of the deceased identify the members of the jury of whom she spoke. The judge had asked those jurors about the allegation and each denied it. He then proceeded with his summing up.

Decision

Lord Hodge held:

> "In the Board's view the judge's method of investigation was inappropriate. He should have asked the jury to withdraw before ascertaining from the prosecution and the deceased's mother the precise nature of her allegations. He would then have put himself in a position to decide whether to question the jurors individually or collectively before deciding on the best course of action... He did not do so."

His lordship concluded that the judge's handling of the allegations did not cause any prejudice to the appellant. The allegations which the mother of the deceased made were far from clear; they were denied by the jurors; and there was no reason to think that the making and the court's handling of the allegations had an improper influence on the jury in the performance of their duty.

Principle

Prejudicial evidence admitted by the prosecution is not necessarily fatal to conviction.

Judicial Committee of the Privy Council

Duporte v The Queen

[2015] UKPC 18

Facts

The appellant was convicted of murder and advanced grounds of appeal which included the ground that a gun (with one spent bullet in the chamber) had wrongly and prejudicially been produced before the jury when there was no evidence of any kind linking that gun to the appellant. The appellant complained that there was heightened sensitivity towards gun crime amongst the local population: and the production of a gun at trial might further heighten the 'fears' of the jury.

It was also suggested by the appellant that the jury could have been placed under the 'stress' of speculating where the particular gun had come from. In such circumstances, it was for the judge to discharge the jury, even though the appellant did not make such an application, or at all events the trial judge should have been given much firmer direction in the summing-up on the issue.

Decision

Sir Nigel Davis noted that the trial judge had asked about the relevance of the gun and that the prosecution were unable to give a clear answer. They stated vaguely that the production of the gun was 'just the completion exercise'. In fact the prosecution were in no position to advance any case that the gun produced by Constable Browne was the gun used to kill the deceased. The prosecution went on to concede that if the gun was not connected either to the killing or to the appellant its production was prejudicial rather than probative. In closing the case, counsel for the prosecution accepted before the jury that the gun used to kill the deceased had not been produced at trial and was not relevant.

His lordship held:

> "In the circumstances of the present case there was no requirement for the jury to be discharged. There may have been heightened local sensitivity about gun crime; but the incontrovertible fact already before this jury was that Shakabee had indeed been shot dead by use of a gun. To produce thereafter at trial a gun – not said to be the actual murder weapon – could have had no further real effect. To say that irremediable prejudice was occasioned by the production of the revolver at court is unjustified. …"

His lordship concluded that the since the jury were, in explicit terms, told that the gun produced in court proved nothing, should not influence their decision and was to be disregarded, there was no reason to think that the jury could not be trusted to abide by those explicit directions. Furthermore, there was no reason to think that the production of the gun at trial of would have encouraged the jury to speculate.

Advice that appeal be dismissed.

Principle

In a case where the jury pool hear a defendant plead guilty to manslaughter (which was rejected by the State) on a charge of murder, the jurors who subsequently hear the trial for murder will not be contaminated where the initial plea and his defence were consistent.

Court of Appeal of Trinidad and Tobago

Wilson v The State

Cr. App. No.31 of 2006

Facts

On arraignment, in the presence of the full array, the appellant pleaded not guilty to murder, but guilty to the lesser count of manslaughter. This plea was rejected by the State. The appellant was convicted of murder and appealed. One of the grounds of appeal argued was that the judge erred in law when he allowed the jury to be sworn in after they had been present when the Appellant pleaded guilty to manslaughter. It was argued that in those circumstances, the jury may have drawn inferences adverse to the appellant and that the judge ought to have empanelled a jury from another array to hear the case.

Decision

Weekes JA noted that in Trinidad and Tobago, it was common for counsel for an accused to indicate to the prosecutor his intention to enter a plea of guilty to a lesser count. The prosecution having indicated whether or not such plea was acceptable, it was then a matter for the defence whether they wished to pursue it in the presence of the array. That decision was an entirely tactical one within the purview of counsel. In any event, even if the plea took the prosecution by surprise, the appellant cannot properly complain as it would have been for him to ascertain the prosecution position before adopting his course.

The learned judge held:

> "The appellant could not have been prejudiced by the jury hearing him plead guilty to manslaughter as his initial plea and his defence were consistent. He never denied that he was responsible for the death of Esther Vidale nor that he had broken into her house with the intention to commit an arrestable offence therein. ..."

Her ladyship concluded that this ground of appealed lacked merit and therefore failed.

SECRECY OF THE JURY ROOM

Principle

The court will not ordinarily enquire into what passes between jurors whether in the jury room or jury box.

Judicial Committee of the Privy Council

Nanan v The State

[1986] A.C. 860

Facts

The defendant was tried on indictment on a charge of murder and, under the provisions of section 16 of the Jury Ordinance the jury were required to reach a unanimous verdict. The judge did not direct the 12 jurors that their verdict had to be unanimous. In the presence and hearing of all the jurors the clerk of the court asked the foreman whether he and the other members of the jury had agreed upon a unanimous verdict and the foreman said they had. The clerk then asked him whether the defendant was guilty or not guilty as charged and the foreman replied that the defendant was guilty. No protest was made by any juror. The clerk did not ask whether the verdict was one on which all members of the jury were agreed.

The defendant was sentenced to death, and he appealed against his conviction on grounds other than non-unanimity of the verdict. The foreman and three jurors subsequently swore affidavits. The foreman of the jury stated that when the clerk of the court asked him whether the jurors had arrived at a unanimous verdict, he thought that the clerk meant a majority verdict; and that although he answered the question in the affirmative, the jury were really divided eight to four in favour of a conviction. He also said that he did not know the meaning of the word 'unanimous.' The other juror informed the registrar that she was one of the four Jurors who had some doubt and that she had given the benefit of the doubt to the accused.

The defendant appealed to the Judicial Committee.

Decision

Lord Goff of Chievely affirmed the well-established general principle that the court does not admit evidence of a juryman as to what took place in the jury room, either by way of explanation of the grounds upon which the verdict was given, or by way of statement as to what he believed its effect to be (Ellis v. Deheer). His lordship noted that the same principle applied to discussions between jurymen in the jury box itself. If a juryman disagrees with the verdict pronounced by the foreman of the jury on his behalf, he should express his dissent forthwith; if he does not do so, there is a presumption that he assented to it. Therefore where a verdict has been given in the sight and hearing of an entire jury without any expression of dissent by any member of the jury, the court will not thereafter receive evidence from a member of the jury that he did not in fact agree with the verdict, or that his apparent agreement with the verdict resulted from a misapprehension on his part.

His lordship noted the policy reasons for the rule namely:the first reason is the need to ensure that decisions of juries are final; the second is the need to protect jurymen from inducement or pressure either to reveal what has passed in the jury room, or to alter their view

The learned judge went on to state exceptions to the general principle:

> "It is, of course, entirely consistent with this principle that evidence may be given that the verdict was not pronounced in the sight and hearing of one or more members of the jury, who did not in fact agree with that verdict, or who may not have done so: see Rex v. Wooler and Ellis v. Deheer. In such a case, the confidence of the jury room can be breached in so far as a juryman outside whose sight and hearing the verdict was pronounced, may give evidence whether he did or did not agree with that verdict. It is also consistent with the above principle that evidence may be given that a juryman was not competent to understand the proceedings in which event, if such evidence is accepted, the ordinary course would be to award a venire de novo…"

His lordship concluded that the affidavit evidence was inadmissible, since that to admit it would have been contrary to the principles stated above. The alleged misapprehension if it existed was of a fundamental kind; but the same could be said of other misapprehensions, for example as to the facts of the case or as to the applicable law, which can likewise lead to an erroneous verdict. In such cases, however, evidence of the misapprehension was equally inadmissible.

Appeals dismissed.

Principle

It is improper for the court, after a jury had returned its verdict, to make any inquiries of jurors as to what was said by individual members of the jury not only during deliberations but at any time after the jury had been empanelled and before it had delivered its verdict.

Court of Appeal

R v Qureshi

[2001] EWCA Crim 1807

Facts

The defendant was convicted in the Crown Court. Three days after the verdicts had been returned a member of the jury claimed *inter alia* that some members of the jury had been racially prejudiced against the defendant and had reached a decision as to his guilt at the outset of the trial. The defendant sought leave to appeal against the convictions, relying in part on the juror's allegations.

Decision

Kennedy LJ held:

> "We observe that the trial took place over seven working days. It is perhaps surprising that the juror did not during that period make her concerns known to the usher or to the trial judge. The matter could then have been investigated… But it is worth emphasising that the investigation would not have involved an interrogation of any individual juror. In the experience of all three members of this court, jurors do take their duties seriously and if they have concerns they do voice them to the usher or to the trial judge."

His lordship concluded that the court would not authorize any further inquiries.

Application for leave to appeal refused.

Principle

A juror's previous friendship with, and knowledge of, one of the witnesses for the prosecution does not automatically mean that the juror would be biased. The question is whether the fair-minded and informed observer, having considered the facts, would conclude that there was a real possibility that the juror was biased.

Judicial Committee of the Privy Council

Tibbetts v the Attorney General of the Cayman Islands

[2010] UKPC 8

Facts

The defendant was tried before a judge and jury in the Grand Court of the Cayman Islands on two counts of assisting another person to retain the benefit of the proceedings of criminal conduct. He was convicted on both counts. He appealed to the Court of Appeal of the Cayman Islands on grounds which included that the verdict had been infected by apparent bias on the part of one of the jurors who had a previous friendship with, and knowledge of, one of the witnesses for the prosecution.

His appeal was dismissed and he appealed to the Privy Council.

Decision

Lord Clarke noted that the appellant's case was that there was a real possibility that one of the jurors was biased in favour of one of the witnesses. His lordship held that the question to be asked was whether the fair-minded and informed observer ('the putative observer'), having considered the facts, would conclude that there was a real possibility that the juror was biased, such that he might have accepted the evidence of that witness as a result. If the answer to that question is yes, the putative observer would also conclude that there is a real possibility that the jury would have done the same.

His lordship stated:

> "In the instant case the juror was Mr Justin Uzzell and the relevant witness was Mr Johan Bjuroe. The question is whether the putative observer would conclude that Mr Uzzell might have accepted Mr Bjuroe's evidence as a result of his previous relationship with and knowledge of him. This raises the question of what is the correct approach to the observer's knowledge of the facts."

The learned judge also held:

> "...The court must approach the issues in two stages. First, it is for the court to find the facts on the balance of probabilities. It is then for the court to decide on the balance of probabilities whether, with knowledge of the facts so found, the putative observer would conclude that Mr Uzzell might accept Mr Bjuroe's evidence as a result of his previous relationship with and knowledge of him."

The learned judge concluded that the critical question was whether, on the facts found, the putative observer would conclude that Mr Uzzell (and thus the jury) might have accepted Mr Bjuroe's evidence because of Mr Uzzell's relationship with him. On the facts of the instant case, the putative observer with knowledge of the facts would not conclude that Mr Uzzell might have accepted Mr Bjuroe's evidence as a result of his previous relationship and conversations with him. It followed that he or she would conclude that there was no real possibility that Mr Uzzell—and hence the jury—was biased.

Appeal dismissed.

MAJORITY VERDICTS

The trial judge has a discretion to accept a majority verdict in all non-capital matters and on the lesser count in capital matters.

Principle

The Judge has a discretion to either further retire the jury after failure to agree or accept the majority verdict.

Court of Appeal of Trinidad and Tobago

Melville v The State

Cr App No T 10 of 2015

Facts

The appellant was convicted and appealed on various grounds. Among those grounds, the appellant submitted that the trial judge erred in recalling the jury before the expiration of the statutory four hour period. He further submitted that the trial judge ought to have sent the jury back to deliberate further in order to ascertain whether it was possible for them to reach a unanimous verdict. Additionally, he submitted that the judge erred procedurally by failing to receive and enter the majority verdict before the jury were asked what was the position of the majority.

Section 28 of the Jury Act Chapter 6:53 as amended states:

"(1) Except in trials for murder or treason, when a jury have been charged and have retired, if at the end of three hours after such retirement the foreman of the jury states to the Judge that seven of the jury are agreed upon a verdict, the verdict of such seven may, at the discretion of the Judge, be received and entered, and if seven are not so agreed, or if the Judge does not think fit to accept the verdict of seven, then the jury may be further directed to retire. However, when the array comprises only eight jurors as contemplated by section 19(3), the verdict of six jurors may, at the discretion of the Judge, be received and entered. ...

(3) The Judge may, on being satisfied that there is no reasonable probability that the jury will arrive at a verdict, discharge the jury at any time after the expiration of four hours from the moment of their first retirement."

Decision

Yorke Soo Hon J.A. noted that in this case the jury deliberated for three hours and when they were recalled the foreman indicated that they were divided 8 to 1. The statutory time limit for the acceptance of a majority verdict is three hours. When this time has elapsed the judge may, in his discretion, send the jury to deliberate further. Upon the expiration of four hours, the judge may discharge the jury if he is of the view that the jury will not arrive at a verdict by majority or unanimity.

The learned judge held:

> "The complaint of counsel for the appellant that the judge should have ascertained the position of the majority before receiving and entering a majority verdict is entirely untenable. It would leave the judge open to an accusation that he disagreed with the majority position, if having heard it, he sent them back to deliberate further. Since a majority verdict

is open to both a guilty and not guilty finding, then, wherever the majority may lie, the judge must accept that position once he accepts the majority verdict. We accordingly dismiss this ground."

The learned judge also stated that the judge was entitled to accept the majority verdict of the eight jurors when the jurors returned. The procedure for accepting the majority verdict was triggered after the expiration of three hours when the trial judge enquired how they were divided and the foreman replied '8 to 1'. The clerk's subsequent enquiry into the majority's view to guilt formed part and parcel of the process and was contemporaneous with the judge's receipt and recording of the majority verdict. That procedure did not violate the statutory requirements nor cause the appellant to suffer prejudice or unfairness.

Principle

After the jury fails to arrive at a verdict and the trial judge makes an order for a retrial, the judge and jury are functi officiis.

Court of Appeal of Trinidad and Tobago

Cummings (Steve) v The State; Paul (Rennie) v The State; Polo (Horace) v The State

(1995) 49 WIR 406

Facts

On a trial at assizes the jury failed to reach a verdict in respect of any of the accused. The trial judge ordered a new trial. Thereupon the foreman of the jury persuaded the trial judge to allow the jury further time in which to reach a verdict. After further deliberation, the jury recorded verdicts of guilty against three of the accused, but failed to reach a verdict in respect of the fourth. The accused against whom verdicts had been ordered appealed against their convictions.

Section 28(3) of the Jury Act provides that:

"The judge may, on being satisfied that there is no reasonable probability that the jury will arrive at a verdict, discharge the jury at any time after the expiration of three hours from the moment of their first retirement.'"

Decision

Hosein JA stated that the issue was whether the judge and the jury became *functi officiis*, when the judge made an order directing that 'the four accused are remanded for retrial at the next sitting of the assizes'. His lordship held that the failure of the jury to arrive at a verdict and, secondly, the pronouncement by the trial judge of an order for a retrial meant that the powers and/or functions of both judge and jury with respect to the trial were spent.

His lordship stated:

> "…there is neither statutory provision nor a rule at common law which gives the judge power or jurisdiction to recall the order made for retrial to permit further consideration of the matter by the jury."

> *Appeal allowed. Convictions quashed; order for retrial.*

The jury's verdict in a non-capital case may be unanimous or the court may accept a majority verdict. In a capital case (in most territories) the verdict must be unanimous.

Principle

It is not a misdirection where the trial judge directs the jury that the verdict must be one upon which they all agree.

Court of Appeal of Trinidad and Tobago

Xavier v The State

Cr A No. 78 of 1988

Facts

The appellant was found guilty of murder after a trial in the High Court. Among his grounds of appeal was that the trial judge erred in directing the jury on the need to return a unanimous verdict. The actual direction was: "Lastly, I must tell you that your verdict must be unanimous. And by unanimous I mean this: That all of you (twelve of you) must be agreed one way or the other –alright? Is that clear?"

Decision

Hosein JA distinguished the case of Raffick Mohammed and others v The State. His lordship was of the view that the directions given were different from those given in the instant case. In that case, the judge directed the jury that in considering their verdict, 'there is no intermediary in this it is either the accused is guilty as charged or not guilty.'

His lordship concluded:

> "In the absence of a verdict in the terms referred to above the 'intermediary' must mean a failure to arrive at a verdict founded upon disagreement. To have been told that there could be no intermediary inescapably meant that they could not disagree. It was on this basis that this court allowed

the appeal and ordered a re-trial. In this case, in our view there is nothing in the circumstances to suggest that in their consideration of their verdict the right to disagree was either suspended or withdrawn."

Principle

It is misdirection where the trial judge suggests to the jury that there is an obligation to agree. This is because the jury has a right to disagree.

Court of Appeal of Trinidad and Tobago

Davis v The State

Crim, Appeal No. 75 of 1988

Facts

The appellant was convicted of a non-capital offence and applied for leave to appeal his conviction. His main ground of appeal was that the trial judge erred when directing the jury on the issue of agreement on a verdict. The judge's direction was: "Your verdict must be unanimous. I am certain you know what "unanimous" means. That is, it means that you must all agree one way or the other. One way or the other, I mean, that he is guilty or not guilty."

Decision

C. Bernard CJ held:

> "It was submitted by attorney for Davis that a direction of this sort tantamounted to a usurpation by the trial judge of the jury's inalienable right to disagree among themselves as to their ultimate verdict…"

His lordship concluded that the direction of the trial judge constituted a serious misdirection.

Leave to appeal granted. Conviction and sentence quashed. Retrial ordered.

CHAPTER SIXTEEN

SENTENCING

The defendant is sentenced following a verdict of guilty. The function of sentencing is carried out by the magistrate or the trial judge as the case may be. Prior to sentence being passed, the defendant has the right to make a plea in mitigation which is aimed at convincing the court to lessen the harshness of the sentence.

THE DISCRETIONARY DEATH SENTENCE

Principle

In cases where a person has either pleaded guilty or been convicted after trial of murder on the basis of the felony/murder rule, the Court is now vested with a discretion to impose the death sentence in appropriate cases.

High Court of Trinidad and Tobago

The State v Alexander Don Juan Nicholas (1) Gregory Tan (2) Oren Lewis (3)

Cr. S. No. 26/06 & No. 109 of 2007

Facts

The accused all pleaded guilty to murder on the basis of the felony/murder rule. Section 2A of the *Criminal Law Act* Chap. 10:04, states:

"(1) Where a person embarks upon the commission of an arrestable offence involving violence and someone is killed in the course or furtherance of that offence (or any other arrestable offence involving violence), he and all other persons engaged in the course or furtherance of the commission of that arrestable offence (or any other arrestable offence involving violence) are liable to be convicted of murder even if the killing was done without intent to kill or to cause grievous bodily harm."

An "arrestable offence" in section 3(1) of the *Criminal Law Act,* Chap. 10:04, refers to capital offences or offences for which a person may be sentenced to imprisonment for a term of five (5) years or any attempt to commit such an offence. The State's case against the three Accused, was that they embarked on a plan to commit the arrestable offence of robbery with violence and/or larceny of a motor vehicle and in the course or furtherance of that offence or those offences, the deceased, Jerry David Boodoo was killed.

Decision

Justice A. Mon Désir stated the law pertaining to felony/murder:

> "In respect of felony/murder it is, therefore, irrelevant *as a matter of liability or guilt,* whether the Accused formed the intent to kill or cause grievous bodily harm. Killing in the course of an arrestable offence with the intent to commit that arrestable offence amounts to murder under the felony/ murder rule."

The learned judge noted that the Privy Council in the case of Nimrod Miguel v. The State was invited to consider whether the mandatory death penalty for felony/murder was unconstitutional. The Privy Council held that because section 2A of the Criminal Law Act Chap. 10:04 was introduced by a 1997 amendment, this provision was not caught by the 'saving law clause' as obtained for section 4 of the

Offences Against the Persons Act Chap. 11:08. The Court, therefore, found that the *mandatory* death sentence for murder on the basis of felony/murder is unconstitutional. His lordship stated that when one reconciles the reasoning in the cases of Khan, Roodal, Matthew and Miguel and follows the progression of the law, it was clear that the Privy Council has effectively decided that the sentence of death is *discretionary* in cases of murder on the basis of felony/murder.

It followed that in cases where a person has either pleaded or been convicted after trial of murder on the basis of the felony/murder rule, the Court is now vested with a *discretion* to impose the death sentence in appropriate cases, whereas before no such discretion existed. In that regard, *the Court may now impose a range of sentences up to and including the sentence of death, in appropriate cases.*

His lordship considered the issue of what was an appropriate case for the imposition of the death sentence where a person has either pleaded to, or been found guilty of murder on the basis of the felony/murder rule. In this regard the learned judge commended the procedure outlined by the Privy Council in R v. White where the death penalty is to be sought in any case where the Court's discretion to impose such a penalty is involved.

In this case it was held that the death penalty should be imposed only in cases which on the facts of the offence were 'the worst of the worst' or 'the rarest of the rare', and that there had to be no reasonable prospect of reform of the offender and that the object of punishment could not be achieved by any means other than the ultimate sentence of death. Furthermore, no judge should reach such a conclusion without the benefit of appropriate reports.

The court in White also strongly endorsed and emphasized the importance of the excellent guidelines for the prosecution, trial and sentencing of accused persons charged with murder set out by Conteh CJ in R v Reyes namely:

(i) from the time of committal, the prosecution should give notice as to whether they proposed to submit that the death penalty was appropriate;

(ii) the prosecution's notice should contain the grounds on which they submitted the death penalty was appropriate;

(iii) in the event of the prosecution so indicating and the trial judge considering that the death penalty might be appropriate, the judge should at the time of the allocutus, specify the date of the sentence hearing which provided reasonable time for the defence to prepare;

(iv) the trial judge should give directions in relation to the conduct of the sentence hearing as well as indicating the materials that should be made available, so that the accused might have reasonable materials for the preparation and prosecution of his case on sentence;

(v) at the same time the Judge should specify a time for the defence to provide notice of any points or evidence it proposed to rely on in relation to the sentence;

(vi) the judge should give reasons for his decision including the statement as to the grounds in which he found that the death penalty had to be imposed in the event that he so concluded and he should also specify the reasons for rejecting any mitigating circumstances.

The court looked at all the relevant authorities and held:

> "The following general guidance may therefore, be distilled from the foregoing authorities: (1) the crime being brutal and heinous itself does not necessarily tip the scale in favour of the death sentence; (2) the death sentence should be reserved for the most extreme and exceptional cases, 'the rarest of the rare' or 'the worst of the worst'; (3) there must be no reasonable prospect of reform; (4) the object of punishment must be incapable of being achieved by any other means than

the ultimate penalty of death; (5) before the imposition of the death sentence, psychiatric reports and social enquiry reports should be obtained and considered; (6) the bad character of the accused ought not to weigh in the scales against him unless his previous conduct is so bad and similar to the index offence that it affects its gravity and/or it is relevant to whether there is a reasonable prospect of reform.

The learned judge concluded that on the facts of this case, this was not a case which was the most extreme or exceptional. Nor could it be appropriately described as falling within 'the worst of the worst' or 'the rarest of the rare' cases for which only the death penalty sufficed. His lordship held further:

> "In the instant case, as wicked and senseless as the actions of the three Accused were, the facts are not nearly as gruesome as in Trimmingham. The facts establish with some sufficiency that although the offence was committed in the furtherance of a robbery, the killing was not planned or premeditated (as distinct from an intention to kill being formed during the course of the robbery). There was no torture of the deceased, no prolonged trauma or humiliation of the deceased prior to death and no weapon, apart from the deceased's own belt, was used in the commission of the offence. In the absence of such aggravating factors this Court would be hard-pressed to impose the death penalty in the particular circumstances of this case."

His lordship therefore declined to exercise his discretion to impose the sentence of death.

Mon Desir J then looked at what sentence would be most appropriate in the circumstances. He held that in cases of this nature, when an Accused had either pleaded guilty to or been found guilty of murder on the basis of the felony/murder rule, where the death penalty is discretionary, the starting point must be life imprisonment. Such an approach not only underscored the sanctity of the human life as a pillar of civilised society, but it also recognised the fact that the offence with which the accused was charged is still that of murder.

The learned judge followed the authority of Allan Henry and Others v The Attorney General and The Commissioner of Prisons in holding that a life sentence in this context means the natural life of the prisoner. He concluded that the argument that a sentence of imprisonment for the whole of natural life is different from life imprisonment and any argument that a life sentence must be less than 20 years were unsupported by authority. He also rejected the argument that life imprisonment has come to mean 12 to 15 years.

His lordship held that a sentence of life imprisonment would be most appropriate in cases where the facts revealed that death ensued as a consequence either of extreme cruelty to the deceased, or of such reckless indifference to human life on the part of the accused. Furthermore, it is only where the imposition of death or life sentences are not appropriate for murder on the basis of the felony/murder rule, that the Court should then go on to consider the appropriateness of a term of years as the sentence to be imposed.

The learned judge stated that a term of years for *the offence of murder,* where a person has either pleaded or been found guilty of murder on the basis of the felony/murder rule, would be appropriate in, *inter alia*, those circumstances where for example death occurs accidentally during the course of the commission of a felony; or where a party to that felony which results in death, so distances himself from the events that lead to or caused the death of the deceased; or could not be said to have foreseen the actions of his co-accused that resulted in death; or took no part in them; or a secondary party to a charge of murder, realised or foresaw that the principal might inflict physical harm falling short of grievous bodily harm and participated in the commission of the felony with that foresight.

SENTENCING METHODOLOGY

Principle

The judge's sentencing structure should generally reflect the following matters:

(i) The calculation of the starting point which takes into account the aggravating and mitigating factors of the offence only; these are the objective circumstances which relate to the gravity of the offence itself and which assist in gauging its seriousness, that is, the degree of harmfulness of the offence;

(ii) An appropriate upward or downward adjustment of the starting point (or dependent on the circumstances, and if there is in effect, a cancelling out, no adjustment at all), which takes into account the aggravating and mitigating factors relative to the offender; these are the subjective circumstances of the offender which in turn inform the degree of the culpability of the particular offender;

(iii) (Where appropriate), a discount for a guilty plea; any deviation from the usual discount requires particularly careful justification and an explanation which is clearly expressed; and

(iv) Credit for the period of time spent in pre-trial custody.

Court of Appeal of Trinidad and Tobago

Aguillera, Ballai, Ballai and Ayow v The State

Crim. App. Nos. 5, 6, 7, 8 of 2015

Facts

The four appellants pleaded guilty to the offence of murder on the basis of the felony murder construct. The death penalty was not considered appropriate since the facts of the case did not constitute a "worst of the worst" scenario. The judge did not consider a sentence of life imprisonment to be appropriate since the appellants were not beyond rehabilitation. The court imposed sentences as follows:

Appellant No. 1 (Lauren Aguillera) - Fourteen (14) years

Appellant No. 2 (Shawn Ballai) - Fourteen (14) years

Appellant No. 3 (Evans Ballai) - Fourteen (14) years

Appellant No. 4 (Richie Ayow) - Twelve (12) years

The appellants appealed their sentences.

Decision

Joint Judgment Delivered by P. Weekes J.A., A. Yorke-Soo Hon J.A. and M. Mohammed J.A.

The court went on to state that the overall sentencing structure should, in general terms reflect the following matters:

1.The calculation of the starting point (established R v Taueki, Ridley and Roberts) which takes into account the aggravating and mitigating factors of the offence only; these are the objective circumstances which relate to the gravity of the offence itself and which assist in gauging its seriousness, that is, the degree of harmfulness of the offence;

2. An appropriate upward or downward adjustment of the starting point (or dependent on the circumstances, and if there is in effect, a cancelling out, no adjustment at all), which takes into account the aggravating and mitigating factors relative to the offender; these are the subjective circumstances of the offender which in turn inform the degree of the culpability of the particular offender;

3. (Where appropriate), a discount for a guilty plea; any deviation from the usual discount requires particularly careful justification and an explanation which is clearly expressed; and

4. Credit for the period of time spent in pre-trial custody.

5. While this is a criminal appeal involving the felony murder construct, it cannot have escaped notice that the adopted definition of the starting point and the recommended structure for sentencing applies across the board to practically all criminal offences, indictable and summary. The modern trend of sentencing requires full transparency which judges and magistrates can best achieve by the adoption of this methodology. ...

The court applied these factors to the facts of the case and held:

> "In this case, the aggravating features relating to the offence are:
>
> – The extent of the planning, from the day before, and the level of premeditation;
> – An underlying offence for gain (robbery);
> – The involvement of multiple attackers;
> – The use of a piece of iron as a weapon;
> – The infliction of a large number of very serious injuries;
> – The use of gratuitous violence; and
> – The concealment of the body.
>
> "There are no mitigating factors relative to the offence."

The court decided that in this case, a starting point of thirty (30) years would be appropriate. This figure reflected the inherent seriousness of the offending as well as the existence of multiple egregious aggravating factors relating to the offence. The court also noted that in a particular case which involved an even greater array of extremely serious aggravating factors relative to the offence, namely, a home invasion, a breach of trust, and the infliction of a very large number of horrific injuries by one person, a starting point of thirty-five (35) years was considered to be appropriate (Fizul Rahaman v The State, oral judgment delivered by Weekes J.A. on 31st May, 2016).

The court concluded that the trial judge in this matter operated from well within the identified starting point, when he arrived at the figure of thirty (30) years, before making deductions for the guilty plea and the time spent in pre-trial custody.

Regarding the levels of involvement of the accused the court held that while that Shawn Ballai, on his account, did not inflict physical violence on the deceased, he nonetheless participated in all the material aspects of planning and executing the crime. At one stage he told his confederates to leave the man alone but he never withdrew from the enterprise which had as its objective, robbery with violence, and during the furtherance of which, extreme violence was employed in his immediate presence. With respect to Evans Ballai, he too was involved in all stages of the planning and execution of the offence. In addition, on his admission, he accepted hitting the deceased in the area of his neck with the piece of iron.

Their lordships held on this issue:

> "In our view, Mr. Khan's contention is without a proper foundation. The judge correctly concluded that in the specific context of this offence, the involvement of the Ballais was not of a relatively limited nature. This is because the offence involved not only an elaborate plan to lure the deceased to a location which supposedly contained scrap metal in some bushes but also involved the intense and vicious beating of the deceased at the said location, which all occurred in the presence of all the appellants at some stage."

As regards the good character of Evans Ballai, the court decided that the judge had before him on the one hand, the good character of

Evans Ballai and on the other, the multiple aggravating factors of the offence. The combination of aggravating factors made the offence so abhorrent, that the good character of this appellant was insufficient to merit a reduction in the starting point. The sentencing judge does not look at one factor in isolation and out of context but rather has to evaluate the entirety of the circumstances of the offence and the offender. The court concluded that the judge was right not to sentence Evans Ballai to a lesser term because of his good character.

The court also addressed the issue of the proper discount for a guilty plea. The court held:

> "We agree with the general reasoning in Hessell v R supra and reiterate what we consider to be some key points for judges to bear in mind during sentencing, when dealing with a guilty plea:
>
> (i) Remorse may be sometimes demonstrated by a guilty plea but it is not necessarily exemplified by it;
>
> (ii) If after a thorough and robust evaluation by the judge, a defendant's remorse is manifest, sentencing credit may be given to it, separate and apart from the guilty plea; while a guilty plea may be an admission of responsibility, in the face of an inevitable conviction, there may in reality be very little remorse for which separate sentencing credit can properly be given – see Najeeb Dawood;
>
> (iii) Precisely when a plea of guilty is entered, is only one of several circumstances that must be evaluated by the judge;
>
> (iv) The usual discount of approximately one-third (1/3) may be properly reduced if it is clear that the plea is motivated by tactical considerations. In this regard, the strength of the prosecution case may, on occasion, be a relevant factor to be

evaluated in considering all the circumstances in which the plea is entered. When a judge considers that this might be a relevant factor, he ought to invite counsel on both sides to address him on the issue. When the judge has found that the prosecution case is a strong one so as to justify a reduction in the usual discount of approximately one-third (1/3), he should give brief reasons for so concluding. Such a reduction in the usual discount must be approached with caution and requires particularly careful justification and an explanation in the reasons which is clearly expressed.

v. It may on occasion be tempting for sentencers to avoid a reduction in sentence for a plea of guilty when the statutory maximum sentence is low or there is some other inhibiting factor and the resulting sentence is considered to be insufficient. This temptation must be resisted.

(vi) Whether a defendant pleads guilty at the first reasonable opportunity is always relevant – this is, however, a matter for particular inquiry rather than formalistic quantification;

(vii) Trial judges should be mindful of the methodology explained in Nadia Pooran v The State (which adopted the reasoning in the decision of Terry Daly v The State Cr. App. No. 1 of 2012 per Yorke-Soo Hon J.A.) for calculating the appropriate level of discount (usually in the order of approximately one-third (1/3)), and at what stage to do so – see paras. 19-26; and

(viii) With respect to (vi) supra, the first real opportunity to plead guilty is upon arraignment. While there is an earlier technical opportunity to plead guilty available at a preliminary enquiry, in the absence of case management rules and given the current state of Court lists, this is not a first opportunity when viewed from any reasonable pragmatic point of view."

The court concluded that the prosecution case in this matter was of a strong nature. Accordingly, the judge acted well within the parameters of the discretion entrusted to him in concluding that because of the strong *prima facie* quality of the prosecution evidence, the pleas were (at least in part), tactical in nature and attracted a reduced discount of twenty-five percent (25%).

Principle

In spite of the difference in privileges afforded to remand prisoners as opposed to convicted prisoners in Trinidad and Tobago, the prevailing conditions on remand in prisons are such that the entire period spent in pre-sentence custody ought to be discounted from the sentence that the trial judge arrives at having taken into account the gravity of the offence, and mitigating and aggravating factors.

Court of Appeal of Trinidad and Tobago

Borneo v The State

Cr. App: 7 of 2011

Facts

The appellant was convicted of murder. He was a juvenile at the time of the offence and was sentenced to fifteen years hard labour. In imposing a sentence of 15 years with hard labour on the appellant, the trial judge expressly stated that she took into account the fact that the appellant had spent more than four years in custody awaiting trial. However, she did not precisely set out how this time was factored into the sentence that she imposed.

Decision

Narine JA noted that in the case of Callachand & anor v. The State of Mauritius, the Privy Council took the view that any time spent in custody prior to sentencing should be taken fully into account by means of an arithmetical deduction when assessing the length of the sentence to be served from the date of sentencing.

His lordship also noted that in R v. da Costa Hall the Caribbean Court of Justice followed the decision in Callachand that pre-sentence time spent in custody should be fully taken into account in imposing sentence. The trial judge should clearly set out what he considered to be the appropriate sentence taking into account the seriousness of the offence, and all the mitigating and aggravating factors. From this sentence, he should deduct any pre-sentence time spent in custody. If the judge decides not to follow the *prima facie* rule of granting substantially full credit for time served prior to sentence, he should set out his reasons for doing so. In the interest of transparency, whether he grants full credit or not, a sentencing judge has to explain how he has dealt with pre-sentence time spent in custody.

Narine JA held further:

> "Accordingly, in spite of the difference in privileges afforded to remand prisoners as opposed to convicted prisoners in this jurisdiction, we are of the view that the prevailing conditions on remand in our prisons are such that the entire period spent in pre-sentence custody ought to be discounted from the sentence that the trial judge arrives at having taken into account the gravity of the offence, and mitigating and aggravating factors. The judge should state the appropriate sentence so arrived at, then deduct the time spent on remand awaiting trial for the offence, showing in a clear and transparent fashion how the sentence to be served is arrived at."

The learned judge decided that the appropriate range of sentence in a matter of the kind before the court was a term of 15 to 20 years. Having regard to the circumstances of this case and the aggravating and mitigating factors put forward, the appropriate sentence was 17

½ years. From the term of 17 ½ years, 4 years and 6 months, would be deducted, being the time spent in custody prior to sentencing.

Appeal against conviction dismissed. Appeal against sentence allowed. Sentence imposed varied to 13 years hard labour, sentence to run from the date of conviction.

SENTENCING UNDER THE PENAL SYSTEM REFORM ACT (BARBADOS)

Principle

In applying the provisions of The Penal System Reform Act in passing sentence, the courts should where appropriate be guided by the pre-sentence report and the expert evidence of the probation officer.

Court of Appeal of Barbados

Cummins v Commissioner of Police

Magisterial Appeal No. 6 of 2011

Facts

The appellant pleaded guilty to four offences and was sentenced by the magistrate. By section 37(4) of the Penal System Reform Act Cap. 139, the Court must obtain and consider such a report. The subsection states that:

"A custodial sentence which is passed in a case to which subsection (1) applies is not invalidated by the failure of a court to comply that subsection but any court on an appeal against a sentence:

(a) shall obtain a pre-sentence report if none was obtained by the court; and

(b) shall consider any such report obtained by it or by that court."

Subsection (1) provides that a court shall obtain and consider a pre-sentence report before forming an opinion that the offence was so serious that only a custodial sentence can be justified for the offence or where the offence is a violent or sexual offence only a custodial sentence would be adequate to protect the public from serious harm from the offender.

A pre-sentence report is defined in section 37(5) as a report in writing which is made by a probation officer with a view to assisting the court in determining the most suitable method of dealing with an offender. Section 34(3) also provides that a court shall obtain a pre-sentence report before forming an opinion as to the suitability for the offender of a community service order or a combination order. A pre-sentence report will generally be helpful in determining the most appropriate sentence in cases other than those in which a custodial sentence is being considered.

Decision

Peter Williams CJ (Ag) noted that the effect of Section 37 was considered by the Caribbean Court of Justice (CCJ) in R. v. Gittens. The comment of the CCJ on the section was to the effect that the Court should obtain and consider a pre-sentence report before imposing a custodial sentence 'unless the Court of Appeal was of the opinion that such a report was "in the circumstances of the case" unnecessary'. It was therefore to be left to the good sense of the Magistrate to decide whether a pre-sentence report was required based on the facts and circumstances of the particular case.

The learned judge noted that in the instant case, the Magistrate took into account the appellant's guilty plea and the Penal System Reform Act, which requires restraint in imposing a custodial sentence unless the offence is so serious as to warrant such a sentence. He was of the view that the sentence should reinforce respect for lawful authority and disdain for attacks on the police. The sentence should also deter the appellant and others from similar offences. His lordship also noted the guideline that rehabilitation is one of the aims of sentencing: section 41(2)1 of the Penal System Reform Act. The learned held that taking all relevant factors into consideration the court should not impose a custodial sentence.

His lordship concluded:

> "We consider a non-custodial sentence appropriate in the special circumstances of the case based on the information disclosed to this Court on the offences and the offender. However, we wish to state emphatically that offences involving physical violence against police officers, public officials who work in institutions, such as doctors and nurses and other persons in authority, will be viewed very seriously by the courts and will generally attract a custodial sentence. It is important for the courts to deter as best they can, attacks on police officers as well as interference with them in the execution of their duties. The importance of respect for law in an orderly society must be maintained."

Principle

In considering the imposition of custodial sentences in the Penal System Reform Act Cap.139 a sentencing judge should explain how he or she has dealt with time spent on remand. Should the judge choose to depart from the prima facie rule of substantially full credit for time served prior to the sentence, he or she should set out the reasons for such departure.

Caribbean Court of Justice

Da Costa Hall v The Queen

[2011] CCJ 6 (AJ)

Facts

The appellant sought special leave to appeal against a decision of the Court of Appeal of Barbados dismissing his appeal against sentence and affirming a sentence of six (6) years' imprisonment imposed on him. He contended that the Court of Appeal erred in law in failing to take into account each day that he spent on remand in custody in reduction of his sentence. As a consequence, his sentence was excessive.

The Court of Appeal considered that the judge had not erred by not taking into account the entire time spent on remand since his arrest, (40 months and 4 days) and that the judge's discount (2 years) for the time spent on remand was reasonable. The Court of Appeal therefore affirmed the judge's sentence of six (6) years' imprisonment.

Decision

Nelson J noted that in Barbados, unlike in the United Kingdom and other jurisdictions there is no statutory provision that makes it mandatory for a sentencing judge to give credit for time spent on remand prior to sentencing. The issue is governed by the common law and the sentencing judge has a discretion as to how to treat time spent on remand.

His lordship stated that in Callachand the Privy Council held that save in exceptional cases or where a difference in local conditions of detention on remand and after sentence existed, the proper approach, was that any time spent in custody prior to sentencing should be fully taken into account, not simply by means of a form of words but by means of an arithmetical deduction when assessing the length of the sentence that is to be served from the date of sentencing.

The learned judge further held on this issue:

> "The Law Reform Commission of Mauritius subsequently expressed the view, based on the evidence of the Commissioner of Prisons in Callachand & Another v The State that the conditions applicable to prisoners on remand were not significantly less onerous than those which applied after sentence, that time spent on remand should be taken into account in the manner indicated by the Privy Council. We endorse this approach particularly where conditions endured by prisoners on remand are more onerous than those after sentence and note that in the instant appeal there is no evidence on the record of any compelling factors that would displace the *prima facie* rule of full credit for time served in pre-sentence custody."

The learned judge acknowledged that the sentencing judge had a residual discretion not to apply the full credit for time served:

(1) where the defendant has deliberately contrived to enlarge the amount of time spent on remand,

(2) where the defendant is or was on remand for some other offence unconnected with the one for which he is being sentenced,

(3) where the period of pre-sentence custody is less than a day or the post-conviction sentence is less than 2 or 3 days,

(4) where the defendant was serving a sentence of imprisonment during the whole or part of the period spent on remand and;

(5) generally where the same period of remand in custody would be credited to more than one offence.

His lordship emphasised that this was not an exhaustive list of instances where the judge may depart from the *prima facie* rule, and that other examples could arise in actual practice. Furthermore the sentencing judge must state his or her reasons for not granting a full deduction or no deduction at all.

The learned judge indicated that the following order would be made:

> "For the reasons given earlier in this judgment, the Court deducts from the notional term 40 months of the period January 23, 2005 to May 27, 2008 spent on remand in custody and substitutes pursuant to section 14 of the Criminal Appeal Act Cap 113A a sentence of 56 months to run from the date of sentence, May 27, 2008. In the result, the Appellant succeeds in his claim for full credit for time spent on remand prior to sentence. The appeal is therefore allowed, and the order of the Court of Appeal set aside."

SENTENCE DISCOUNT FOR A PLEA OF GUILTY

Principles

1. *In determining the level of discount for a guilty plea, the discount should be something of the order of one-third. There may be situations where no discount will be appropriate. There may be circumstances in which a discount of approximately one-third may be reduced and there are also very limited circumstances, where a judge can properly apply a discount of more than one-third.*

2. *In cases where two sets of "deductions" are to be made, for both a guilty plea and time spent on remand, the order of the deductions must be considered. If the starting point is the "but for" or the notional sentence, that is the sentence that would otherwise have been imposed given the mix of aggravating and mitigating factors, it is entirely logical that the discount for the guilty plea should*

come first before the calculation where credit is given for the time spent on remand.

Court of Appeal of Trinidad and Tobago

Pooran v The State

Criminal App. No. 32 of 2015

Facts

The appellant Nadia Pooran (who had been indicted for Murder jointly with three other persons – Shelly-Ann Anganoo, Nicholas Ali and Tesfa Jones), pleaded guilty to the offence of manslaughter. At the hearing of the plea in mitigation, the judge enquired as to the basis upon which the guilty plea to the lesser count of manslaughter had been accepted by the State. Anganoo had also pleaded guilty to manslaughter. Counsel for the prosecution responded that the acceptance of the guilty plea was occasioned by the appellant's statement under caution, which comprised the only evidence against her. In that statement, she had minimized her role, as had Anganoo. Each confederate had, in 'textbook' fashion, sought to cast far more substantial blame upon the other confederates while severely minimizing her or his own role.

Decision

Mohammed J.A. noted that at the time of the appellant's sentencing in June of 2008, and before the decisions were rendered by the Judicial Committee of the Privy Council in Callachand and Anor v The State of Mauritius and by the Caribbean Court of Justice in Da Costa Hall v R there was no consistent approach in this jurisdiction with respect to judges performing the sentencing exercise, granting full credit for the time spent by a convict on remand. By the time she was ready to be sentenced, the appellant had spent approximately five years on remand.

His lordship further noted that the sentencing judge had concluded that the killing did not appear to be premeditated, but one that had spiralled out of a robbery. The judge also took account of the fact that the appellant had no previous convictions and considered that the appellant had given a voluntary statement to the police. She considered that both prisoners had already been incarcerated for a period of five years. In weighing up the relevant considerations, the sentencing judge considered the most notable factor in favour of the appellant to be that she had pleaded guilty, thus taking responsibility for her actions and not wasting precious judicial time.

By way of the aggravating features which attended the matter, the sentencing judge noted that the case appeared to be one involving the use of gratuitous violence. The judge referred to decisions of the Court of Appeal which examined sentences imposed in cases which involved a callous level of brutality.

The learned judge then set out the authorities dealing with sentencing discounts for guilty pleas.

1. In Jaggernath and Kanhai v The State, Cr. App. Nos. 16 and 18 of 2007 at para 39, Weekes J.A. noted that as a general principle, an offender who pleads guilty may expect some credit in the form of a reduction in the sentence which would have been imposed if he had been convicted by the jury on a plea of not guilty.

2. In R v Paul Edward Buffrey (1993) 14 Cr. App. R (S) 511 CA Lord Taylor C.J. suggested, only as general guidance, that something of the order of one-third would very often be an appropriate discount from the sentence which would otherwise be imposed on a contested trial.

3. In Daly v The State it was held that in determining the level of discount for a guilty plea, the judge must bear in mind that in the ordinary course of events, the discount should be something of the order of one-third. There may be circumstances where the

court may properly deviate from this very general yardstick. There may be situations where, for example, because of the egregious or exceptionally depraved nature of the offence, no discount will be conceivably appropriate. There may be circumstances in which a discount of approximately one-third may be quite properly reduced, for example, where it is clear that the timing of the plea is made for solely or primarily tactical reasons.

One situation where this may arise is where a statement contains the only evidence against an accused and its admissibility is challenged after the entering of a not guilty plea; the statement is subsequently allowed into evidence after a *voire dire* is conducted and a guilty plea ensues only at this stage. This is not to necessarily say that a post arraignment guilty plea automatically deprives a convict of an approximate one-third discount.

His lordship further held:

> "Further, we are of the view that there are circumstances, very limited though they may be, where a judge can properly apply a discount of more than one-third. An example is when an accused person, from the time of first being confronted by the police with the allegation against him, gives an indication of guilt, continuing to do so through committal proceedings and thus evincing an unequivocal desire to take responsibility for the offence charged, from very early on and consistently so after that. In such an exceptional case, especially when viewed against the background of an overburdened criminal justice system where trial time is becoming increasingly limited and is indeed a precious commodity, a discount above the level of one-third might well be considered appropriate. All of the considerations referred to in paragraphs (19) and (20) above may be relevant to the sentencing judge's exercise of his discretion whether to allow a discount at all or in ascertaining the level of such discount since he or she is in

the best position to make an informed assessment in all of the circumstances."

His lordship held that in the instant case, the judge did not follow the methodology which was prescribed in Daly. To simply state that the guilty plea was "The most notable factor" in favour of the appellant was insufficient according to the reasoning in that case. The judge was required to go a bit further.

Mohammed J then turned to the issue of a case which necessitated two sets of sentence deductions. He held:

> "There is one other point which warrants brief mention. In cases where two sets of 'deductions' are to be made, for both a guilty plea and time spent on remand, the order of the deductions must be considered since different orders of consideration yield slightly different results. If the starting point is the 'but for' or the notional sentence, that is the sentence that would otherwise have been imposed given the mix of aggravating and mitigating factors, it is entirely logical that the discount for the guilty plea should come first before the calculation where credit is given for the time spent on remand. In Da Costa Hall v R at paragraph 42 of the judgement of Wit J., the concept of time spent on remand being properly considered as a 'set off' and not a reduction supports our conclusion that credit for time spent on remand must be the final calculation."

His lordship then proceeded to detail the sentence methodology appropriate to the instant case. He held that an appropriate discount in the vicinity of one-third of the sentence for the guilty plea should be given. Then the full amount for the time spent on remand has to be credited. His lordship took a starting point of twenty five years at the upper end of the scale, because of the extreme gratuitous violence involved. He then applied the one third discount given the appellant's guilty plea. This resulted in a rounded off figure of approximately seventeen years.

This would have been the sentence that would have been appropriate given the mix of mitigating and aggravating factors (the 'but for' or the notional sentence). Furthermore, full credit was given for the time spent in pre-trial custody which amounted to five years. This produced a final figure of twelve years.

Appeal on sentence allowed. Sentence set aside and a sentence of twelve years substituted to run from the date of the Guilty Plea entered.

CHAPTER SEVENTEEN

CRIMINAL APPEALS FROM THE HIGH COURT

Criminal appeals from the High Court/ Supreme Court are heard in the Court of Appeal. The appellate procedure is statutory and is supplemented by rules. In Barbados, Guyana, Belize and Dominica the final appellate court is the Caribbean Court of Justice while the Privy Council remains the final appellate court for the other Commonwealth Caribbean territories. The appellate process is initiated by the appellant filing a notice of appeal, notice of application for leave to appeal or notice of application for an extension of time to appeal.

THE NOTICE OF APPEAL

Principle

The appellant's failure to sign the notice of appeal may in certain circumstances amount to no more than a technical non-compliance with the rules, and may be accordingly waived in the interests of justice.

Judicial Committee of the Privy Council

Pollard (George) v R

(1995) 47 WIR 185

Facts

The appellant was convicted of murder and sentenced to death. He applied for leave to appeal to the Court of Appeal but his application was refused as he had not signed the notice of application in accordance with rule 44(1) of the West Indies Associated States Court of Appeal Rules 1968. Counsel for the appellant arranged for another notice of application to be prepared and signed, but the Court of Appeal refused to admit this out of time on the ground that it had no jurisdiction under section 48(2) of the Eastern Caribbean Supreme Court Act to extend the time in such a case for filing a notice for application for leave to appeal.

Section 48(1) and (2) of the Eastern Caribbean Supreme Court Act ('the Act') provides that:

"(1) Where a person convicted desires to appeal under this Act to the Court of Appeal or to obtain the leave of the court, he shall give notice of appeal or notice of his application for leave to appeal, in such manner as may be directed by rules of court, within fourteen days of the date of conviction.

(2) Except in the case of a conviction involving sentence of death, the time within which notice of an application for leave to appeal may be given, may be extended at any time by the court."

The form of notice is provided for in rule 44(1) of the West Indies Associated States Court of Appeal Rules 1968:

"Every notice of appeal or notice of application for leave to appeal or notice of application for extension of time within which such notice shall be given shall be signed by the appellant himself, except under the provisions of paragraphs (4) and (5) of this rule."

The appellant appealed the decision of the Court of Appeal.

Decision

Lord Jauncey of Tullichettle held that there is a general dispensing power conferred on the Court of Appeal by rule 11 of the 1968 Rules which states:

'Non-compliance on the part of an appellant in any criminal cause or matter with these Rules or with any rule of practice for the time being in force shall not prevent the further prosecution of his appeal if the court considers that such non-compliance was not wilful, and that it is in the interests of justice that non-compliance be waived. The court may, in such manner as it thinks right, direct the appellant to remedy such non-compliance, and thereupon the appeal shall proceed.'

The learned judge was of the view that given the unequivocal terms of section 48(2) of the Act, the Court of Appeal had no alternative but to refuse the appellant's application to extend the time for lodging a notice. His lordship noted the appellant's submission that although rule 11 could not be applied to override specific statutory provisions such as the time limit in section 48(2), it could be applied to waive non-compliance with requirements which derive solely from the Rules such as the failure to sign the notice.

His lordship held:

> "Their lordships consider that Mr Emmerson's submissions are correct. A notice which does not comply with a particular rule but in respect of which that non-compliance has been subsequently waived under another rule is nonetheless a notice 'in such manner as may be directed by rules of court' within the meaning of section 48(1) of the Act. The waiver validates the notice from the date of its lodging and does not merely bring into existence for the first time a valid notice when rule 11 is applied."

Lord Jauncey concluded that the lack of the appellant's signature on the notice amounted to no more than a technical non-compliance with the rules. It clearly was not wilful on the part of the appellant and, given that the appeal of the co-accused John on similar if not identical grounds was to proceed, it would have been in the interests of justice that the appellant's non-compliance should have been waived so that his appeal could be heard at the same time.

The learned judge also stated that it was also relevant to the appeal that after the Court of Appeal refused the appellant's application the conviction of the co-accused John, who had appealed on similar grounds to that advanced by the appellant had been quashed.

His lordship concluded:

> "In these circumstances, there are compelling reasons in the interests of justice why rule 11 should be applied to relieve the appellant of his technical non-compliance with rule 44(1). Their lordships, therefore, apply the rule with the result that the appeal was validly constituted and the Court of Appeal have the jurisdiction to hear and determine it."

Advice that appeal be allowed.

EXTENSION OF TIME

Statute in most Commonwealth Caribbean jurisdictions allows for an extension of time to file a notice of appeal.

Principle

Substantial grounds must be given for the delay in filing a notice of appeal before the Court of Appeal will exercise its power to extend the time. This notwithstanding, the court would intervene in a case where the trial judge exceeded his jurisdiction in imposing a sentence or did not have jurisdiction to impose the sentence.

Court of Appeal of Trinidad and Tobago

Ali v R

(1969) 15 WIR 399

Facts

On 5 May 1969, SA was convicted of unlawful wounding and sentenced to three years hard labour and ordered to receive ten strokes with the birch. He gave notice of appeal against conviction on the same day. When the application came on for hearing on 24 November, counsel informed the court that SA no longer wished leave to appeal against conviction but, instead, desired leave to appeal against sentence. The application was out of time. The reasons for the delay in making the application were (a) that the applicant was unrepresented and failed to appreciate the distinction between an appeal against conviction and an appeal against sentence; and being in custody he was unable to retain counsel; (b) that through the agency of his son counsel was retained.

Decision

Mc Shine CJ noted that by s 50 (1) of the Supreme Court of Judicature Act, No 12 of 1962, where a person convicted desires to appeal or to obtain leave to appeal he must do so within 14 days of the date of conviction. And except in the case involving sentence of death the Court of Appeal may by sub-s (2) extend the time within which notice of appeal or notice of an application may be given. His lordship also referred to the learning found in Archbold's Pleading, Evidence And Practice in Criminal Cases which stated that when an application is made for extension of time, 'Substantial grounds must be given for the delay before the court will exercise its power to extend the time'.

The learned judge concluded:

> "In the circumstances we find that there has been no substantial reason such as excuses the delay advanced before us that would enable us to grant an extension of time. The rules are of importance and are to be followed and one of the requirements is that substantial grounds are shown before

any extension of time may be granted. To have delayed from May to November on the ground that he did not understand the distinction between an appeal against conviction and an appeal against sentence is in our view wholly insufficient and in the circumstances this application for extension of time to appeal against sentence must be refused."

Application refused.

Principle

Time for the purposes of filing the notice of appeal begins to run from the date of sentence.

Caribbean Court of Justice

Appellate Jurisdiction

Rambarran v The Queen

[2016] CCJ 2(AJ)

Facts

A jury had returned verdicts of guilty against the applicant and other appellants who appealed. The DPP raised the point that the applications for leave to appeal against conviction had been filed out of time and so could not be heard.

All of the notices seeking leave to appeal against conviction were filed more than 21 days after the verdict of guilty had been pronounced (35, 195, 200 and 215 days, respectively). The Court of Appeal accepted this point in its judgment of 5th February 2015 dismissing the applications.

Section 19(1) of the Criminal Appeal Act Cap 113A, which came into effect on 1st September 1983 states:

'19.(1) Subject to subsection (2), a person who wishes to appeal to the Court, or to obtain the Court's leave to appeal, must give notice of appeal or his application for leave to appeal, in the manner provided by rules of court within 21 days of the date of conviction, verdict or finding appealed against, or,

'(a) in the case of an appeal or application for leave to appeal against sentence, other than a sentence of death, within 21 days of the date on which sentence was passed; or

'(b) in the case of an appeal or application for leave to appeal where the sentence is death, within 14 days of the date on which sentence was passed; or

'(c) in the case of an order made or treated as made on conviction, within 21 days from the date of the making of the order.'

Decision

The Rt. Honourable Sir Dennis Byron, President and The Honourable Justices Jacob Wit and David Hayton

The court interpreted the relevant statutory provision and held:

> "It has been seen that the main body of section 19 prescribes three separate non-overlapping events from which the time for filing a notice of appeal or an application for leave to appeal can be reckoned: a 'conviction', a 'verdict' and a 'finding', while section 19(1) (a) deals with a sentence other than a sentence of death, (b) deals with a sentence of death and (c) deals with an order made or treated as made on conviction. In our view, construing section 19 in context, the date of a 'conviction' is the date of the judgment consummating the

verdict of guilty or a guilty plea by a sentence or order, the date of a 'verdict' is the date of a verdict of not guilty by reason of insanity and the date of a "finding" is the date of a finding of unfit to plead.

Paragraphs (a) to (c) of section 19(1) deal with cases where an appeal is only against a sentence or order. Thus, in the usual case of an appeal against a determination of guilt and the sentence, an appellant has until 21 days from the date of that sentence entailing the determination of guilt. Where an appeal is only sought against a 'sentence' or 'order' the position is spelled out in paragraphs (a) to (c) as 21 days from the date of the sentence or order. ...

If, unusually, the appellant seeks to appeal only the determination of guilt he has until 21 days after the date of the sentence. Thus, he can put in an early appeal or application for leave to appeal, though it will not be heard until sentence has been passed, the date of which will be well before the application is listed for a date for hearing, taking account of the length of the list of criminal appeals. ..."

The court further stated that an ordinary prisoner would naturally expect to seek to appeal once the proceedings were completed by a sentence since no proceedings on the appeal would normally occur between the guilty verdict and the sentence. Their lordships noted that in the definition section, section 2, 'conviction' was not defined, but 'sentence' was defined to include any order on conviction with reference to the person convicted, or his wife or children. The use of the preposition 'on' instead of 'after' suggested that, for the purposes of the Act, the sentencing process was to be regarded as part of the conviction process.

Their lordships stated that the court, on hearing an appeal against conviction, had the power to quash the sentence and pass another sentence in substitution. This implied that the appeal against conviction gave the court power to vary the sentence. It would therefore be logical that the appeal against conviction be filed once the sentence had been passed.

The court held in this regard:

> "It follows, therefore, that we do not agree with Lord Bingham's conclusion that the word 'conviction' was unambiguous and that it was therefore unnecessary to examine the context in which it had been used to determine the meaning to be attributed to it. We have done such an examination and are satisfied that, in the context of section 19(1) of the Barbados Act, the statutory intention was to use the term conviction in the sense of final adjudication by sentence or other order and not simply the pronouncement of guilt by a guilty verdict."

In addition the court made it clear that Legislative interpretation involves the application of legislation to the well-being of the community. It followed that it was more beneficial to the administration of justice for time to appeal against a conviction only to expire when 21 days had elapsed since the date of sentence. This made the system practical, clear and less dependent on judicial discretion for extensions of time, reflecting natural expectations of prisoners. The court found that this approach was consistent with the practice in several other Commonwealth Caribbean countries such as in Jamaica, the Judicature (Appellate) Jurisdiction Act, 1962, section 16(4), the Bahamas, the Court of Appeal Act, 1965, section 17(3) and in Dominica, the Eastern Caribbean Supreme Court (Dominica) Act, 1969, section 46(3).

The court concluded that in the circumstances, the time for filing a notice of appeal or an application for leave to appeal against a conviction pursuant to section 19(1) of the Act expires when such a notice or application has not been given within twenty-one days of the date of sentence.

Principle

Criminal appeals in capital cases under the Eastern Caribbean Supreme Court Act carry a discretionary time limit. The Court of Appeal may grant extensions of time to appeal in capital cases where properly appropriate to do so.

Court of Appeal of the Eastern Caribbean States

Cannonier v Director of Public Prosecutions Isaac and others v Director of Public Prosecutions

Eastern Caribbean Supreme Court (Appeals) HCRAP 2008/002

Facts

The Appellants were convicted of murder and sentenced to death. Their notices of appeal were filed late. The issue was whether the court having jurisdiction to extend time for filing notice of appeal. The Eastern Caribbean Supreme Court Act at Section 52 states as follows:

"52. *Time for appealing*

(1) Where a person who is convicted desires to appeal under this Act to the Court of Appeal or to obtain the leave of the Court of Appeal, he or she shall give notice of appeal or notice of his or her application for leave to appeal in such manner as may be directed by rules of court within fourteen days of the date of conviction.

(2) Except in the case of a conviction involving sentence of death, the time within which notice of appeal or notice of an application for leave to appeal may be given may be extended at any time by the Court of Appeal."

Decision

Mitchell JA (AG) explained that the traditional rationale for fixed time limits in which to seek leave to appeal in capital cases was that the court had no power to extend the time within which to appeal a conviction involving sentence of death because the mere giving of a notice of appeal had the effect of postponing the date of the execution.

The inflexible time limit for appealing in capital offences dated back to the period when executions were expected to be carried out quickly after sentence, namely within a matter of weeks. The rule was intended to facilitate that process.

The learned judge noted however that the ability of defendants in the Federation of Saint Christopher and Nevis to apply to the Privy Council meant that executions could no longer be carried out within such a short time frame. Execution dates were no longer set immediately after sentence in St Kitts and Nevis.

Defendants who alleged they had been denied a merits review of their conviction and sentence in the Court of Appeal because of inflexible procedural rules had the right to apply to the Board for conservatory orders and stays of execution while the application for leave to appeal was being prepared, as was demonstrated in the instant case. In England, where the death penalty was long abolished, appeals after a delay of 12 years were not unknown.

The principle of inflexible time limits was expounded in Twynham's case. His lordship noted that the rule had long been applied in Saint Vincent so that in the case of Pollard the Privy Council held that the Court of Appeal had no alternative but to refuse a defendant's application to extend time for lodging a notice, and they referred to Twynham's case.

Mitchell JA further held:

> "The issue of proportionality arises. The correct approach to proportionality was set out by Lord Clyde in the de Freitas case on appeal from Antigua and Barbuda. There, he observed that in determining whether a limitation by an Act, rule or decision is arbitrary or excessive the court should ask itself—
>
> *'whether: (i) the legislative objective is sufficiently important to justify limiting a fundamental right; (ii) the measures designed to meet the legislative objective are rationally connected to it; and (iii) the means used to impair the right or freedom are no more than is necessary to accomplish the objective.'*"

The learned judge stated that the authorities established that a statutory restriction must be shown to be reasonably justifiable in a democratic society. There must be shown to be a sufficiently important objective for the restriction, a rational connection with the objective, the use of the least drastic means, and no disproportionately severe effect on those to whom the restriction applies. The provision under challenge must be shown not to be arbitrarily or excessively invasive of the enjoyment of the guaranteed right according to the standards of a society that has a proper respect for the rights and freedoms of individuals.

His lordship acknowledged that criminal defendants in St Kitts bringing appellate proceedings faced very real difficulties. Some of these difficulties were recognised by the House of Lords in Weir's case as follows. A defendant unsuccessful in the Court of Appeal may well be in prison and experience difficulty in giving instructions, obtaining legal aid and perhaps instructing different solicitors and counsel for an appeal to the House.

His lordship concluded:

> "Appellate review of convictions and sentence of death is obviously of especial importance given the final and irrevocable nature of the penalty. Having regard to the discretionary nature of the death penalty in St Kitts, appellate review by the Court of Appeal is also important to ensure the consistent application of the death penalty and to safeguard against arbitrariness and excessive use. The fixed 14-day time limit in s 52 serves no legitimate purpose, but has the capacity to cause very real injustice. The rule therefore fails to satisfy the first of Lord Clyde's criteria in the de Freitas case."

The learned judge on the facts of the instant case held that the inflexible 14-day time limit had infringed Cannonier's right of access to a court more than was necessary in order to achieve the aim of speedy appeals. The rule had operated in a way which absolutely prevented him from having the Court of Appeal review his conviction and sentence, even though no fault or blame attaches to him for the failure of his attorney to comply with the time limit and the notice was lodged only one day outside the time limit....Furthermore, the need for expeditious disposals of appeals in capital cases could be equally met by a discretionary time limit, where extensions would be granted where appropriate to do so.

Leave granted to appeal against conviction and sentence.

FRESH EVIDENCE

Statute in the Commonwealth Caribbean allows for the admission of the evidence of a witness at the hearing of the appeal i.e. fresh evidence even though that evidence was not led at trial.

Principle

The Court of Appeal's discretionary power to receive fresh evidence represents a significant safeguard against the possibility of injustice. This discretionary power ought to be exercised if, after investigation of all the circumstances, the court thinks it is necessary or expedient in the interest of justice to do so.

Court of Appeal of Trinidad and Tobago

Hernandez (also called Redman) v The State

Cr. App. No. 63 of 2004

Facts

The appellant was convicted on two counts of murder and sentenced to death. The Court of Appeal dismissed his appeal and affirmed his convictions and sentences. No psychiatric evidence was adduced on behalf of the appellant and no psychiatric assessment was conducted. By supplemental petition for special leave to appeal dated 30th January 2008 the appellant sought leave to admit fresh evidence in the form of a neuropsychological report of Dr. Alistair Gray a Clinical Psychologist. Section 47 of the Supreme Court of Judicature Act Chapter 4:01 of the Laws of Trinidad and Tobago confers upon the Court of Appeal hearing a criminal appeal the power to receive fresh evidence "if it thinks it necessary and expedient in the interest of justice".

Dr. Gray concluded from his assessment of the appellant that he presented two distinct psychological profiles, namely a depressive of long standing and a level of cognitive functioning that represents a learning disability. Dr. Gray noted that the assessment tools he used were developed in research settings in Europe and North America and validated for clinical use in those locations. There were no appropriate locally validated assessment tools.

Decision

R. Narine, J.A. summarised the principles that applied to the exercise of the discretion to admit fresh evidence:

a. The evidence that it is sought to call must be evidence which was not available at the trial.

b. It must be evidence relevant to the issues.

c. It must be evidence which is credible evidence in the sense that it is well capable of belief; it is not for this court to decide whether it is to be believed or not, but it must be evidence which is capable of belief.

d. The court will after considering that evidence go on to consider whether there might have been a reasonable doubt in the minds of the jury as to the guilt of the appellant if that evidence had been given together with the other evidence at the trial.

His lordship held further:

> "In Benedetto v The Queen, the Board explained that the Court of Appeal's discretionary power to receive fresh evidence represents a very significant safeguard against the possibility of injustice. This discretionary power ought to be exercised if, after investigation of all the circumstances, the court thinks it is necessary or expedient in the interest of justice to do so.

The learned judge in applying the principles enunciated earlier held that

(i) the fresh evidence was relevant;

(ii) it was capable of belief;

(iii) it was not available at trial, since neither the prosecution nor the defence considered that the mental condition of the appellant brought him within the Mc Naghten rules, or within the statutory definition of diminished responsibility, hence no psychological assessment was carried out before or at the trial and

(iv) the evidence ought to be admitted in the interest of justice.

The court accordingly exercised their discretion to admit the report of Dr. Gray.

Principle

Under the Eastern Caribbean Supreme Court Act, the Court of Appeal is required to receive fresh evidence unless it is satisfied that the evidence if received would not afford any ground for allowing the appeal. At the hearing of the appeal, the court would decide whether the evidence affected the validity of the conviction.

Judicial Committee of the Privy Council

Director of Public Prosecutions (Appellant) v Nelson (Respondent)

[2015] UKPC 7

Facts

The appellant was convicted of murder. Before the Court of Appeal, the defendant sought leave to adduce a new witness statement from an ambulance emergency officer, Mr Greenidge, who had been called out in the early hours of the morning to the scene of the shooting. The court granted leave to adduce the evidence, but on examining it concluded that it could not affect the safety of the conviction. The appellant contended that in so concluding the Court of Appeal illegitimately arrogated to itself the fact-finding function which is exclusively committed to the jury, and moreover deprived the defendant of his constitutional right to the verdict of the jury.

He contended that once the fresh evidence was received by the Court of Appeal, the only possible consequence, unless the evidence were such as to demonstrate unequivocally the innocence of the defendant, is that a re-trial be ordered to enable the jury to perform its task in assessing the whole of the evidence, including the new.

Decision

Lord Hughes referred to the Canadian case of R v Stolar. In that case the Canadian Supreme Court addressed the test in Canada for the reception at appeal level of fresh evidence. His lordship noted that the statute (section 610(d) of the Criminal Code) merely permitted the Court of Appeal to receive any fresh evidence if it was in the interests of justice to do so. The case law of Canada, establishes that a two-stage process is, or is normally, adopted. The first question is whether the evidence should be admitted. At this stage the test includes asking whether the evidence is such that, if believed, it could reasonably be expected to have affected the result of the trial. In Stolar the Court of Appeal had, at the first (admission) stage, resolved by a majority that the fresh evidence was such as might reasonably have been expected, if accepted, to affect the outcome of the trial.

Upon appeal, the same court had, by a different majority, determined that the case against Mr Stolar had been so strong that the new evidence could not have altered the jury's conclusion. The Supreme Court held that it was impossible so to reason when the opposite conclusion had been reached and announced at stage one.

His lordship noted that the test set out in section 45 of the Eastern Caribbean Supreme Court Act requires the court to receive the evidence 'unless it is satisfied that the evidence if received would not afford any ground for allowing the appeal'. The learned judges stated that this clearly left open the question, for determination at the appeal, whether the evidence affected the validity of the conviction, including whether it would, if accepted, be such as might reasonably have affected the outcome of the trial.

Lord Hughes held further:

> "The procedure conventionally adopted by the English Court of Appeal, Criminal Division, under the differently expressed section 23 of the Criminal Appeal Act 1968 is comparable, namely in most cases to receive the fresh evidence (if the other conditions for doing so are met) *de bene esse* and then to examine in the context of the appeal as a whole whether it is such as to impact adversely on the safety of the conviction."

The learned judge concluded that nothing in Stolar imposed on the Eastern Caribbean Court of Appeal the obligation to determine at the stage of receiving the evidence that it would be expected, if accepted, to have affected the outcome of the trial, and generally it was both permissible and sensible to receive the evidence on the basis that its possible impact on the trial would be examined during the hearing of the appeal.

Advice that the appeal of the Director of Public Prosecutions should be allowed and the conviction for murder and sentence restored, whilst the cross appeal of the defendant should be dismissed.

Principle

The court may exercise its jurisdiction to give leave to withdraw a notice to abandon an appeal where it is shown that circumstances are present which enable the court to say that that abandonment should be treated as a nullity.

Court of Appeal, Criminal Division

R v Medway

[1976] QB 779

Facts

The applicant applied for leave to withdraw a notice of abandonment of his application for leave to appeal against a court order made under ss 60 and 65 of the Mental Health Act 1959 whereby it was ordered that the applicant be admitted to and detained in a hospital subject to restrictions on his discharge.

Decision

Lawson LJ noted that under the rules, whether of 1908 or of 1968, when a notice of abandonment has been given the application or appeal of which it is the subject is disposed of. It followed that after abandonment the court was *functus officio* and there was no longer any proceeding extant before the court in relation to which its jurisdiction could be exercised.

His lordship added that the court possessed jurisdiction to give leave to withdraw an abandonment where it was shown that circumstances were present which enabled the court to say that the abandonment should be treated as a nullity.

According to the learned judge, the kernel of the 'nullity test' is that the court is satisfied that the abandonment was not the result of a deliberate and informed decision, in other words that the mind of the applicant did not go with his act of abandonment. His lordship listed some instances when the court would exercise its jurisdiction. This included mistake, fraud, wrong advice, and misapprehension.

The learned judge held that on the facts of the instant case there was no element of mistake in the appellant's decision, and that further, the decision was considered and deliberate.

Application refused.

APPEAL FOLLOWING A PLEA OF GUILTY

An appellant who pleaded not guilty may appeal his conviction and sentence after being found guilty by a jury. An appellant may also appeal severity of sentence following a plea of guilty. In limited circumstances an appellant may appeal his conviction following a plea of guilty.

Principle

Where a defendant has been convicted on his own plea of guilty the court may allow an appeal against conviction provided that the court is satisfied that under all the circumstances of the case the conviction is unsafe or unsatisfactory.

Court of Appeal, Criminal Division

R v Lee

[1984] 1 All ER 1080

Facts

The applicant who was deemed fit to plead, pleaded guilty to a number of offences. He subsequently applied for leave to appeal citing grounds which included the claim that the applicant was of low intelligence and of a deprived and institutionalised background and that his pleas of guilty were prompted "not by any acknowledgment of his guilt but out of motives of a desire for notoriety and publicity".

Section 2(1) *(a)* of the Criminal Appeal Act 1968 provided as follows:

'Except as provided by this Act, the Court of Appeal shall allow an appeal against conviction if they think—*(a)* that the verdict of the jury should be set aside on the ground that under all the circumstances of the case it is unsafe or unsatisfactory ... and in any other case shall dismiss the appeal ...'

Decision

Ackner LJ held that as originally drafted, s 2(1) *(a)* was confined to the 'verdict of the jury'. The word 'conviction' was substituted by s 44 of the Criminal Law Act 1977 following the decision of the House of Lords in R v Shannon where the court drew attention to the failure to give the court power to intervene where the accused had pleaded guilty. His lordship approved of dicta of Salman LJ in that case which was to the effect that the 1968 Act was intended to extend the powers conferred by the Criminal Appeal Act 1907. Section 4(1) of the 1907 Act, amongst other things required the Court of Criminal Appeal to allow an appeal (subject to the proviso) if they thought "that on any ground there was a miscarriage of justice."

On the facts of the instant case his lordship concluded that the fact that the applicant was fit to plead, knew what he was doing, intended to make the pleas he did, and pleaded guilty without equivocation after receiving expert advice, although factors highly relevant to whether the convictions on any of them were either unsafe or unsatisfactory, could not of themselves deprive the court of the jurisdiction to hear the applications.

Principle

A plea of guilty to an offence is no bar to an appeal providing that it would have been impossible for the defendant to have been lawfully convicted of the offence.

Court of Appeal, Criminal Division

R v Whitehouse

[1977] QB 868

Facts

The accused was charged on indictment with incitement to commit incest. The particulars disclosed that the accused had incited his daughter then aged 15, to have sexual intercourse with him, but she had refused. At his trial the accused pleaded guilty. He appealed against sentence, but was then given leave to appeal against conviction.

Decision

Scarman LJ held that the issue to be decided was whether the court, in the face of a guilty plea had jurisdiction to entertain an appeal against conviction. The learned judge stated that the appeal would be allowed only if it could be properly said that there was a wrong decision of law or a material irregularity in the course of the trial. If it was that there was no offence known to the law as charged, it would be a wrong decision of law for the judge to accept a plea of guilty; and *a fortiori* it would be wrong for the judge to allow the matter to proceed to judgment.

His lordship concluded:

> "We have therefore come to the conclusion, with regret, that the indictment does not disclose an offence known to the law because it cannot be a crime on the part of this girl aged 15 to have sexual intercourse with her father, though it is of course a crime, and a very serious crime, on the part of the father. There is here incitement to a course of conduct, but that course of conduct cannot be treated as a crime by the girl. Plainly a gap or lacuna in the protection of girls under the age of 16 is exposed by this decision. It is regrettable indeed that a man who importunes his daughter under the age of 16 to have sexual intercourse with him but does not go beyond incitement cannot be found guilty of a crime.... The girl's notional crime, because she never did commit it, is unknown

to the law and therefore there can be no offence by him, the inciter."

Appeals against conviction allowed. Appeal against sentence allowed; sentence varied.

THE PROVISO

Commonwealth Caribbean jurisdictions have legislation which allows the Court of Appeal to apply the proviso and dismiss an appeal even where the court finds merit in the grounds of appeal.

Principle

The criterion for the application of the proviso is whether, if the jury had received the appropriate directions, they would without doubt have convicted the appellant on a consideration of the whole of the admissible evidence, omitting from consideration evidence which clearly the jury did not believe.

Court of Appeal of Trinidad and Tobago

John v The State

Cr. App. No. 39 of 2007

Facts

The appellant was found guilty of three counts of rape and sentenced on two counts to 25 years hard labour and 10 strokes with the birch and on the third count to 25 years hard labour. He was also found guilty and sentenced for other counts arising out of the same incident as the rape. He appealed against his convictions and sentences for rape. Section 44(1) of The Supreme Court of Judicature Act. Section 44(1) provides:

'The Court of Appeal on any such appeal against conviction shall allow the appeal if it thinks that the verdict of the jury should be set aside on the ground that it is unreasonable or cannot be supported having regard to the evidence, or that the judgment of the Court before whom the appellant was convicted should be set aside on the ground of a wrong decision on any question of law or that on any ground there was a miscarriage of justice, and in any other case shall dismiss the appeal; but the Court may, notwithstanding that they are of opinion that the point raised in the appeal might be decided in favour of the appellant, dismiss the appeal if they consider that no substantial miscarriage of justice has actually occurred.'

Decision

P. Weekes, JA held:

> "In Stafford and Carter v The State the Privy Council stated that the criterion for the application of the proviso is whether, if the jury had received the appropriate directions, they would without doubt have convicted the appellant on a consideration of the whole of the admissible evidence, omitting from consideration evidence which clearly the jury did not believe."

The learned judge concluded that while the jury was not adequately assisted on the issues pertinent to the identification parade, when the totality of the State's case against the appellant was considered, the court was satisfied that even if an adequate direction had been given, the jury would have indubitably come to the same conclusion. The evidence against the appellant was overwhelming and in this context, the judge's error was not fatal to the convictions. It followed that this was a proper case for the application of the proviso.

Appeal dismissed.;

www.ingramcontent.com/pod-product-compliance
Lightning Source LLC
Chambersburg PA
CBHW020624220526
45464CB00001B/16